Princes in the Making

By the same Author

*

PUBLIC SCHOOL SLANG
Constable

UNIVERSITY SLANG
Williams & Norgate

WHITE HORSES AND OTHER HILL FIGURES
Country Life

A HISTORY OF FOOTBALL
Secker & Warburg

SHANKS'S PONY
Dent

PRINCES
IN THE MAKING

A Study
of
Royal Education

MORRIS MARPLES

FABER AND FABER
24 Russell Square
London

First published in mcmlxv
by Faber and Faber Limited
24 Russell Square London WC1
Printed in Great Britain by
Ebenezer Baylis & Son Limited
The Trinity Press, Worcester, and London

The art of reigning is the profession of a prince.

HANNAH MORE

Theory and experience both teach us that the education of a Prince can be but a poor education and that a royal family will generally have less ability than other families.

WALTER BAGEHOT
(*The English Constitution*)

Be not over solicitous about education. It may be able to do much . . . It may mould and direct character, but it rarely alters it.

LORD MELBOURNE
(to Queen Victoria)

The fault lay not in my stars but in my genes.

H.R.H. THE DUKE OF WINDSOR

Acknowledgments

Plates I, II, IV, VI are reproduced by gracious permission of Her Majesty the Queen from originals in the Royal Collections. I am indebted for permission to use Plate III to the Trustees of the National Portrait Gallery, and for Plates V and VIII to the Radio Times Hulton Picture Library. Plate VII is reproduced by permission of Mrs. M. Prance and the Editor of the *Cornhill Magazine*, for whose further help I am also grateful.

For the subject matter of this book I am wholly indebted to the authors or editors of the fifty or so works listed at the end; but it would not have been possible to write at all, in the somewhat inaccessible place where I live, without the cooperation of the London Library, whose officials I would like to thank for so promptly sending me what I wanted.

Most of all I thank my wife, for her patience in listening to the whole book read aloud and her always down-to-earth criticisms.

January 1965   MORRIS MARPLES

7

Contents

Illustrations

Preface

Until the Queen and Prince Philip made their momentous decision to send the Prince of Wales and Princess Anne to boarding school, almost every English prince or princess for 500 years or more had been educated in private. The boys had tutors, and so also did the girls, until the Hanoverians took to employing teaching governesses as well; and around these revolved a host of lesser functionaries, who taught modern languages (in which royalty have always excelled), music, dancing, deportment, equitation and other accomplishments.

Inevitably one asks oneself, how did this old and outdated system work? This book attempts to supply an answer.

Starting with Henry VIII (during whose childhood the Renaissance first began to influence English educational methods, I have tried to find out how English royal children were educated—what they learnt, how they were treated, who taught them. This is not a piece of historical, or even educational, research, neither of which would I be qualified to undertake. But as a former working teacher of long experience, I have looked at the subject with a mainly pedagogic and practical eye. For this purpose I have used standard biographies, and sometimes, where available, published diaries and collections of letters. The list of books on pp. 198-9 consists simply of those I have consulted, and makes no claim to be an exhaustive bibliography.

It has been amusing (thought not surprising) to find among these royal pupils, their parents and their teachers, all the same problems which confront pupils, parents and teachers in grammar or public schools today.

The range of ability and educability among English kings and queens and their families over the last 500 years has been wide indeed—at one extreme those intriguingly brilliant scholars Lady Jane Grey, Queen Elizabeth I, Edward VI and James I (two girls among them, we note), who were so easy to teach, and who, in a

Preface

modern context, would all have won open classical scholarships to
Oxford or Cambridge; at the other extreme, difficult and troublesome pupils such as the Hanoverian princes (who to me often recall
the inmates of the old-fashioned Army class) and problem children
like George III, Princess Charlotte and Edward VII, who were a
perpetual anxiety to all concerned.

Royal parents, we find, have been just as prone as any other
parents to mishandle their sons and daughters, perhaps even more
so than most, owing to the issues at stake – pressing them too hard
like Queen Victoria and Prince Albert, disciplining them too
harshly like George III, or disapproving too obviously like George
IV with his daughter Charlotte.

As a schoolmaster, one looks with special interest at one's professional colleagues, the royal tutors – a long and remarkable series
of men. We begin with Henry VIII's eccentric preceptor, the poet
John Skelton. Next those Renaissance scholars, as brilliant as their
pupils, like Sir John Cheke and Roger Ascham (tutors respectively
to Edward VI and Elizabeth I); finally, after a long line of bishops,
come the lesser clergymen and dons of the nineteenth century. All
these men were classical scholars, most of them in holy orders, few
of them, after the sixteenth century, professional teachers. Many of
them were confronted with appallingly difficult tasks. It is with
fellow feeling that one studies their efforts to control the recalci-
trance of princes, and with applause that one greets the strong
measures they sometimes took to do so.

In the teaching of princes almost everything depends on the man;
but curricula, time-tables and text-books also play their part, and
I have looked into these matters when possible, keeping modern
practice in mind for comparison.

I have also taken particular note of treatises dealing expressly with
the education of princes. Since it was first put forward in Renaissance Italy that the aim of royal education must be to produce the
perfect ruler, there have been many attempts, both here and abroad,
to define and realize such an ideal. The first to be made in England
was by John Skelton, the last perhaps by Prince Albert, though the
best known works on the subject are those of James I in the seventeenth century and of Hannah More in the nineteenth. These have
all been referred to in the appropriate place.

Finally I have been interested, as any schoolmaster is with his own
pupils, to see how these royal children turned out in the end – how

14

much they owed to heredity, how much to their education and upbringing, how they overcame or outgrew the often very considerable
shortcomings revealed in them as children. For this purpose it has
been necessary sometimes to be briefly biographical; but I have tried
to look at the royal personages concerned as men and women rather
than as rulers, and have kept clear of history in the wider sense.

If there is a moral to this book, it is the obvious one that, however
hard you try – and royal parents and royal tutors have often tried
harder than most – you cannot alter a child's basic character, though
you can help him to develop and control it; and that the worldly
wise Lord Melbourne was right, when he wrote to Queen Victoria:

'Be not over solicitous about education . . . It may mould and
direct character, but it rarely alters it.'

Introduction

When the Renaissance first began to take shape in Italy of the fifteenth century under the impact of Greek learning and literature, philosophers were much concerned with formulating the concept of the Perfect Man – the many-sided man (*l'uomo universale*), who could do everything and do it well, who was at the same time man of action and man of culture, poet and soldier, scholar and athlete, artist, musician and man of affairs; and as a corollary to this, natural in a land of petty princedoms, there was an interest also in the ideal of the perfect ruler, who should combine all the qualities of the many-sided man with others peculiar to a prince – such royal virtues as magnificence, nobility, open-handed generosity, kindliness, justice and mercy, combined with the humility and the philosophic outlook of Plato's philosopher king.

Nor were these ideals the product of mere theorists or visionaries, out of touch with life. There were many men – and women too – who tried to realize them in their own lives, and some who succeeded to a degree which has never been possible since; and there were princes too who conceived themselves in the rôle of the ideal ruler – men like Lorenzo the Magnificent in Florence, Lodovico Gonzaga at Mantua, Federigo da Montefeltre at Urbino. The whole educational system of the day, now based firmly on Greek as well as Latin learning, was geared to the production of men and women who possessed these admired qualities; and it was not confined to those of royal or noble birth – children of humble origin deemed capable of profiting by such a training were readily admitted, and the great schools of the period, like La Giocosa at Mantua under Vittorino da Feltre, contained a mixture of social classes.

As this ferment of new ideas and new values spread west and north from Italy, the concepts of the perfect man and the ideal ruler became widely accepted throughout western Europe as a practical aim for education. Royal and noble families had their sons and daughters taught Greek; treatises were written expounding and expanding the ideas first put forward in Italy; tutors on the Italian pattern were found ready to impart them privately; and western rulers did their best to realize in their persons, or the persons of their heirs, the princely qualities of a Medici.

The Renaissance was slower to influence our remote island. But its breath was beginning to be felt in the reign of Henry VII; and his sons, Prince Arthur (who died young) and the future Henry VIII, were the first English princes to be given a Renaissance education, albeit without Greek.

Thereafter, until the middle of the seventeenth century, every child born into the English royal house, Tudor or Stuart, was educated in accordance with principles laid down in Italy of the Quattrocento. All of them were taught Greek and were well grounded in classical learning, and all, even the girls, were subjected to a formidably comprehensive course of training, not only intellectual, but moral, musical and physical as well, as recommended by the best Italian authorities. Some of them, most of all Elizabeth I, showed some of the qualities of the ideal monarch of the Renaissance.

After that the original impulse began to fade, and, in royal education at least, was soon lost, though its consequences remained till within living memory in an educational system for the intellectually élite based on Greek and Latin.

I

Tudor Princes

THERE HAD BEEN EDUCATED RULERS IN ENGLAND BEFORE HENRY VIII. Alfred the Great was distinguished for his learning amid a largely unlearned people. Henry I himself said that an unlettered king was a crowned ass and took care not to be one. Henry II was reputed to know every language spoken between the Channel and the Jordan. Henry VII was soundly if soberly educated. But with Henry VIII the education of English princes and princesses enters a new phase.

Henry himself, smug and sophisticated as we see him in his portrait as a child, had all the Tudor precocity, which came out so strongly in his own family, and began his serious education at an age when modern children are still in the nursery or the infants' school. When people saw that, like his brother Arthur, the heir to the throne, he was to be given a classical education (though without Greek), there were rumours that he was destined for the see of Canterbury. Englishmen were not yet familiar with the notion of an educated layman. But in fact Henry VII was already moving with the times, and his aim was to give both princes the sort of upbringing which their contemporaries abroad were now enjoying.

Yet he did not accept the new order wholeheartedly. The boys' tutors were chosen in the old way. They were not specially appointed university graduates, like the royal tutors of the next and subsequent generations, but men already employed at court for their special learning or talents. One of them was Bernard André, a blind poet from Toulouse, who was an Augustinian friar, and held the office of royal historiographer. Another Frenchman, Giles d'Ewés, who spent a lifetime in the royal service as librarian, taught the young princes French (and was in due course to teach Henry's daughter, Mary). There were probably others. But their best known tutor was the poet, John Skelton.

Tudor Princes

This curious character, around whose reputation many apocryphal stories have accumulated, was a Cambridge man and a good scholar, renowned for his own Latin verses, at a time when topical Latin verse composition was very much in vogue, and the author of several grammars. But he was of the old order in one important respect – he had no Greek; indeed, following the Roman satirist Juvenal, he despised Greek as the language of a decadent people, and thought learning it a waste of time, since it had no practical use – a man could not order hay for his horse in Greek, he said. His fame rested, and rests, on his poetry. As the leading English poet of his generation, he had enjoyed the status of unpaid laureate at court since 1488; and had been honoured also for his poetry at the universities of Oxford and Cambridge. As soon as the young princes were old enough, he became their tutor; and continued to be responsible for them till the death of Prince Arthur in 1502.

His subsequent career is typical of the man. On his retirement from court (when it seems he was superseded by another tutor, William Honne) he took orders and became rector of Diss in Norfolk; but his habit of clowning in the pulpit roused criticism, and the fact that he was living with a woman (to whom in fact he was secretly married) scandalized his parishioners, with the result that he was suspended by his bishop. So at any rate it is said, though it may not be true.

Meanwhile his fierce satire, directed particularly at the clergy, was making him many enemies. His bold and outspoken comments touched even Wolsey himself, who failed to silence him with threats, and perhaps dare not send him to the Tower. The King does not seem to have moved either for or against his former tutor, by this time back at court as *orator regius*, whose sallies doubtless appealed to his sense of humour, as they had done in earlier years. But Skelton took the precaution of settling in lodgings within reach of sanctuary at Westminster Abbey, where, despite a reconciliation with Wolsey, he remained till his death in 1529.

This was the man responsible for young Prince Henry's education from the age of eight. As he himself wrote:

> *'The honour of England I learned to spell,*
> *I gave him drink of the sugared well*
> *Of Helicon's waters crystalline,*
> *Acquainting him with the Muses nine.'*

Possibly his idiosyncrasies had not yet fully emerged at the time of his appointment, for he was still only in his thirties. But it was a strange choice, and we may wonder why the sober-minded King picked on such an eccentric, however able, to tutor his sons.

Yet Skelton took his duties very seriously. He composed several moral treatises for his pupils – on how to behave, how to speak well, how to avoid sin, even how to die; and he was the first royal tutor in England to follow the continental fashion by writing a comprehensive manual of guidance for the two princes, which he called *Speculum Principis, A Prince's Mirror*. This contains many pieces of advice to which the adult Henry paid singularly little heed.

'Above all else abhor gluttony,' says Skelton, among other things. 'Cultivate sobriety and self-restraint. Avoid drunkenness. Eschew luxury. Shun the company of lewd women. Defile not your marriage . . .'

But more important in its effect than these moral commonplaces was Skelton's personal influence on the young Prince. We have noted his anti-clerical views. These may not have become dominant until later, but he surely held them during the period of his tutorship, and just as surely they must have made some impact on his pupil, unless – which is highly unlikely – he preserved that colourless impartiality on vital issues which is sometimes recommended to teachers today. The germs of the King's anti-clerical policy of later years, with all its profound consequences in English history, may even – who knows? – be found in the caustic comments of a tutor.

Environment, too, as it must do with every child, played a dominant part in moulding the mind and character of this Prince. Though the English court under Henry VII was already sensitive to the new spirit of the Renaissance, the King himself was a product of the old order. He was studious rather than learned. He read a good deal in French, and was well acquainted with Latin, in which he conducted some of his correspondence. But he had none of the qualities of the Renaissance prince. His youth had been hard, and the task which fell to him, of consolidating royal power in England, called for the resources of a businessman and an administrator, rather than a scholar or man of culture. There was little time for music or poetry or philosophy, perhaps not even much for theology. Yet Henry was not ill disposed to the new learning, and welcomed scholars, divines and poets to his court, though he could hardly meet them on their own ground, as later sovereigns did.

One of the strongest influences which governed this practical-minded king and encouraged his patronage of learning was that of his mother, Margaret Beaufort, Countess of Richmond, whose advice he constantly sought. This remarkable lady, who had been thrice married, but in later life had taken monastic vows and lived in seclusion, was herself a tremendous patron of learning, though from strongly religious motives. Caxton himself and possibly also Skelton were among her protégés. She founded colleges at Cambridge, primarily for the teaching of Greek, Latin and Hebrew (including St. John's, which soon became a veritable nursery of royal tutors); endowed professorships in divinity at both universities; possessed a considerable library at a time when books were rare and costly, and few English ladies owned more than one or two; and herself entered the field of devotional literature with translations from the French. Her influence was present in the background throughout Henry's childhood, and may have weighed with his father in planning the young Prince's education. She died in the same year as her son.

The boy thus grew up in an atmosphere of learning and piety, into which the lively spirit of the Renaissance was already penetrating. He was not by nature a scholar, though he had the ability to become one. For mathematics he is said to have shown a 'remarkable docility'; but his main gift was probably for languages, though as a grown man he knew only French and Latin really well. As the common coin of international relations, the latter in particular was essential for a ruler, and Henry acquired a sound working knowledge of it at a very early age: indeed, there is an anecdote which implies that his command of the language as a small boy was unusual. In 1499, when Henry was nine, Sir Thomas More took his friend Erasmus to see the young prince, who was under Skelton's care at Eltham Palace. The great scholar was highly impressed with the boy's talent; and it is said that, exchanging a Latin correspondence with him afterwards, he could not believe that the letters he received were a child's work until he was shown the rough drafts corrected in Henry's own hand (at which point the cynic will remark that there was nothing to prevent Skelton from dictating the corrections). For the rest of his life Henry used Latin freely in his intercourse with foreigners, very few of whom at that time thought it worth while to learn English.

In addition to French and Latin, he had some Italian, doubtless acquired from one of several Italians at his father's court, and an imperfect knowledge of Spanish dating probably from his betrothal to Catherine of Aragon. In his ignorance of Greek he resembled most Englishmen of his generation. The language was not yet regarded as an essential part of a polite education in England; and did not become so till the next generation, when all Henry's children, including the girls, learnt it, and prodigies like Lady Jane Grey were reading Plato in the original for pleasure.

Like his daughter Elizabeth, Henry had a vigorous command of his own language, and, in the fashion of the day, diverted himself with writing verse. He is one of the very few English monarchs whose poems still appear occasionally in anthologies. Skelton may be allowed the credit, which he claims, of inducing the young Prince to taste the sugared waters of Helicon. Yet Henry's work and Skelton's are worlds apart. Skelton, with his 'ragged, tattered and jagged rhymes', as he calls them, belongs poetically to the Middle Ages. The affinities of Henry's verse, in poems such as

> '*Pastime with good company*
> *I love, and shall until I die,*'

are with the new poetry of the Elizabethan age which was soon to break.

With his passionate interest in music also Henry was a man of the new era. He was extremely well taught musically, and thanks to a combination of talent and technical virtuosity he was a genuinely outstanding performer on the harpsichord and the lute, which were the fashionable instruments of the day, as well as a skilful organist. He practised his playing, we are told, both day and night. He could sing too, reading a part fluently at sight, and had some gift for musical composition, both vocal and instrumental. His reputation here is no product of courtly flattery; he is still recognized as a minor composer of merit, and some of his music, particularly his anthem 'O Lord, the Maker of all thing,' is still occasionally performed.

In music, as in everything else which attracted him, Henry indulged his taste to the full, as soon as he was sufficiently his own master to do so. Even as a boy he maintained a troupe of minstrels. Later, as king, he took great interest in the choir of the chapel royal, scouring the country for choristers. Among works they performed were masses composed by himself. His organist was Dionysius

Memo, whom he attracted to England from St. Mark's, Venice, and whose duties included both teaching and entertaining the King. It is said that Henry would sometimes listen to an organ recital by Memo for hours at a time, while the non-musical members of his entourage endured in silence.

A versatile talent for sport was another of Henry's Renaissance traits. Familiarity with the gross, unwieldy figure of later years obscures for most people the fact that as a boy and young man he had all the qualifications of the natural athlete – a fine physique, a keen eye, a quick hand and unbounded energy; and he delighted to use them. No doubt he had the advantage of coaching from the best available performers. But whether in archery or wrestling, hunting, hawking or jousting, horsemanship, tennis or dancing, he was exceptional among the youths of his class and generation. Foreign observers, rather carried away by the spectacle of so princely a prince, wrote rapturously of his prowess. Giustinian, the Venetian ambassador, who thought him the handsomest monarch in Europe, found it the prettiest thing in the world to see him play tennis, 'his fair skin glowing through a shirt of the finest texture'. Another who watched him in single-handed combat with his brother-in-law, the Duke of Suffolk, was reminded of the epic fight between Hector and Achilles, though it would not have done to press the analogy too far. A third noted that he could draw the bow with greater strength than any other man in England. These comments were not for the King's eye, and any exaggeration there may be in them springs not from flattery, but from the genuine admiration which Henry inspired so readily as a young man.

To Englishmen who remembered only Henry's rather glum father it must have seemed as if England at last had a king who could match the brilliant princes of Europe. The future seemed bright indeed. 'What may we not expect,' exclaimed Sir Thomas More – and for us there is a tragic irony in his words – 'from a king who has been nourished by philosophy and the nine Muses?' But our concern here is not with the fading of Henry's own image (though he remains on any count a great king), but with his children.

By the time the question of their upbringing arose, the pattern of humanistic education, now including Greek, was fully established in this country, and this became the basis for the education of the royal children. How it was applied in the case of the girls, Mary and Elizabeth, will be considered in the next chapter. For Edward, the long awaited male heir, born at last when his father was well advanced into middle age, Henry planned, or got someone else to plan for him, a broad course of training, of which the logical conclusion would have been once more the ideal ruler. Fate willed that these ambitious schemes should never reach their conclusion. But one result of Edward's early death is that more is known about his youth than would probably have been put on record if he had reached maturity, so that we are able in his case to follow the education of a prince and a king in much greater detail than is usually possible in that period.

Henry's solicitude for his infant son was obvious from the moment of his birth. Precautions were taken to see that everything about him was kept hygienically clean, that no infection came near him, that his food was free from taint. Responsibility for these matters was placed in the hands of Lady Bryan, who had won the King's regard as lady governess to the Princess Mary. Edward's own mother had of course died in child-bed, but Queen Catherine Parr was a kindly stepmother to all the royal children. Henry himself took an active personal interest in this baby boy on whom so much depended, carrying him about, playing with him, showing him to visitors or to the crowds outside his windows.

The serious business of his education began prematurely even for those days, when Edward was only three. Perhaps it was no bad thing that it was interrupted for a time almost at once by an illness. But it was resumed as soon as possible with an intensity which would seem most improper nowadays, but at that time was normal with high-born infants. It seems to have done Edward no harm, either then or later.

The tutors Henry chose for his son were recognized teachers and scholars, men of a different stamp from his own tutors. The first was Dr. Richard Coxe, a man of humble origin (never at that time a bar to preferment), who had been a scholar of Eton and a fellow of King's, Cambridge, and at the time of his appointment was headmaster of Eton. One cannot help wondering why the King chose an eminent headmaster, who at forty-four must have already been somewhat set in his ways, to instil the elements of Greek and Latin into his infant son; but at any rate it marks the importance he attached to the task. Coxe was by no means as non-plussed as a modern headmaster of Eton might be if transferred to an infants' school. He seems to have made a successful effort to adapt his methods to so young a pupil, using what would perhaps now be called the play-way. This, as described in a report which Coxe made to a member of the King's Council on relinquishing his appointment, consisted in making a sort of military game out of the struggle to master grammar and syntax. In this the parts of speech became the enemy, whom the young Prince was to attack and overthrow, as his father had over-thrown the French at Boulogne. The idea worked well at first, and Edward got to the stage of producing compositions described by his proud tutor as 'pretty Latins'. But when fresh realms to conquer began to loom ahead in the shape of Cato, Aesop and other authors thought appropriate for the infant scholar, the ex-headmaster found himself confronted, first with boredom, then, as he tried to get his pupil to memorize selections from the Book of Proverbs and listen to his own moral discourses, with open revolt. At this point the play-way was temporarily abandoned, and Coxe, somewhat against his principles, fell back on corporal punishment. Edward had not ex-pected this, and the results were immediate. Coxe himself having successfully defeated Captain Will, his pupil went on with better heart to face yet another adversary in the shape of Captain Oblivion.

Coxe's final summing up was a favourable one: the young Prince, he thought, was 'a vessel apt to receive all goodness and learning, witty, sharp and pleasant'—a school report of which anyone might be proud. But it may be that Henry was not altogether satisfied with Coxe himself—or perhaps he thought the time had come for a man of even greater distinction to take over. At any rate in 1544, when Edward was six, Coxe ceased to be responsible for his education, and assumed the still very important function of almoner in his house-hold. No disgrace or demotion was involved in this change: Coxe remained with the Prince for another five years, and continued to teach him from time to time. The two were fond of one another. When Coxe was away ill, Edward wrote to him in Latin inquiring about his health, and introducing classical and biblical allusions in a way which he knew would please his old tutor. Coxe for his part, reporting to Cranmer in 1546, when Edward was nine, called him 'a singular gift sent from God, and an imp worthy of such a father', and referred to his 'towardness in learning, godliness, gentleness and all honest qualities'.

'He hath learned almost four books of Cato,' he went on, 'to con-strue, to parse, and say without book. And of his own courage now, in the latter book, he will needs have at one time fourteen verses, which he conneth pleasantly and perfectly, besides things of the Bible, the Satellitium of Vives' – of which more will be said later – 'Aesop's fables, and Latin-making.'

The conquest of new territory seems to have been proceeding according to plan. But the direction was now in the hands of the new tutor, John Cheke. This distinguished scholar had already reached the head of his profession, when no more than twenty-six, as the first Regius Professor of Greek at Cambridge, where he was the leading figure among a group of scholars, mostly St. John's men, of protestant sympathies. Both Elizabeth's tutors, William Grindal and Roger Ascham, belonged to this coterie: so too did Lady Jane Grey's tutors, John Aylmer and John Haddon. Cheke's influence was thus predominant in the upbringing of three children who were in the line of direct succession to the throne; and that in matters of religion it was a protestant influence had a bearing on future events. Only Mary, much older than the others, and tutored by an Oxford man, under the powerful control of her Catholic mother, was brought up differently.

Henry paid Cheke a very high compliment in appointing him tutor to Edward, his 'most noble jewel', on whom all his hopes for the continuance of the dynasty rested; and it was an excellent choice, for Cheke, despite his university background, soon showed that he knew how to get the best out of a clever small boy, who was also a prince. His secret seems to have been that to Edward he was always the scholar, the lover of learning, sharing the delights of language and literature with his pupil, never the courtier or the pedagogue. He took it for granted that Edward was capable of understanding anything he might put before him, even though it might seem beyond a child, as for example the philosophy of Aristotle. Unquestionably these methods worked; and Edward's attainments in classical scholarship soon reached a level of maturity beyond his years.

By a lucky chance several of Edward's exercise books are still in existence, with a number of letters in Latin probably composed under the eye of his tutor, and more than a hundred so-called orations on set themes in Greek and Latin. These give us a fascinating glimpse of the schoolboy at work; and by modern standards it must be confessed they are remarkable. Occasionally we are reminded that small boys of the sixteenth century were not fundamentally different from those of the twentieth. Like any ten-year-old beginning Greek at his preparatory school, Edward sometimes amuses himself by writing English words in Greek characters. Once we catch him out shirking the use of the dictionary, and wildly guessing the meaning of words entered in his vocabulary notebook, instead of looking them up. He often leaves projects uncompleted, as children do; and good resolutions are sometimes soon forgotten.

But his sheer linguistic virtuosity is impressive, outclassing anything a modern schoolboy of his age could do. At fourteen he had reached a standard in languages, though not one must emphasize in anything else, comparable with that of Oxford and Cambridge open scholarship candidates today.

At the risk of dwelling over long on the details of Edward's work in Greek and Latin, it is worth considering how this was achieved. It was not as if Edward devoted all his time to these languages, as we shall shortly see. The explanation certainly lies in the fact that Latin, the lingua franca of educated Europe, was being taught with a practical purpose, in fact as a means of expression; and the same methods were applied by analogy to Greek. Edward learned to speak both from an early age, Latin with great fluency; and his written work in both consisted of free composition rather than the translation on which stress is so heavily laid today. When he was a very small boy he wrote to his friends and relations in Latin. It may be guessed from the absence of mistakes and the rather stilted language that the surviving letters are fair copies written under supervision; but nevertheless they were not motiveless, abstract compositions. Later, following a practice recommended by Erasmus, he was taught to compose discourses in Greek as well as Latin, on controversial themes or topics of the day set by his tutor. This again meant that he was expressing his own thoughts in the language of the moment. They may not have been very interesting or original thoughts; but the weekly exercise of setting them down, at considerable length, in Greek or Latin, must have helped to clarify them, and at the same time gave him a ready command of his medium. As to this, we have the opinion of the Princess Elizabeth's tutor, Roger Ascham, expressed in a letter of 1550, when Edward was thirteen, to his great friend Sturm, rector of the gymnasium at Strasburg. 'Latin he understands with accuracy,' says Ascham, 'speaks with propriety, writes with facility combined with judgement.' As for Greek, he goes on, 'He has proceeded so far in that language that he readily translates the Latin of Cicero's *Philosophia* into Greek.'

The range of Edward's classical reading was equally impressive. Cheke seems to have believed in the virtues of studying ancient philosophy at an early age, at any rate for a prince. In the letter just quoted, Ascham mentions that Edward had completed what he calls the *Dialectic* of Aristotle, and was now going on to his *Ethics*. When he asked Cheke why he had set his pupil to this rather than a practical treatise like Xenophon's *Education of Cyrus*, the reply was, in effect, that it was better to study the first principles of moral philosophy before looking at particular instances. A few years later, when Cheke was seriously ill, and did not expect to live, he particularly urged his pupil in a farewell letter to read two chapters of Aristotle's *Politics*, which had a special bearing on monarchy. It is a measure of Cheke's genius as a teacher that he could attempt to study such works with a pupil of no more than fourteen or fifteen.

But Cheke naturally did not limit Edward's reading to the philosophers.

'I would have a good student pass rejoicing through all authors, both Greek and Latin,' he wrote to Ascham. 'But he that will dwell in these few books only, first in God's Holy Bible, and then join with it Tully, Plato, Aristotle, Xenophon, Isocrates and Demosthenes must needs prove an excellent man.'

He must have read all these authors (in part) with Edward, and especially Demosthenes, who was his own favourite.

A further clue as to Edward's reading is to be found in a list quoted by an early seventeenth-century eulogist of the books he was reputed to have studied with Ascham himself. These include Melanchthon (a contemporary German theologian, then highly regarded, but now forgotten), all Cicero, a great part of Livy, selected speeches of Isocrates (two of which he rendered into Latin), the tragedies of Sophocles and the Greek Testament. This is almost identical with the list of books Ascham read with the Princess Elizabeth, and may represent his particular taste.

Finally it is worth noting what classical books Edward had in his library; though their presence there does not of course mean that he read them. A collection of books which belonged to him is still kept together at the British Museum. There are about a hundred works in all, mostly theology; but among them are six classical authors – Herodotus, Thucydides, Ptolemy's Geography (in Italian), Galen, several volumes of Cicero and, finally, Plutarch. Of these, apart from Cicero, we only know from correspondence between Cheke and

Ascham, that Edward read Plutarch (or some of him), whose *Lives of the Noble Greeks and Romans* had important object-lessons for a prince.

Striking a balance between the languages in these several lists, we get a proportion of twelve Greek to three Latin authors. Superficially this may seem to be no more than the natural bias of a Regius Professor of Greek. But, versed as he was in both languages, Cheke had a genuine conviction that Greek literature or philosophy had more to offer his pupil than Latin. With this the modern scholar will be disposed to agree. At the same time the absence of poetry or drama (apart from Sophocles) will strike him as peculiar. Where are Homer and Vergil, or Horace and the Roman elegiac poets, to name only some of the principal omissions? And why Sophocles but not Euripides? We know that Cheke read all Homer and all Euripides with his pupils at Cambridge. The explanation probably is that Edward's reading was deliberately planned by Cheke to stress, firstly the practical use of language in prose-writing and oratory, secondly the application of history and philosophy to the requirements of a ruler. Other considerations were largely ignored.

The sheer bulk of Edward's alleged reading is astonishing. It is very difficult to imagine how any small boy, even with Cheke beside him, could have read all Cicero and most of Livy, together with even a selection from the works of the other authors named. We must not forget that he had other subjects to study, and many other things to do. Yet his performance does not seem to have been abnormal in that generation. His half-sisters were both tremendous readers. Elizabeth herself is said to have read most of Cicero and Livy. Lady Jane Grey, who died at sixteen, and the future James I must have covered at least as much ground as Edward, for they were formidable classical scholars. We are almost led to the conclusion that royal children in the sixteenth century were a species of superman. But in fact the explanation probably is that their capacity actually to think in Greek and Latin enabled them to read those languages far faster than students normally can today.

For a period of seven or eight years John Cheke was the strongest influence in Edward's life, not only as the chief of his tutorial staff, but as the man with whom he was in closest personal contact day by day. This must have been specially so after his accession, when Cheke continued to treat him as a boy rather than a king, and was one of the few members of his entourage who dared to approach him without any of the elaborate ceremony then customary, which even Mary and Elizabeth observed. For the rest of his life Edward liked and admired his tutor more than most other men. Questions of discipline probably did not often arise between them. One anecdote tells of an occasion when, shortly after coming to the throne at the age of nine, Edward was heard using bad language; and on being questioned by Cheke said that one of his companions had told him that kings always swore. Schoolmasterly inquiries having revealed the culprit, it would have been appropriate that both boys should have been punished. But Cheke, so we are told, though it seems inconsistent with his character, did not like to chastise the Lord's anointed, so beat the other boy in Edward's presence, with the warning that the King would not escape so lightly, if he offended again. This story seems to have given rise to the legend that Edward had a 'whipping boy', a companion whose function was to serve as scapegoat and suffer the King's punishments on his behalf. But in fact the employment of whipping boys seems to have been obsolete by this time.

A good deal of Cheke's time with his pupil must have been spent, not in classical studies, but in awakening his interest in the modern world, and directing his thoughts to the problems of government and of international relations, which he would shortly have to face for himself. This was the evident purpose of the journal or record of events, which at Cheke's suggestion Edward began to keep at the age of thirteen, and which he continued till within seven months of his death. Cheke also seems to have thought, and quite rightly, that it would be good for his pupil to meet men different from those who ordinarily appeared at court, and from time to time introduced interesting personalities to him – foreign scholars, his own friends from Cambridge, originals like the famous antiquary Leland. He encouraged his interest also in scientific questions, particularly those connected with his own hobby, astronomy, in which Edward became so knowledgeable that he was able to hold his own in argument as to the origin of comets with Cardano, the celebrated Italian mathematician, physician and astrologer, who visited him to present a copy of a work he had dedicated to Edward. Cheke himself seems to have taught Edward history and geography, which were recognized as important subjects for a ruler. The textbooks would of course be in Latin, but the ideas modern. Foxe the martyrologist, writing enthusiastically in 1563 of Edward's geographical knowledge, gives us a glimpse of its practical character. The young King, he says, could 'recite all the ports, havens and creeks, not within his own realms only, but also in Scotland and likewise in France, what coming in there was, how the tide served in every haven or creek, moreover what burden or what wind served the coming into the haven.' Edward, it seems, could almost have piloted his own ships into port.

There was one contemporary who disapproved of the way Edward was being taught. In 1551 William Thomas, clerk to the Council, who seems to have felt that the King's education was too narrowly linguistic and that he personally was the man best qualified to redress the balance, wrote secretly offering to instruct Edward in policy and statecraft, and enclosing a list of eighty-five topics on which he was prepared to submit papers for study. Edward, on his own initiative, accepted tentatively, and asked for essays on several of Thomas's topics, for example, foreign relations, the reform of the coinage, and one or two more abstract propositions, such as 'whether it is better for a commonwealth that the power be in the nobility or the commonalty'. It does not appear how Cheke took this implied criticism of his methods; but some of the subjects put forward by Thomas were among those which he himself had set his pupil several years before for treatment in Greek or Latin, and since then they had studied the history, the laws and the constitution of England together, so he probably smiled and said nothing.

Cheke certainly had enemies at court and in government circles (though Thomas was not necessarily one of them), for his closeness to Edward sometimes made him an obstacle to the schemes of ambitious men. But, though he was in temporary disgrace and retired to Cambridge for a short period in 1549 as a result of accepting a gift of £15, which might have been interpreted as a bribe, from Seymour, the Lord High Admiral, just before his fall and execution, he was soon back in favour, and received several special marks of the King's regard. He became provost of King's College, Cambridge, was given a grant of land, and—a curious and original tribute—was accorded certain shooting rights normally confined to noblemen. He was appointed a privy councillor and gentleman of the bedchamber. Finally, in 1552, Edward paid him the highest possible compliment by knighting him. It was shortly after this that Sir John fell seriously ill; and when the King was informed that he was not expected to live, 'No,' he replied, 'he will not die at this time, for this morning I begged his life of God and obtained it.'

1   EDWARD VI: school of Holbein

2   PRINCESS ELIZABETH (Elizabeth I), aged 13: by an unknown artist

Cheke did in fact make a complete recovery, and shortly after-wards became Clerk of the Council and a Secretary of State. He served Edward faithfully to the end, and was with him when he died. But the sequel is a sad one. Like so many of the leading protestant scholars of his day, he found himself in trouble when Mary succeeded: in his case there was a specific cause of offence, for he had served as Lady Jane Grey's Secretary of State during her abortive reign. He was at first not treated harshly; and, after a spell in prison, was allowed to go abroad; but having foolishly stayed out of the country beyond the stipulated time, he was kidnapped by the Queen's agents and brought back to the Tower, where to save his life he made a public recantation. He was released; but shortly afterwards died, it is said, of shame, at the early age of forty-three.

One of Cheke's responsibilities during the happier days before Edward's fatal illness was to supervise the rest of his educational staff. His own immediate colleague had been Dr. Coxe, who, on his retirement in 1549, had been succeeded by Sir Anthony Cooke, a man of proved pedagogic skill, acquired in the process of educating his own four sons and five daughters, of whom some of the latter, says Fuller, were 'learned above their sex in Greek and Latin'. Nothing is known of his impact on Edward. There was also the Princess Elizabeth's tutor, Roger Ascham, a familiar figure in the household of Catherine Parr, who must also have done a good deal of reading with Edward, though officially he seems to have been employed as librarian and also as a writing master. Strange though it may seem in a distinguished classical scholar, Ascham had a great reputation as a calligraphist. He did not of course actually teach Edward how to write. That had already been done by a man of humbler status, an Italian named Vannes. Ascham was concerned only with the finer points of penmanship, and we may imagine him instructing Edward in the two sophisticated styles of handwriting then in vogue among educated people, the Roman or Italian hand for ordinary everyday use, and the more involved engrossing style for special purposes, both of which he also taught to Elizabeth. To judge from specimens which survive, Edward never became as skilful as his half-sister in either style.

Edward's French tutor, as he himself records in his journal, was John Belmaine. Though always more at home in Latin, he learnt French quickly and easily. How well he could write it at the age of eleven appears from a lengthy composition entitled 'Treatise against the supremacy of the Pope', which he drew up in French under Belmaine's guidance, and of which a manuscript copy, with corrections, certified by Belmaine as Edward's own work, is to be found among his literary remains. Thus early did the youthful king take up the theme with which his father is so strongly identified. Belmaine was later rewarded for his services with the grant of a manor, and settled in England. He was among the mourners at Edward's funeral.

It is not known who taught Edward Italian and Spanish. No exercises or letters of his in these languages survive; but contemporary accounts show that by the time he was thirteen or fourteen he was using them freely in conversational exchanges with foreign ambassadors; so it can be assumed he had been skilfully taught and spent much time in oral practice. How it was possible to find the time for this, remains a puzzle. But it was the same with the Tudor princesses and with James I: all of them seem to have learned modern languages effortlessly, while devoting most of their time to the classics.

As for German, like English, it was not one of the languages which cultivated Europeans thought it necessary to learn; and no one would have suspected Edward of learning it, were it not for the fact that Fuller, a century later, mentions a mysterious personage, Randolph the German, among his entourage. But there is no evidence that Randolph taught German; and none that Edward learnt it.

In addition to the teachers of languages there were the musicians. All Henry's children inherited some of his talent for music, and though Edward could not rival his father, or perhaps even his half-sisters, he became a skilful lutanist; and when in 1550 negotiations were going on for his betrothal to Elizabeth of France his advisers evidently considered his proficiency a point in his favour, and arranged for him to give a recital for the French envoys. Musical virtuosity was of course considered at this time an essential part of the equipment of a cultivated gentleman and the lack of it a mark of barbarism. It would have been unthinkable for a prince to be uneducated musically. Edward was taught music mainly it seems by Philip van Wilder, a Fleming or Dutchman who was chief court musician under Henry VIII (for which his salary was 66s. 8d. a month), and had previously taught the Princess Mary. The leading musicians of the day, who had enjoyed his father's patronage, took Edward's interest for granted. One of them, Dr. Tye, set a metrical version of the first fourteen chapters of the Acts of the Apostles to music specially for him, with the expressed hope that he would play it instead of 'songs of wanton love'. Another, Thomas Sternhold, who had been a particular favourite with Henry, dedicated a metrical version of the Psalms to the young King, to take the place of the *'amatoriae et obscoenae cantiones'*, which he seems to imply had previously been popular at court. But by the time Edward received them, he was too weakened by the onset of his final illness to do more than toy with them. One of Sternhold's psalms was sung at his funeral.

Proficiency in sport and in the arts of war remained as much as ever a qualification of the ideal prince, and room had to be found for practice and instruction on these in Edward's programme. Like his father and most of his contemporaries, he enjoyed open-air activities wholeheartedly, though even before his fatal illness began he was not robust and had none of his father's prowess. Archery and jousting, running at the ring and tennis, with hunting and hawking, were still the sports of the day. Apart from jousting, in which only the toughest could excel, and from which he was perhaps tactfully dissuaded on account of his weak physique, Edward took part in them all, though without much success. The one he liked best was riding at the ring; but even in this he had little skill; nor indeed, it seems, had his friends. At a tournament in 1551, which Edward mentions in his diary, his team did not succeed in striking the ring at all in 120 courses, while his opponents, the winners, struck it only twice. Some of the other performances he records were very little better. Few of Edward's eulogists have attempted to describe him as a good athlete, though he was acknowledged to be a keen one.

It was generally agreed in this period that princes should share their education and their sports with a group of other boys of about the same age, not more than eight in number nor less than four according to the best authorities, who should be chosen for their good qualities regardless of birth. This practice was followed in Edward's case, and he spent a good deal of his time in the company of a group of young noblemen, two of them interestingly enough Irishmen, chosen in the first instance by his father. The chief of these, the Duke of Suffolk, was older than his fellows, in fact seven years older than Edward, and must have been the natural leader. He was exceedingly able – a rather fulsome letter he wrote from Cambridge to the young King, then aged thirteen, survives as proof of his brilliant command of Latin—and we may think of him as a sort of model or pattern for Edward to copy. Unhappily he died shortly after this of the sweating sickness. Another very talented boy, also older than Edward, whom the King much admired, was Sir Henry Sidney, father of Sir Philip. But his favourite was one of the Irishmen, Barnaby Fitzpatrick, a lively, likeable but rather irresponsible boy, traditionally identified as the King's whipping boy—though in fact, as we have seen, he probably did not have one. To Barnaby Edward wrote affectionately in English rather than Latin, and sometimes in the tone of a Dutch uncle, when his friend was absent on a mission to France. These youths were allowed and encouraged to treat the King informally; and it must have been very good for a boy cut off, as Edward was, from normal human contacts, to have to stand on his own legs for a while each day among his contemporaries, even if there were only six or eight of them. No one in England had yet thought of sending a prince to school or university, which would have been better still.

It is not clear to what extent Edward's companions shared his actual lessons. Most accounts seem to imply that he was given private tuition by Cheke and others. This may well have been the case most of the time. But there must surely have been some communal work with those who were not too old or too advanced; conversational practice would have been more fruitful with a little group of pupils, and for Edward himself the competition would have been a stimulus. Though we are not told exactly how things were managed, we should probably visualize something like a small and select school, with Cheke at its head, and several other tutors and instructors in attendance, teaching groups of boys or individuals, as required. Edward perhaps got more attention than the others. But his companions, we must remember, were being educated too; and to judge from the Latin prose of the young Duke of Suffolk, when he went up to Cambridge, the tuition they received must have been as good as anything which Edward himself enjoyed.

When we come to consider the effect on Edward's mind and character of an upbringing to which so many men of high ability and high character had contributed, we are struck at once by the formidable difficulties confronting one who was at the same time a pupil and a king. Edward came to the throne when he was nine. From that moment, and increasingly so as he grew older, his life was dislocated not only by the requirements of court ceremonial and the essential

duties of a king, but by personal demands upon his time and attention. His uncle, the regent Somerset, should have given him fatherly
guidance; but he was tactless in his handling of the young King and
there was little sympathy between them. In the circumstances
Edward owed everything to the steadying influence of Cheke, who
quickly became his confidant and friend. When court ceremony
threatened to engulf him, it was Cheke who insisted that the
proper place for a boy of nine during working hours was the classroom; and when he needed advice and guidance in performing his
royal functions or facing the claims of other people, it was Cheke who
gave it. If it had not been for this kindly and understanding man
Edward would not have been half the boy he was, and might have
gone far astray in the bewildering turmoil of events around him.

This was the background of Edward's formal education; and his
achievement and that of his teachers must be judged against it. It
will have been obvious all through this account of his upbringing
that Edward's tutors and instructors were exceptionally competent.
Despite all the distractions, which must have occurred in spite of
Cheke, they were almost unbelievably successful. Certainly they
had a very able and willing pupil, which is not given to all tutors.
But without their professional skill Edward would never have been
able in the short ten years allowed him, to acquire such a command
of two ancient and at least three modern languages beside his own;
nor yet have reached that general level of knowledge and understanding which enabled him at fifteen to play his part in councils of
state and hold his own in conversation with learned men of all
nations. If Edward was remarkable, so were his teachers.

Equal care had been given to his religious education, probably in
part by the same men, and with equal success. Like all children at
that time, he was brought up to take his religion very seriously, and
it played a much bigger part in his life than the religion of any
modern child, however pious. His father, despite his own continued
adherence to a nominal Catholicism, had seen to it that his chaplains
and tutors were all of the new protestant persuasion; and Edward
grew up with a strong anti-Catholic bias, which, among other
things, caused strained relations with his Catholic half-sister, Mary.

As most people did at that time, he genuinely enjoyed sermons,
took notes of all he heard, and tried to follow the advice they gave.
His quick and sincere response on one occasion to a sermon preached
by Bishop Ridley filled the bishop with amazement and admiration

that a king so young should take his words so much to heart. He
liked too to listen to and engage in the popular game of theological
discussion; and if it was sometimes no more than a game, yet there
were times when, for example on such questions as the doctrine of
transubstantiation, he held passionately to one or other opposed
views in a way which seems to us almost inconceivable in a child. In
all this it is clear that his training had decisively moulded his
character, on lines his father would have approved.

Perhaps the greatest handicap a young king had to face in that
period was the consciousness of being different. All his life it was
constantly impressed upon Edward, sometimes in so many words,
more often by implication, that he was set apart fo fulfil, under God,
a unique function. Like that other juvenile King, James VI and I, he
believed in his divine mission at a very early age, but with this
difference—Edward, unlike the youthful James, had a strong sense
of duty, and took his responsibilities seriously. His resolve to be a
good king is evident from a document he drew up at the age of
thirteen, with the little 'Discourse about the Reformation of Many
Abuses', in which with charmingly naïve idealism he puts forward
his proposals for setting the world to rights. His more realistic, if
more cynical, advisers of course quietly suppressed it: and in this
sort of treatment lay his tragedy. Though he was conscious of being
king, and was treated like a king, with all the outward show of
deference, he neverthless felt himself frustrated, because he was
powerless to carry out his purposes, and knew that the real power
lay with the scheming politicians who surrounded him, men like his
uncles, Somerset and Seymour, or, when they had gone the way of
scheming politicians, the wily Northumberland.

In the ordinary social exchanges of court life Edward was gracefully at ease from a very early age. A great deal of time, of which we
hear nothing, must have been devoted to his training in the essential
arts of social intercourse, not merely such things as dancing and
music, but the complicated formalities of conduct, the conventions
observed at court in conversation, at meals and in receiving foreign
visitors. In the sixteenth century protocol and ceremony were
notoriously more elaborate at the English court than any other.
Edward faced it all with an aplomb, which, though the result of
careful training, seems to have come easily. He obviously enjoyed
pageantry and ceremonial, especially when he was the centre of it,
as he usually was; not surely out of mere vanity, but rather perhaps

because to ride in silver and gold at the head of a gorgeous cavalcade, or sit in state surrounded by his councillors, satisfied his
feeling of what a king should be.

But a natural reaction came when he was released from the restraints of acting the part of king in public. At the shooting butts, on
the tennis court or in the tilting yard quite a different boy was seen;
and here once more we may observe the wisdom of those who
planned the King's day. He was given plenty of time for relaxation;
with the result that, though he worked hard at his books and never
neglected his royal duties, he does not seem to have suffered from
overwork, like that other youthful sovereign, James VI and I, with
whom one cannot help comparing him.

There was a tendency in the fifteenth and sixteenth centuries to
look upon royal children as infant prodigies; the natural result
perhaps of the feeling that they were being educated to conform
with an ideal conception of the perfect prince. Almost every recorded
account of Edward is a eulogy. Foreign ambassadors noted with
admiration his grasp of affairs; foreign scholars resident in England
wrote wonderingly of his talents; while patriotic Englishmen were
inclined to become lyrical over the virtues of their youthful monarch.
Thus William Thomas, clerk of the council, a year after Edward's
accession:

'If ye knew the towardness of that young prince, your heart
would melt to hear him named, and your stomach abhor the malice
of them that would him ill: the beautifullest creature that liveth
under sun, the wittiest, the most amiable and the gentlest thing of
all the world. Such a spirit of capacity for learning the thing taught
him by his schoolmasters, that it is a wonder to hear say. And finally
he hath such a grace of port and gesture in gravity, when he cometh
into any presence, that it should seem he were already a father, and
yet passeth he not the age of ten years. A thing undoubtedly much
rather to be seen than believed.'

And Bishop Hooper, writing to the German scholar, Bullinger,
in 1550, when Edward was thirteen:

'Believe me, my much esteemed friend, you have never seen in
the world for these thousand years so much erudition united with
piety and sweetness of disposition. Should he live and grow up with
these virtues, he will be a terror to all the sovereigns of the earth.'

Eulogies such as these have their counterparts in portraiture. One
of these is the well-known painting by an artist of the school of

Holbein, which shows Edward in the character of the ideal prince – brilliant, elegant, self-confident.

The truth of course falls short of these idealized versions of the King's image. But from factual evidence alone it is clear that Edward was distinctly above the average in ability and character, to put it no higher; and, as we have already noted, his tutors had been most successful in developing his natural good qualities. No one can say what unexpected traits, what flaws perhaps, adolescence would have revealed: he was only just sixteen when he died. But the omens were favourable, and the chances were that, if Edward had lived, though he might not have been a terror to the kings of the earth, he would have been a ruler to be reckoned with in his own right.

2

Tudor Princesses

WHETHER WOMEN SHOULD BE EDUCATED OR NOT WAS A MATTER of some controversy during the sixteenth century, and not least during the reign of Elizabeth I, herself one of the best educated women in history. The dispute was a relic of the Middle Ages, when, broadly speaking, only women destined for the religious life were given a genuine education. The idea that all women of good birth (who alone were concerned in this debate) should share in the life of culture open to men was slowly reviving after a lapse of many centuries. But there must still have been some, perhaps many, who doubted the wisdom of such a course. An extreme view was that of a writer who declared that giving a woman education was like giving a madman a sword. There were others who felt, or at any rate said, that women could not be trusted with education. If they learnt foreign languages, wrote the Italian Giovanni Bruto in 1598, it would merely open the way for them to read the amorous tales of Boccaccio or the more improper works of Ovid. If they studied music, their moral characters would be corrupted, if not by the music, then by the music-master. Male tutors for girls were in any case to be avoided, lest (like Hortensio in *The Taming of the Shrew*) they should turn out to be lovers in disguise. The safest plan in the circumstances, it seemed, was to train women only for housework.

Despite the hazards implied in these cynical views, a great many girls of high birth or liberal-minded parentage were being educated in much the same way as men, wherever the breath of the Renaissance was felt throughout Europe. This applied no less to England. English educational writers took a sane and tolerant view of the problem. Richard Mulcaster, a contemporary of Bruto, whose opinions on all educational questions were liberal and advanced, wrote strongly in favour of educating girls. A considerable number of the most enlightened parents had long been of the same opinion, and there were many families where the girls spoke several languages and could hold their own intellectually with men. Instances are often quoted. An early and celebrated example is that of the family of Sir Thomas More, whose three charming blue-stocking daughters, with their kinswoman, Margaret Giggs, who lived with the family, are brought vividly to life in their father's correspondence, and so impressed Erasmus that he likened the household to the Academy of Plato. But these girls were far from unique, even in the early decades of the century.

Henry VIII, who was well aware that many of the daughters of contemporary rulers, not to mention the aristocracy, throughout Europe were being educated in much the same way as their sons, probably had no second thoughts, when the time came, about giving his daughters, Mary and Elizabeth, a full academic education. If he was aware of arguments against the education of women, he ignored them. There was of course already a tradition of feminine learning in the English royal house, going back three generations to Henry's grandmother, Margaret Beaufort. But even if there had not been, the rising fashion of the day would have ensured that the two princesses should not only be taught such graceful accomplishments as music and dancing, but should learn Greek and Latin, as their half-brother Edward later did, and be equipped with the full array of modern languages then current in the courts of Europe.

In one respect Edward's education went further than theirs. For whatever reason, whether because they were girls, or because he did not really anticipate that they would ever succeed to the throne, Henry did not apparently have his daughters instructed, as Edward was, in modern history or political theory and statecraft. When the time came, they had to pick up what they needed for themselves; and Elizabeth at least did not need much prompting.

Henry's first wife was as committed to the education of girls as her husband. Catherine of Aragon had been born and reared in one of the most brilliant and enlightened of European courts, where the cultural equality of men and women was normal. In Spain at this time there were women who were great patrons of learning; others who rivalled men in literature; and even women professors in two of the Spanish universities, of Latin at Salamanca and of History at Alcala, a phenomenon scarcely heard of again until our own time. No queen with such a background could have contemplated anything less than the full Renaissance education for her own daughter.

Catherine herself had been solidly grounded in humanistic learning, though, like Henry, she had no Greek. Her education had been supervised by her mother, the strong-minded Isabella, who brought foreign scholars to Spain to teach her. There were no concessions to feminine weakness. She began Latin as an infant, and in due course added French, English and Flemish to her repertoire of languages. In theology likewise she was well and thoroughly instructed, and throughout her life was noted for her piety. Erasmus himself, whose opinions on his contemporaries have so often been preserved, thought her exceptional, and said that she was educated in the humanities beyond the point of being merely 'a miracle of her sex'. Her other virtues were as solid as her learning; she was strong, sober and, as events proved, courageous.

When Mary was born in 1516, there was no hesitation about what should be done: the Queen took charge, and sent immediately to Spain for guidance. The most noted Spanish educationist, a man with a European reputation, best known today under the Latinized form of his name as Ludovicus Vives, was deputed to advise her.

Perhaps with an eye to some such preferment, Vives had dedicated his commentary on St. Augustine's *De Civitate Dei* to Henry. Henry responded by inviting him to England, and he took up residence in 1522 at the newly founded Corpus Christi College, Oxford, one of the first of the many great scholars that small foundation has nurtured; here he was admitted to the degree of D.C.L., and lectured on philosophy. It is said that his honeyed eloquence caused bees to hive in the roof of the college, as they had swarmed on the lips of Pindar. But a good part of his time must have been given to completing the task for which he had come to England. In the next few years he produced two works on the education of women, and a manual for the personal use of the Princess Mary, all written, we must presume, at Catherine's bidding.

His treatise on *The Instruction of a Christian Woman*, intended for mother rather than daughter, came out in a Latin edition in 1523 and was dedicated to Catherine. Of the three parts, dealing respectively with the unmarried woman, the wife and the widow, only the first has anything to say about the immediate problem which confronted the Queen.

Somewhat unexpectedly Vives recommends a régime of almost Puritan austerity. The properly brought up young girl, he says, must eschew worldly pleasures. For her there can be none of those things which delight the female heart. Nice clothes (and especially low-necked dresses), make-up, jewellery, scent, tasty foods, wine, dice, cards, modern dancing – all are banned, with the sole concession that she may drink ale or beer instead of water, if she pleases. Even sleep, laughter and talk must be restrained, and especially the last two in the presence of young men. As a further precaution, when she goes out, a young girl must be veiled, she must walk neither too fast nor too slow, and of course avoid the eyes of the young men. In fact it is better that she should spend most of her time at home, working or reading good books, in the company of her mother or a trustworthy chaperone, or with selected companions of her own age.

If this appears reactionary, we must remember that it was not long since the sole aim of woman's education had been the religious life, and monastic ideals were slow to fade. In practice young girls may have been brought up strictly, as Catherine herself was; but loving parents generally made sure that severity should be tempered with affection. This happened in Mary's case. Though Catherine may have accepted Vives's thesis as theoretically orthodox, she rejected his harsher recommendations for her own daughter; in which she was doubtless backed by Henry, who in these early days had not yet abandoned the rôle of indulgent parent. Mary was brought up strictly but lovingly under the eye of her mother, whose own high principles and strong religious faith she unconsciously absorbed in early youth. In these lay the source of the strength with which in years to come, though still only a child, she resisted her father's attempts to push her into the background in favour of a male heir yet unborn; here also were to be found the seeds of that bigoted and misguided obstinacy, with which she stuck to her principles as queen. In happier circumstances these qualities might have matured to form a more balanced character of noble strength and independence.

In view of his general attitude it is a little surprising to find that Vives comes out strongly in favour of giving a full academic education to women of ability; but any other opinion would have been difficult to sustain in contemporary Spain. He supports it with the argument that history has proved that learned women are invariably virtuous, in proof of which doubtful proposition he quotes many instances. Nevertheless he is conscious of the risk of a possible Hortensio, and recommends that girls should be taught by women, or, if none is available, by elderly or staid married men.

His advice on reading could offend no one. Young girls, he says, should not be allowed to read books on war, extravagant romances or vicious and lascivious tales (of which he lists a selection, none of them in English): in place of these let them study the scriptures, the Christian fathers, Plato, Cicero and Seneca, to which in another work he adds a somewhat curious selection of verse—Lucan (but why not Vergil?), Seneca's tragedies (but no Greek drama) and some Horace, together with various Christian Latin poets now largely forgotten. The emphasis is strongly on Latin. Unless we are to assume the inclusion of the Greek testament, or some of the Christian fathers who wrote in Greek, the only Greek author mentioned is Plato. This probably represents orthodox opinion as to the relative importance of Latin and Greek at the time when Vives wrote. Mary was born too soon in fact to feel the effects of the swing towards Greek even then gathering force in England among the younger scholars at Cambridge,[1] of which Elizabeth and Edward, as yet unborn, were to gain the full benefit.

But the reading list probably suited Mary's taste very well. Frivolous romances, which were popular at the time, had little appeal for this serious-minded girl; and when in later years she could not sleep for anxiety and took to reading in bed, we may be sure she turned to classical Latin authors and devotional works, as recommended by Vives.

In the same year as his exhaustive treatise on a woman's whole duty Vives published a guide to the teaching of Latin, spoken and written, called *A Plan of Study for Girls*, also dedicated to Catherine. The author describes this as no more than an outline, to be elaborated by Mary's tutor, to whom he refers, though not by name, in complimentary terms. But in fact it contains a great deal of wise advice and many practical suggestions, most of them still relevant today. There is nothing about it peculiarly applicable to girls, except that more stress is laid on devotional reading than in the companion volume for boys, which Vives also wrote.

For Mary herself Vives next produced a little tract of moral guidance, which he called *Satellitium—Bodyguard*; a collection of 239 wise saws and modern instances in Latin, none of them more than five words long, and each accompanied by a brief commentary,

---

[1] As well as at Vives's own college of Corpus Christi, Oxford, founded in 1516, the first Oxford college to give full weight to Greek.

a sort of thumbnail sermon. This was very much in accordance with current tastes, and must have pleased the little Princess, who was about nine years old when the work was presented to her in 1524. In his dedication Vives explains that the maxims and mottoes in the collection will stand as bodyguard to Mary's soul, and he advises her to make sure they are always about her. We may be certain she took his advice seriously – her mother would have seen to that; and some of these tags of wisdom must have stuck in her mind for life, gathering new meaning from her unhappy experiences. Here are a few of them: 'War upon vice', 'No complaints' (the motto of Vives himself), 'It is not how long, but how well we live that matters', 'Nobility lies not in birth but in virtue', 'The more fortune smiles, the less she is to be trusted'. More than twenty years later the young King Edward, himself nine years of age, was using Mary's *Satellitium*.

Meanwhile one of Henry's most eminent subjects, the learned Thomas Linacre, who had been tutor to the King's elder brother, Arthur, and now held the office of royal physician, was bringing out a specially revised English edition of his well-known Latin grammar for Mary's use, under the title *Rudimenta Grammatices*. This was a graceful compliment from a great scholar, who had been closely connected with the royal family for a long time. Linacre was now an old man, and rich in distinctions. After a brilliant career at Oxford, where he was elected a Fellow of All Souls, and at Padua, where he took his doctorate in medicine, he had been one of the pioneers of the new learning in this country. His own versatility gives him some claim to be regarded as an example of the 'universal man' so much admired in Renaissance Italy. He was a first-class Greek scholar, whose fame as a teacher in earlier days attracted pupils of the calibre of Erasmus (only six years his junior) and Thomas More. At the same time, as founder of the Royal College of Physicians he is remembered as one of the great names in English medical history. It is not likely that he actually taught the Princess Mary; but in dedicating his grammar to her, while apologizing for not being able to attend her as physician owing to his own infirmity and advancing years, he expresses the hope of making some contribution to the enrichment of her mind. Mary's own copy of the grammar is still to be seen at the British Museum, and there is every reason to suppose that she used it.

The Princess's formal education began at what was then the normal age of four. Even before that she had learnt to play the virginals; and on one occasion, deputizing for her parents, who were absent at the summit conference known as the Field of the Cloth of Gold, she entertained three noble French visitors with a performance on that instrument, at which they marvelled greatly. Her own mother, helped perhaps by Vives's *Plan of Study* and Linacre's grammar, gave her a solid grounding in Latin. But it soon became necessary to appoint a full-time tutor and other instructors to cover all the subjects with which the heir to the throne must be acquainted. One might have supposed that Vives would have been the obvious choice for the office of principal tutor. But probably his being Spanish debarred him from such a post in England; and in any case he may not have wanted it, for it would have been no sinecure. Instead the post went to a relatively obscure Englishman, Richard Fetherstone, chaplain to the Queen, and of course a Catholic. This must have been the man to whose competence Vives paid tribute in the introduction to his *Plan of Study*. He seems to have been undistinguished as a scholar; but events proved him a good and faithful teacher, and in the end revealed that he had the strength of character to die for his principles.

It became customary about this time for royal children to be placed in infancy under the care of a sort of guardian, known as a governor or governess, according to sex. The feminine word at any rate has slipped downhill semantically over the centuries. For originally these were men and women of noble birth: and the office was an honourable and perhaps honorary one. They were chosen for their personal good qualities; and among other things were required to teach manners and deportment, to supervise instruction in social accomplishments like dancing and horsemanship, and in general to relieve royal parents of the burden of training their own children. As soon as the royal infant was considered old enough to have a separate household, which was often at a very early age, the governor or governess took charge of its management.

Mary's first governess was Lady Margaret Bryan, a kindly and conscientious woman. After a short interval she was replaced by Margaret, Countess of Salisbury, a lady of considerably higher rank. This was evidently no reflection on Lady Bryan, for years later she became governess in succession to both Henry's other children. But Lady Salisbury was unquestionably a woman of far greater distinction, who must have done much to fortify the young Princess's character as well as school her conduct. Her quality may be judged from the way in which, many years later as an old woman, she faced the executioner without flinching.

Mary's French tutor was Giles d'Ewés, who had taught her father and grown old in the royal service; a man of some wit and humour, who, when gout prevented him from attending the Princess, sent her 'an epitaph on the death of French'. He too wrote a manual specially for his royal pupil, called 'Introductory for to learn to read, pronounce and to speak French truly', containing dialogues in which real people featured, including Mary herself. There must have been other language teachers, for she learnt some Italian; and as a Spanish princess's daughter naturally possessed a good knowledge of Spanish, much of it perhaps picked up from her mother, which must have eased a situation difficult enough for other reasons when later she came to marry a Spanish King.

She had the Tudor talent for music, performed elegantly on the fashionable lute and virginals while still only a child, and learnt also to play the small portable organ called a regal. This last was surely at the instigation of the King, who must have enjoyed seeing his own virtuosity as an organist reproduced in his daughter. Though Mary had her own teachers for these instruments – a certain Giles, for example, was her lutanist at this time at a salary of 40s. a month – there is no doubt she must have been helped and encouraged a good deal by her musical father, who took pride in her skill and liked to display it to visitors.

Little is known of the details of Mary's education; nothing of her daily round at this time. She was an able and industrious pupil, though not as brilliant as Elizabeth, and needed little persuasion to work hard at her lessons. One can imagine her, with Fetherstone at her side, conscientiously following the very down-to-earth and practical hints for learning Latin, which Vives sets out in his *Plan of Study* – to learn something by heart every day, to go over it last thing at night and try to recall it early in the morning; to have her dictionary constantly at hand; to make full use of her notebook; to lose no chance of talking Latin; and many more, including one unexpected but useful tip, which must have shocked Ascham the calligraphist, when he came to read Vives – to write for speed, not elegance.

As Princess of Wales and heir to the throne Mary was given a separate establishment and council of advisers when she was no more than nine, and took up residence on the Welsh border at

3   JAMES I, aged 7, in 1574: by an unknown artist

4 HENRY, PRINCE OF WALES: from a miniature by Isaac Oliver

Ludlow Castle. There was little break in the routine of her life. Lady Salisbury remained in charge of the domestic arrangements. Richard Fetherstone continued to supervise the Princess's education. A directive, in which the hand of Henry may be recognized, especially in its emphasis on hygiene, was issued for the guidance of Mary's governess and councillors, who were instructed to have 'most tender regard to all such things as concern the person of the said Princess, her honourable education and training in all virtuous demeanour. That is to say, at due times to serve God from whom all grace and goodness proceedeth. Semblably, at seasons convenient, to use moderate exercise for taking open air in gardens, sweet and wholesome places and walks . . . And likewise to pass her time, most seasons, at her virginals or other instruments musical, so that the same be not too much, and without fatigation and weariness, to intend to her learning of Latin tongue and French; at other seasons to dance, and amongst the residue to have good respect unto her diet, which is mete to be pure, well prepared, dressed and served with comfortable, joyous and merry communication . . . likewise unto the cleanliness and well wearing of her garments and apparel both of her chambers and body, so that everything about her be pure, sweet, clean and wholesome, and as to so great a Princess doth appertain; all corruptions, evil airs and things noisome and displeasant to be foreborne and eschewed.'

It would be interesting to know what Vives thought of this rejection of the Spartan régime he recommended.

A letter addressed to Mary by her mother surviving from about this time draws the curtain aside for a moment on a human situation. The Queen had evidently been giving writing, as well as Latin, lessons to her daughter, and is sad at the prospect of handing her over completely to Fetherstone.

'As for your writing, I am glad ye shall change from me to Master Fetherstone, for that shall do you much good to learn by him to write right, but yet sometimes I would be glad when ye do write to Master Fetherstone, of your own inditing, when he hath read it, that I may see it, for it shall be great comfort to me to see you keep your Latin and fair writing and all.'

She was now old enough to play the part of princess gracefully; and like most royal children in that century she was regarded as something of an infant prodigy. To some commercial envoys from Flanders, who addressed a complimentary speech to her in Latin,

D   49

when she was nine, she replied elegantly in the same language 'with as much assurance and facility as if she had been twelve years old' (which incidentally throws light on what might be expected of twelve-year-olds at that time). A little later, when negotiations were going on with a view to her possible marriage to the French King, Henry, who was well aware of the impression she would create, presented the French envoys to her in person, and allowed them to put her through her paces. They tried talking to her in French, Italian and Latin, and were amazed to find that she was at home in all three, undisturbed apparently, though we are not told so, by the notorious difference of pronunciation between English Latin and continental Latin; after which she entertained them on the virginals. One of them said afterwards that he thought she was the most accomplished child he had ever met – the stock response to displays of royal precocity.

More concrete proof of Mary's genuine ability survives in the translation of a prayer of St. Thomas Aquinas, which she made at the age of eleven, and which reveals an unusual command of both Latin and English. Lord Morley, who had himself translated some of the writings of St. Thomas, spoke very highly of it in dedicating one of his works to Mary:

'. . . You were so ripe in the Latin tongue,' he wrote, 'that rarely doth happen to the woman sex, that your Grace not only could perfectly read, write and construe Latin, but furthermore translate any hard thing of the Latin into our English tongue, and among all other your most virtuous occupations, I have seen one prayer translated of your doing of St. Thomas Aquinas that I do assure your Grace is so well done, so near to the Latin, that when I look upon it . . . I have . . . marvel at the doing of it!'

and indeed it has a feeling for words and phrasing unusual in the work of a child.

It must have been about this time that Mary (and her mother) went out of favour with the King, with whom the need for a male heir outweighed all other considerations, and the clever little girl, once her father's pet, found herself branded as illegitimate and thrust into the background. She was cut off from her mother; her household was reduced; and though her education continued after a fashion, her father was no longer interested. For a time Richard Fetherstone retained his post; and Lady Salisbury, of her own accord, stood firmly by the Princess in her misfortune. These two, the humble tutor and the aristocratic lady governess, were alike in their disapproval of the King's matrimonial manœuvres at this time and in the future, and both in the end paid for it with their lives.

The staunchness with which Mary herself faced this persecution, though separated from her mother, she owed very largely to her early training and the strong religious faith it had given her. She was fortified also by reading, to which more and more she had recourse as she grew older. Antoine Crispin, a Frenchman living in England, noted her studious habits as a young woman of twenty in 1536, the year of her mother's death and her own final submission to the King. At that time her day was roughly divided into three; the first part given to the scriptures; the second to the study of languages, ancient and modern, including Greek, or to natural philosophy and mathematics; the third to music. We know that she still had her own music teachers at this time, Mr. Paston for the virginals, Philip van Wilder (who was also Edward's teacher) for the lute; gifts to these two are recorded in her account-books, as well as frequent items for the tuning and repair of instruments. But she seems to have had no tutor; and we have to imagine her deep in her solitary reading, helped at times perhaps by her chaplain. It remained a consolation to her for the rest of her life.

Vives, who was still in England, stood loyally by Catherine and Mary in their misfortune, and as a good Spaniard openly criticized Henry's treatment of his patroness and her daughter. This naturally aroused the displeasure of the King, who put him under house arrest; but, as a foreigner, he was shortly allowed, or perhaps encouraged, to leave the country, and so passed from the English scene. His influence remained, strongly but incalculably, with Mary, and over a wide field through his educational works, which were read and imitated. One of them even enjoyed a brief revival in modern times, when a volume of dialogues illustrating school life, first published in 1529, was reissued almost exactly 400 years later as one of a series of texts for the teaching of Latin by the conversational method which Vives himself had used.[1]

The King had now remarried; and his second daughter was born in 1533. Elizabeth's brilliance of intellect is well known: it was, as her tutor thought, a masculine intelligence. Along with her red-

[1] In the Lingua Latina series, 1931, edited by the late Dr. W. H. D. Rouse, headmaster of the Perse School, Cambridge, who revived the old method of learning Greek and Latin through conversation, known today as the Direct method.

gold Tudor hair, it was perhaps the most striking of the gifts she inherited from her father. Certainly none of it came from her mother, who was cunning rather than able. With it went an insatiable capacity for hard work and an excellent memory. The combination of the three could have led to real distinction in classical scholarship; but from that Elizabeth was barred, both by convention as a woman, and by her own circumstances as third in succession for the throne.

She was fortunate that her childhood and early adolescence passed in comparative tranquillity, with none of the emotional stresses and strains to which Mary had been exposed from the age of nine. Her mother's execution, which took place when she was not yet three, can scarcely have affected her, if she knew of it at all. She enjoyed her father's favour; and her early upbringing by the same Lady Bryan who had been Mary's governess gave her a background of happy security. Later her stepmother, Queen Catherine Parr, looked after her with as much care and affection as if she had been her own daughter. It was not till Mary came to the throne, when Elizabeth was twenty, that as a possible rival she first faced danger, uncertainty and imprisonment.

Nothing seems to be known, curiously enough, of Elizabeth's early education. She must certainly have been well grounded in Latin as an infant; throughout life her command of the language was exceptional for a woman. At ten she was learning French and Italian, the latter taught by Giovanni Battista Castiglione, who spent a period in the Tower on a charge of sedition under Mary, and was later rewarded for his services to Elizabeth by appointment as a gentleman of her privy chamber. Her earliest surviving letter is one written in Italian to Queen Catherine Parr, when she was eleven. The same year she made a translation from French of Margaret of Navarre's poem *The Mirror of a Sinful Soul*, which, with a painstakingly composed introduction, she presented to her stepmother in an embroidered cover she had worked herself. This may seem strong meat for a little girl; but children in that age were not kept so much in isolation from serious things as they are today.

At this stage Elizabeth was being taught by Edward's tutor, John Cheke, though the gap of four years between the two children makes it unlikely that they were taught together. In 1544 she was given her own tutor. The choice fell on a young Cambridge man named William Grindal (probably of Cumbrian stock, like the future archbishop, Edmund Grindal), who seems to have combined charm of manner with high standards of scholarship and in particular a fine command of Greek. In the eighteen or twenty years which had passed since Mary began her classical studies, the lead in English scholarship had for the time being passed from Oxford to Cambridge, where Edward's tutor Cheke, Regius Professor of Greek and a leader of protestant opinion, reigned supreme among the younger scholars. Grindal was the favourite pupil of Roger Ascham, one of the most brilliant of this group (later famous as author of *The Schoolmaster*), with whom he worked for seven years, perfecting his scholarship and nursing a vocation for teaching. It was probably Ascham who recommended Grindal for the royal service. His charm and enthusiasm soon won the co-operation of Elizabeth, who made rapid progress. Watching the two at work together, Ascham remarked that he did not know which to admire most, the ability of the pupil or the diligence of the tutor. Unhappily Grindal died of the plague in 1548; but in the four years at his disposal he had carried his pupil far and deep into the world of classical learning, where he was so much at home himself. Elizabeth was already showing herself so devoted a scholar that she was coming to be thought of as almost unnaturally learned for her age.

During Grindal's tutorship the Princess had become friendly with Ascham, who was also Edward's writing master and probably often to be seen at court and in the household of Catherine Parr, and had started a correspondence with him in Latin. When Grindal died she asked specially that Ascham might succeed him. Queen Catherine Parr had other ideas; but she gave way to the Princess, and Ascham was appointed. Like his pupil Grindal, he was a man of attractive character and a very able scholar, a humanist who at the same time rejected the influence of Italy. He had gone up to St. John's, Cambridge, at fifteen (quite a normal age in the sixteenth century), and was elected in due course to a fellowship. Versatile like most of his contemporaries, he lectured on mathematics as well as classics, cultivated a talent for music, and won a reputation for the beauty of his handwriting, which, as we have already noted, led to his becoming the writing master of both Edward and Elizabeth. With all this he combined an interest in archery, a subject of serious national importance at that time, on which he wrote a book called *Toxophilus* –'English matter in the English tongue for English men,' as he says –and a more frivolous liking for dice-play and for cock-fighting, on which he planned a book that was never written. It was perhaps due to these last two addictions that he was always notoriously in financial difficulties. His weaknesses, such as they were, proved no bar to preferment in the royal service, in which he continued, off and on, for life. He was more successful than his master Cheke in adapting his religious beliefs to circumstances – or perhaps not important enough for his opinions to matter – and, despite the Protestantism which he had professed at Cambridge, even became Latin secretary to Mary, a post which he retained under his pupil, her successor.

It must have been agreeable work for him teaching a pupil so intelligent, so eager and so well grounded as Elizabeth. Some years later, when Elizabeth was queen, Ascham gave thanks to God for his good fortune in having had a share in the education of so able and learned a monarch. That this was what Ascham really felt, and not mere courtier's language (such as might have come naturally from a man who depended on patronage for his living), we may guess from a letter which he wrote to his friend, Sturm, when Elizabeth was just sixteen:

'It is difficult to say whether the gifts of nature or of fortune are most to be admired in my distinguished mistress. The praise which Aristotle gives, wholly centres in her; beauty, stature, prudence, and industry. She has just passed her sixteenth birthday and shows such dignity and gentleness as are wonderful at her age and in her rank. Her study of true religion and learning is most eager. Her mind has no womanly weakness, her perseverance is equal to that of a man, and her memory long keeps what it quickly picks up. She talks French and Italian as well as she does English, and has often talked to me readily and well in Latin, moderately in Greek. When she writes Greek and Latin, nothing is more beautiful than her handwriting. She delights as much in music as she is skilful in it. In adornment she is elegant rather than showy . . . I am inventing nothing, my dear Sturm; there is not need.'

Perhaps allowance must be made even here for a tutor's pardonable enthusiasm over a royal, and, one must add, a feminine pupil. But Ascham's opinion was shared by others who knew or met Elizabeth. Bishop John Hooper, whose eulogy of Edward has been quoted, for example, wrote in 1549 as flatteringly as Ascham himself of her remarkable command of Greek and Latin, and the facility with which she was able to defend the true religion in argument against all comers.

Ascham's book, *The Schoolmaster*, for which he is best known, was written some years later, and not published till after his death. In it he describes how it arose from an after-dinner argument in 1563, while he was dining at Windsor, where the court had gone because of the plague, with Sir William Cecil, Secretary of State, and others of the Queen's ministers. Some boys had recently run away from school at Eton for fear of a flogging, and the discussion turned on the value of corporal punishment. Ascham, who was strongly against it, and believed in gentle methods, was urged to set forth his theories in a book, and agreed to do so.

He himself was educated in a nobleman's household, and had probably never been to school. Nor was he acquainted with the harsh realities of teaching in school–his experience had been exclusively with university students or private pupils, who (like Elizabeth herself or William Grindal) were much above the common average. *The Schoolmaster* in consequence looks at education mainly through the eyes of the tutor rather than the class teacher. But there is a warm humanity about the book, and an insistence on the delights of learning and true scholarship, which make it much more than a mere treatise on the art of private tuition, or a diatribe against punishment; and it is for this that the book has always been admired, and is still valued today.

As a teacher Ascham modelled himself on Cheke, and his methods were persuasive and enticing. But, like all teachers, he naturally had his technical tricks. In his classical teaching he made much use of what is called double translation, by which the pupil was required first to translate a Greek or Latin author into English, then back again into the original tongue. There must have been a good deal of drudgery in this; but for an eager pupil like the Princess Elizabeth, who did not mind hard work and could concentrate for long periods, it was obviously effective.

As Ascham's pupil, Elizabeth spent her mornings at Greek, reading first from the Greek testament, then from some classical author, such as Isocrates, Demosthenes or Sophocles, who seem to have been Ascham's favourites. In the afternoons she worked at Latin, and in due course read with Ascham almost all Cicero and a great part of Livy; a formidable achievement indeed, but matched by that of other royal pupils in the same century. There was even time to read some theology in Latin to supplement the Greek testament, for example St. Cyprian among the early fathers and Melanchthon representing the moderns. Meanwhile Elizabeth of course kept up her French and Italian, and later added Spanish and even a little German. Apart from Castiglione for Italian, the names of her tutors seem to be unrecorded.

Ascham himself refers to her delight in music, for which she certainly had the Tudor talent. Like all her family, she became more than ordinarily proficient with lute and virginals, and as queen was adept at using music to supplement the arts of diplomacy. She was also an enthusiastic and by all accounts a most beautiful dancer, who nearly sixty years later was still dancing, and still charming those who watched.

After only a year – a year of political anxiety for Elizabeth, who was suspected of complicity in the intrigues of the Lord Admiral Seymour – Ascham had an unfortunate quarrel with members of her household, and resigned his post as tutor. He may even have been estranged from the Princess herself; but, if so, it did not last long. She continued to regard him as her director of studies. In 1555, when she was twenty-two, and beyond the normal age of dependence on tutors, she resumed her Greek reading with him for the sheer delight of studying in his company. Even as queen, when Ascham's official status was that of Latin secretary, she continued this practice; and in 1562 was reading Greek with him after dinner every day, as a relaxation from the cares of government. Was it altogether a coincidence that, at a time when Elizabeth's mind was somewhat preoccupied with Philip of Spain, the authors chosen should be Demosthenes and Aeschines, no less preoccupied themselves with Philip of Macedon?

Ascham remained immensely proud of his royal pupil, and in *The Schoolmaster* holds her up as an example to the 'young gentlemen of England'.

'It is your shame,' he writes, 'that one maid should go beyond you all in excellency of learning and knowledge of divers tongues. Point forth six of the best given gentlemen of this Court, and all they together shew not so much good will, spend not so much time, bestow not so many hours, daily, orderly and constantly, for the increase of learning and knowledge, as do the Queen's Majesty herself. Yea, I believe that beside her perfect readiness in Latin, Italian, French and Spanish, she readeth here now at Windsor more Greek every day than some Prebendary of this Church doth read Latin in a whole week. And that which is most praiseworthy of all, within the walls of her privy chamber she hath obtained that excellency of learning, to understand, speak and write, both wittily with the head and fair with the hand, as scarce one or two rare wits in both the Universities have in many years reached unto.'

The end to this almost ideal partnership came prematurely and tragically. In 1568, sitting up all night to write a New Year poem for the Queen, Ascham, now fifty-three and in chronically poor health, caught a chill which proved fatal. On hearing the news, Elizabeth cried out that she would rather have cast £10,000 into the sea than lose her Ascham.

She remained a lover of learning for life, her interest fresh and lively to the end. In 1601, two years before her death, on receiving an account of the records in the Tower from the Keeper, who was the antiquary William Lambarde, she read the work carefully, and asked many questions, remarking that

'she would be a scholar in her age, and thought it no scorn to learn during her life, being of the mind of that philosopher, who in his last years began with the Greek alphabet.'

How easy it would have been for a monarch to accept such a gift with a few smooth compliments and a perfunctory glance.

That Elizabeth understood the value of learning for others also is shown by her patronage of education. Most of the so-called Queen Elizabeth's Grammar Schools dating from her reign owed their existence not so much to the Queen's own action, though of course she approved, as to the general tenor of the age, which induced wealthy men to come forward as founders or benefactors. But Westminster was the Queen's own creation.[1] This school she cherished with loving care; and among other things she was responsible for the inauguration of the Westminster Latin play, which has been performed annually with scarcely a break for over 400 years, and still preserves in its pronunciation the barbaric Latin accent of Elizabethan England, which foreigners (including Scotsmen) found so deplorable.

In practical terms the Queen's proficiency as a linguist proved immensely useful to her, for she was always able to converse direct with foreign envoys, who of course had no English, in one or other of the languages at her command. It was important for a ruler who meant to rule not to have to rely on intermediaries, and Elizabeth's position was greatly strengthened by the fact that she never needed to do so.

[1] It is interesting to note that Ascham sent his son to Westminster.

One of the numerous anecdotes about Elizabeth tells how in 1597, when a Polish envoy was reading aloud to the Queen a somewhat arrogant letter from the King of Poland, which was of course in Latin, Elizabeth suddenly leapt to her feet, and reprimanded the man for his insolence with the utmost fluency in the same language, to the delight of the listening court. Ascham himself records how on one occasion she replied successively with extempore speeches in Italian, French and Latin to the addresses of three ambassadors delivered to her in those languages.

It was well known too how at the universities of Oxford and Cambridge, and at the public schools she visited, especially Westminster, she particularly enjoyed the ceremonies conducted in Latin and the plays staged for her amusement in that language, and was quick to reply in the same tongue to addresses of welcome. These displays of learning in a woman made a great impression, and helped to build up the mystique of the nonpareille queen, the '*unica phoenix*' of Elizabeth's own motto.

But in speaking of the Queen's facility in foreign tongues we must not forget that she was a mistress of her own tongue, that idiom which we very aptly call Elizabethan English. To modern tastes her prose style, like that of most Elizabethan prose writers, seems mannered and obscure. It was admired at the time of course, for the fashion of the day favoured an artificial and involved manner of expression. Ascham himself praises Elizabeth's 'modest metaphors and comparisons of contraries well put together and contrasting felicitously with one another'. But taste in these matters has moved far. It is otherwise with the spoken word, in its most direct form. What Elizabeth said, to her parliament or her people, still has the power, even on the printed page, to rouse men's feelings, as it moved the hearts of her listeners 400 years ago. That proud speech she made to the army at Tilbury, when a Spanish invasion was expected, has a Churchillian ring. Here is just one sentence:

'I know I have the body of a weak and feeble woman, but I have the heart and stomach of a king, and of a king of England too, and think foul scorn that Parma or Spain, or any prince of Europe should dare to invade the borders of my realm.'

There was the famous Golden Speech too, which she made to the House of Commons only a year or two before she died. Again a sentence will show how precisely she knew what to say and how to say it:

'What you do bestow on me, I will not hoard up, but receive it to bestow on you again; yea, my own properties I account yours, to be expended for your good, and your eyes shall see the bestowing of it for your welfare.'

This command of the spoken tongue was in part a family trait; in part an expression of character, like the English of Churchill himself, or of Queen Victoria, neither of whom owed anything directly to Cicero or Demosthenes; but in part also it came from her early and long familiarity with the language and rhythms of the Greek and Roman orators, which she had absorbed in reading with William Grindal and Roger Ascham.

Even more intellectually brilliant than Elizabeth was the nine-days Queen, Lady Jane Grey. It is difficult to get a clear picture of this unusual girl. The dramatic circumstances of her brief, unwilling reign and her execution have distorted the image. She was not the paragon some of her admirers, writing centuries after her death, have supposed, though her steadfast faith and her strength of character must be given full weight. But there can be no doubt of her outstanding ability; of that there is ample contemporary evidence. No other woman of the blood royal in English history, except only Elizabeth, can be compared with her. Ascham, who was in a better position than anyone else to know, thought her superior to Elizabeth, and only equalled among contemporaries by one of the daughters of Edward's tutor, Sir Anthony Cooke, who afterwards married Sir William Cecil, later Lord Burleigh, Elizabeth's Secretary of State.

Lady Jane was born in 1537 (the same year as Edward VI), eldest daughter of Lord and Lady Dorset, created Duke and Duchess of Suffolk in 1551 when the original title became extinct with the death of the Duke who was Edward's fellow pupil. Her mother was a grand-daughter of Henry VII, whom she thus shared as a common ancestor with the three children of Henry VIII. Neither of her parents was of more than average ability, and neither had much interest in learning or scholarship. Jane was in fact something of a misfit in her own family, and, though the social circumstances were of course totally different, reminds one at times of those brilliant working-class boys sometimes thrown up by the educational system of today, who move on a different intellectual plane from their own parents. Like some of these boys, Jane found relief from the lack of interest and understanding shown by her parents in a world of reading and in friendship with her teachers;

and, as parents sometimes do when this happens today, hers resented it and took it out of her. Yet, though her mother lacked intellectual gifts of her own, it must have been through her that Jane inherited them from the same source as the three royal children and the King himself. Ability in this case had leapt a generation or two.

Though Jane's parents showed little affection and treated her badly, they went to considerable expense and trouble to give her what was literally an education fit for a queen. Ranking next after the three royal children and her own mother, Jane was fifth in line of succession for the throne; and her parents, from purely selfish motives, were determined that one day she should reach it, either – what seemed a rather remote possibility – in her own right, or, as they secretly hoped, by marriage with Edward. This is not the place to unfold the sordid web of intrigue which was woven around Jane during the next fifteen years. Let us only remember that for a brief spell the plot succeeded, at the cost to the duke of his own life as well as his daughter's.

For Jane in early childhood it meant first-class tutors and a life given up almost entirely to learning and devotional exercises, in which worldly pleasures played little part. It suited her admirably. She was happy in her work, and there was discord only when her parents intervened.

Her first years were passed in seclusion on the Dorsets' estate of Bradgate in Leicestershire, where we may presume she worked to a daily routine with her tutors. As an infant she was already learning a formidable battery of languages – Latin, Greek, Spanish, Italian and French, all of which were introduced to her by the time she was six. This was a much heavier concentration than Mary, Elizabeth or Edward had to face. It would be interesting to know whether in these early stages she got them confused, as infant linguists sometimes do, and whether she replied in one language to questions in another, or conversed bilingually without being aware of it.

Jane's first tutor was Thomas Harding, a Devonian and a Wykehamist, later professor of Hebrew at Oxford, a considerable linguist himself, if he taught all these languages, as he probably did, conversationally. It may seem surprising that he did not teach her Hebrew also; but perhaps it was not thought to be among the essentials for a ruler, though it was now being taught in some English schools. When later she realized its importance for biblical studies, Jane learnt it for herself, together with some Arabic and the variety of Aramaic at that time called Chaldee.

Harding was shortly succeeded by John Aylmer, a remarkable man in his way, like many of the royal tutors of that age, who remained with Jane almost to the end. He was a member of an old East Anglian family in somewhat straitened circumstances, who would have missed a university education had not Dorset come to hear of his youthful talent, and sent him to Cambridge at his own expense. There he joined the protestant or reformist group headed by John Cheke, and in due course took holy orders and became a fellow of Queen's. He ended his career in the Church, after a period of exile during the reign of Mary, as Bishop of London under Elizabeth. But though he had been a gentle and kindly man in his youth—we have Jane's word for it— he became a harsh and uncompromising one in his age, and was noted for his severity towards his religious opponents. With Aylmer was associated another Cambridge man, James Haddon, the Duke's chaplain, a fellow of Trinity College, who also suffered exile for his religion.

All these three were strong in the protestant faith, to which the Duke and Duchess adhered, and must have been largely responsible for moulding Jane's religious beliefs to the same pattern. But Jane soon left them all behind in the fervour of her devotion and in her antagonism to Catholicism; and when one of them, Thomas Harding, whether from conviction or for reasons of expediency, abandoned his Protestantism on the accession of Mary, he was scathingly denounced for cowardice and treachery by his former pupil, sixteen years old by then, whose own faith, even in the Tower, and even in the face of death, when a recantation would have meant reprieve, remained steady as a rock.

The letter Jane wrote on this occasion is a ferocious piece of invective indeed to come from one so young:

'I cannot but marvel at thee and lament thy case,' she wrote, 'who seemed sometime to be the lively member of Christ, but now the deformed imp of the devil; sometime the beautiful temple of God, but now the stinking and filthy kennel of Satan; sometime the unspotted spouse of Christ, but now the unshamefaced paramour of anti-Christ . . . When I consider these things I cannot but . . . cry out upon thee, thou white-livered milksop . . . sink of sin . . . child of perdition . . . seed of Satan:'

and much more which must have made Harding wince. Some have

thought that this has been touched up by editors; but to most it rings true.

But this incident was in the future. A happy interlude opened for Jane, when her parents, in the furtherance of their plans, arranged that she should enter the household of Queen Catherine Parr. Jane was about eight when she left home to join Elizabeth and Edward under the mild direction of the Queen Dowager. It was the first time she had really been mothered, and she began to respond to sympathetic handling in a way which might have transformed her if it had continued. She benefited too, there is no doubt, from the company of the two royal children, whose daily life she shared, and whose wits were almost as sharp as hers. Probably she worked at times with Edward and his tutor: Elizabeth, five years older, must have been well ahead of them both in learning. This congenial way of life was not interrupted by the death of Henry VIII and the succession of Edward. But a year later it all came to a sudden end, when Catherine, having secretly married her old lover, Thomas Seymour, the Lord Admiral, died in childbed; and Jane had to return home.

Her old tutors were still in charge, and had been kept on despite some friction with their employers. (What part they played while Jane was with the Queen Dowager we do not know.) Both of them were friends of Elizabeth's tutor, Roger Ascham, and it was through them, and perhaps also through Elizabeth, that Jane also became his friend and a mutual admiration developed. Ascham himself tells the story of a conversation he had with her, not by any means the first, but one which led to a close understanding between them, though they never actually met again. On relinquishing his appointment as Elizabeth's tutor, he had gone to Bradgate probably to see Aylmer and Haddon before leaving on an official mission to Germany. Everyone was out hunting, except Jane, who was alone in her room reading Plato's *Phaedo* in Greek, 'with as much delight,' says Ascham, 'as some gentlemen would read a merry tale in Boccaccio.' They were able to have a long private talk during which Jane unburdened herself to the sympathetic Ascham, who skilfully brought into play once more his particular talent for winning the confidence of young girls. The substance of what she said Ascham reproduces in his book, ostensibly in Jane's very words:

'One of the greatest benefits that ever God gave me is that he sent me so sharp and severe parents and so gentle a schoolmaster. For when I am in presence either of father or mother, whether I speak, keep silence, sit, stand, or go, eat, drink, be merry, or sad, be sowing, playing, dancing or doing anything else, I must do it, as it were, in such weight, measure, and number, even so perfectly as God made the world, or else I am so sharply taunted, so cruelly threatened, yea, presently sometimes with pinches, nips and bobs and other ways, which I will not name, for the honour I bear them, so without measure misordered, that I think myself in hell, till time come that I must go to Mr. Aylmer, who teacheth me so gently, so pleasantly, with such fair allurements to learning, that I think all the time nothing, whiles I am with him. And when I am called from him, I fall on weeping, because, whatsoever I do else but learning is full of grief, trouble, fear and wholly misliking unto me: and thus my book hath been so much my pleasure, and bringeth daily to me more pleasure and more, that in respect of it all other pleasures in very deed be but trifles and troubles unto me.'

Of course there is exaggeration here: with so sympathetic a listener Jane could scarcely fail to embroider her story, and Ascham himself may have heightened the atmosphere. But even on the best interpretation there was obviously an unhappy cleavage between parents and daughter, revealed again in Jane's pitying comment on her parents' preferring sport to Plato: 'Alas, good folks,' she sighed, 'they never felt what pleasure meant.' Ascham's response was to take Jane's side entirely. He would have done better to adopt a more judicial attitude. But as usual he seems to have been rather carried away by contact with feminine precocity, and his one thought was to help and encourage this brilliant child, regardless of her parents.

He wrote learnedly to her from Germany, and also introduced her to a number of Swiss and German scholars and theologians, best known among them the Zurich reformer, Heinrich Bullinger, with a view to an exchange of letters. Her parents, rather surprisingly, but doubtless for reasons of their own, raised no objections. It may be wondered why such men should think it worth while to correspond at some length, as they did, with this fourteen-year-old girl; and the answer of course is that they had a double interest in her, first as a prodigy of learning, but most of all as an ardent protestant, who, they were assured, would shortly be Queen of England.

Jane herself took great pleasure in this unprecedented correspondence. Her letters to Bullinger and others, all in Latin with some quotations in Greek, are long and learned. The range of ideas and command of language, though conventional, are remarkable for a child, the Latin itself not only correct but stylish.

Ascham himself was delighted with the situation he had created, and was as proud of Jane as if she had been his own pupil. In a letter addressed jointly to Aylmer and Jane, 'Happy Aylmer,' he wrote, 'to have such a pupil, and you, Madam, such a master–all joy to you both.'

Most remarkable among Jane's gifts was the speculative bent which she began to show at about the age of thirteen, and which at that time, encouraged by Aylmer and Haddon, flowed naturally into theological channels. It is difficult today to enter sympathetically into the mentality of our sixteenth-century forebears who found so much satisfaction in a theological discussion. But we must accept the fact that they did; and that to most of them questions of religious dogma seemed vitally and pressingly important. Jane was a child of her age. But even in the sixteenth century few girls were theologians at thirteen, and it is understandable that the eminent scholars and divines, with whom she corresponded, should be impressed. Jane herself took it all very seriously indeed, and as adolescence approached she came to find in religion the chief incentive of her life. In biblical knowledge and the art of apt quotation from the scriptures she was the equal of any man; and when it was a question of defending her protestant stand-point, no considerations of tact, or good manners, or, it must be added, of self-interest, prevented her from saying just what she thought, as emphatically as she could say it. Her classical reading, particularly in philosophy, must have been strongly coloured by her religious beliefs, and we may surmise that her interest in Plato's *Phaedo* lay in the fact that it deals with death and immortality in terms broadly acceptable to a Christian.

Certainly Lady Jane Grey was a most remarkable child. Though we may not altogether admire her character, and though at times we may think her priggish, egotistical, arrogant, intolerant, obstinate, narrow–a puritan before there were any Puritans–she remains on any count remarkable. With her gift of tongues, her philosophical bent of mind, her religiosity, she seems in herself to be the epitome of Tudor education, a living example of what might be accomplished, given the perfect pupil. Her tutors themselves thought her unsurpassed.

'I do not think,' wrote Haddon, 'that among all the English nobility for many years past there has arisen a single individual, who to the highest excellencies of talent and judgement has united so much diligence and assiduity to the cultivation of every liberal pursuit.'

Subsequent generations have continued to look back at her with a kind of awe.

How she would have matured we can only guess. If she had remained queen, she would unquestionably have been driven by her conscience, as Mary was, to excesses in defence of her faith, and the persecution of Catholics might have begun earlier and reached a greater intensity than it did. She would never have developed the flexibility and statecraft of Elizabeth, nor yet her power to command men's devotion. She would have been a lonely queen. But as Elizabeth did, she would have filled the background of her life as queen with reading; and with her the escape would have been into philosophy and religion.

But as the intrigues wove themselves round her, and she found herself, first a reluctant wife, then after the death of Edward a reluctant queen, then a prisoner, these possibilities faded.

3

The Wisest Fool

THE MEN WHO HAD THE UPBRINGING OF YOUNG JAMES VI OF Scotland, destined thirty-five years later to become James I of England, had a unique opportunity to test the truth of the theory that, if you have complete control of a child for the first seven years, you can mould him for life. They did not succeed in doing so, defeated, as all teachers must be from time to time, by the effects of heredity and environment, and also partly because they tried so hard. But the attempt was not altogether in vain. James owed much to his early teachers, though they could not change his character.

Almost from birth he had been, to all intents and purposes, an orphan. His father, Darnley, had been murdered within a few months of his birth. His mother, the Queen of Scots, had abdicated in his favour when he was scarcely one year old: her efforts to maintain contact with him had been suppressed, and he never saw her again. He thus owed nothing, or hardly anything, directly to their influence. But who can say what ineradicable combinations of qualities came to him with the genes he inherited from two parents so lacking in princely virtues? His father, the vain and dissipated Darnley, had nothing worth inheriting save his good looks, and these he failed to transmit. The Queen certainly had qualities which have often been found in rulers, though they were hardly virtues – egotism, selfishness, obstinacy and a love of pleasure were among them – together with a strong consciousness of royal blood. All these she passed on to her son. Her one great quality, the blazing courage which did not desert her even on the scaffold, he did not inherit. In one respect he received more than either of his parents had to give. In intellectual ability he far outstripped his father, and was superior even to his mother, herself a woman of no small intelligence and highly educated also.

66

The Scottish Privy Council thus found themselves faced with the problem of educating a king almost from the cradle. Whatever we may think of them as men, these rather rough and uncouth lords took the responsibility very seriously. Plans were made for the little King's secular education to be in the full Renaissance style; and in fact at all points his upbringing resembled that of young Edward VI in England, except that few of the refinements and elegances of a Renaissance court were to be found in Scotland.

In 1567, shortly after his baptism, James had been lodged by his mother at Stirling Castle in the care of the Earl and Countess of Mar, whose family enjoyed a sort of hereditary status as guardians of the royal Princes of Scotland. This arrangement was allowed to continue after Mary left the country; and when, a few years later, Mar himself died, his brother, Sir Alexander Erskine, took his place, while Lady Mar still attended to the King's physical needs.

Sir Alexander, says Sir Thomas Melville, who was his contemporary, was 'a nobleman of a true, gentle nature, well loved and liked of every man for his good qualities and great discretion'; if this is a true description, he was the right man to be the governor of a young king. Lady Mar for her part looked after the King well and provided him with the secure background an infant needs. But he seems to have had respect rather than affection for her; and it may be that she was rather stern and forbidding, and kept the young King as well as his household under firm control. Certainly there seems to have been a lack of feminine softness in James's upbringing, which cannot have been without effect on his character. Yet, looking back in later years on this period of his life, he seems to have approved, for he put Lady Mar in charge of his own son.

When James was four years old, the Council appointed the necessary educational staff. There were to be two tutors, two instructors for horsemanship and other manly accomplishments, and two court musicians; two other tutors for French and Italian; and probably a dancing master also. The energies of eight or nine picked men were thus to be directed almost wholly upon this one small boy; for though, as recommended by the best authorities, several other boys of noble birth were chosen to share his nursery and schoolroom, he must have felt himself to be in fact the real target of this educational attack, and in any case he was probably often taught alone.

There was an obvious candidate for the post of principal tutor to the King. George Buchanan, greatest of Scottish scholars, was then at the height of his fame. This dour but brilliant man was one of the most accomplished Latinists of his own or any other generation. He had a European reputation as a writer, and, according to Dr. Johnson, was 'the only man of genius his country ever produced,' which, coming from Johnson, was a compliment indeed. He was virtually trilingual, being as much at his ease in Latin or French as in his own native Scottish dialect. He was naturally well versed in Greek also. But Latin was the language he preferred, and his writings in it, both prose and verse, were seriously compared by his contemporaries with the work of Livy, Horace and Vergil. If subsequent generations have come to modify that exaggerated judgement, it remains true that he had an amazing facility in Latin, which he wrote and spoke as a living tongue in a distinctive but authentic style of his own. In his lifetime and for long after, his works were read all over Europe. If they are now forgotten, it is partly because the controversies with which they deal are dead, partly because the minority who can read Latin nowadays seldom go beyond what the Romans themselves wrote during the brief golden age of their literature. But Buchanan's occasional verse has something to offer those who enjoy Martial or Catullus, his dramas are as readable – or as unreadable – as those of Seneca, and his rendering of the Psalms into the metres of Horace is a *tour de force* which modern scholars may admire, even if they have no desire to imitate it.

This was the man, a great Scotsman indeed, whom the Council put in charge of the infant King's education. Buchanan was not without experience as a teacher. He had been private tutor to several eminent persons; first in Scotland to Lord Cassilis; then to one of the illegitimate sons of James V; and finally to Mary herself, though he had since become one of her bitterest enemies. He had also held various university posts in different parts of Europe. (Among his pupils during a brief period at Bordeaux had been Montaigne, whose proficiency in Latin at a tender age roused even his admiration.) At the time of his appointment he was principal of St. Leonard's College in the University of St. Andrews. But he was already sixty-four; his health was beginning to fail, and his temper with it; and he was much preoccupied with his own literary work. One may doubt whether, for all his eminence, he was the right man to take charge of a small boy just out of the nursery.

Perhaps the Council had some doubt about him on the score of age, for they gave him as colleague a much younger and hitherto unknown man, Peter Young by name, who had little or no teaching experience, and had only just completed his own studies at Geneva. In the eyes of these Scottish lords, hostile as they were to Catholicism, a strong point in his favour was that he had come under the influence of teachers close to Calvin himself, and had a thorough grasp of the Calvinistic theology, which they themselves favoured.

Young was personally more attractive than Buchanan, as well as having the advantage of youth. The grim régime, under which he must have lived in Calvinistic Geneva, had not set its mark upon his character. He was a cheerful and friendly man, who handled his pupil with the sympathy and understanding of a natural teacher. It is pleasant to find that, despite his own harsh and domineering manner, Buchanan approved of these gentler methods, and always held Young in high esteem.

James himself naturally became fond of Young rather than Buchanan; and, whereas Buchanan's career ended with his tutelage of the King, for Young in his early twenties the post of royal tutor was an auspicious beginning. After his services as a teacher were no longer required, James continued to employ him. For some years he was chief almoner in the royal household, and was sometimes entrusted with delicate missions, such as the inspection of prospective brides for James, surely an unusual proof of the King's regard for his old tutor. In 1604 James paid him another compliment by appointing him tutor to his son Charles, who needed sympathetic handling. In due course Young was knighted, received a pension for his services, and retired to his estate in Scotland, where he died at the age of eighty-three. By contrast with the bachelor and by this time misogynist Buchanan, Young was three times married and the father of twelve children.

Though the two were so far apart in age and so unlike in character, they co-operated successfully in planning a curriculum for James. The broad outlines were of course by now almost standard; but there was room for disagreement over details, and the situation called for some tact and diplomacy from Peter Young, for Buchanan was a man of vehement opinions. However, the two tutors had no difficulty in agreeing as to their one overriding purpose, to make the King a real scholar. Buchanan himself took the view that a king should be the most learned man in his dominions. If few monarchs in history have come within measurable distance of achieving this, it was thanks to Buchanan and Young that James was one of those who did.

If this purpose was to be achieved, a good library was essential. James was far better provided for in this respect than young Edward had been in England thirty years before. The initiative came from Peter Young, who applied to the Council successfully for funds; and a collection of about 600 volumes was gradually got together for the King's use. It was probably the largest library in Scotland at that time. The titles themselves, covering almost the whole field of contemporary learning, epitomize the breadth of interest which an enlightened prince was expected to possess.

The Greek and Latin classics predominated, both in the original tongues, and in French, Italian or English translations, together with the accompanying apparatus of grammars and other works in pure linguistics. The fables of Aesop and Phaedrus and a collection of the pithy sayings attributed to Cato, all popular school texts of the day, must have been among the first of these to be used by the young King. But there were many contemporary works, most of them in Latin, which was still the main vehicle of modern thought, many in French, some in Greek, Spanish, Italian or English. Among these history, political theory and historical biography were well represented, no doubt by the special wish of Buchanan, an historian himself, who believed that princes should be well grounded in history. As in most libraries at that time and for long afterwards, theology bulked large. The presence of most of the best Renaissance writers on the education of princes and on the training of young men of birth and breeding (among them Castiglione's *Courtier*, Sir Thomas Elyot's *Book named the Governor* and the recently published *Schoolmaster* of Ascham) is particularly interesting. If these were in the library from the beginning, they were obviously meant primarily for the teachers rather than the taught, and indicate quite clearly the sort of results at which they were aiming. Later, when James came to write a manual of guidance for his own son, he drew on them heavily. Finally, there were works on a wide variety of subjects of general and current interest–mathematics and science generally, including geography, cosmography and zoology; logic and dialectics; the art of war; hunting; even magic; and a number of volumes appealing more to the imagination, salvaged by Peter Young from Mary's library at Holyrood, consisting mainly of medieval romances and French and Italian poetry.

James was thus surrounded by books from infancy, and his tutors took care that he should accept their importance and learn how to use them. The effect this emphasis on book-learning had on his character and mentality, for better or worse, will become clear as we follow his development. Meanwhile he was beginning to show 'great towardness in learning', and even in infancy gave promise of being an outstanding scholar. At this stage much depended on the fact that he had a good memory and enjoyed using it. Probably he was one of those little boys, known to all teachers, who seem to have an unfathomable capacity for learning things by heart. Sixteenth-century schoolmasters had no inhibitions about letting pupils use their memories. James was stuffed full of learning. There were signs of strain. That he was a neurotic and highly strung little boy one may guess from that rather pathetic portrait of him in the National Portrait Gallery of Scotland, in which the pale, pasty face and tired, disillusioned eyes tell their own tale. But fortunately he had the capacity to stand up to it. While a less gifted pupil might have cracked under such heavy pressure, James came through successfully.

Peter Young has left a note of the young King's routine, when he was about ten. This was certainly exacting, but not abnormally so for the period. The day began with morning prayers, which cannot have been later than about 5.30. Then followed a long session of Greek, during which (at the time covered by Young's account) James read first from the New Testament, then from Isocrates and the Apophthegms of Plutarch, with practice in the rules of grammar. This ended with breakfast. How long the Greek session lasted we are not told; but if the practice in English schools at about the same time may be taken as a guide, it may have been three hours, from 6 to 9. The modern method of dividing the school day into seven or eight short periods had not yet been thought of. After breakfast and for the rest of the morning, probably another three hours, the subject was Latin, with reading from the inevitable Cicero and Livy, together with the obscure Roman historian, Justin, and various contemporary Scottish and foreign historians. These last were doubtless chosen by Buchanan, and may have included some of his own writings, which were once read in many English schools and sometimes even prescribed in the statutes, as at St. Bees. His actual *History of Scottish Affairs*, dedicated to James, but denounced by him (after Buchanan's death) as an 'infamous invective' because of its verdict on his mother, was not yet published.

Latin was of course still the foundation of all higher education, and the man of culture still needed to speak and write it fluently. Buchanan believed that it was destined for an even greater future, as the universal language of mankind. We may be sure it was drummed into James almost from the cradle. A pathetic note scribbled in his copy-book shows that even the victim noticed a lack of balance here: 'They gar me speik Latin ar I could speik Scotis.' But the means were justified in the result; James acquired a genuinely fluent command of the language, for which he was later grateful.

After dinner came a period of composition, presumably in Latin or Greek. Then for the rest of the afternoon, if time allowed, the King worked at his subsidiary subjects – arithmetic, cosmography (including geography and astronomy), dialectics or rhetoric; by which time his attention must have begun to flag. There is no mention of French and Italian, which, like other royal children of the sixteenth century, James learnt and learnt well: they may have been fitted in when there was a moment to spare, and were perhaps practised as a social accomplishment during the King's leisure hours.

This time-table, or a variation of it, was probably followed on most days, but certainly not every day; for, apart from recreation, there were other things to be attended to. A king still needed to be an expert horseman, proficient in all things connected with the chase and in the skills of warfare; and music and dancing were still essential accomplishments for every man of culture. Two relatives of James's governor, the Earl of Mar, David and Adam Erskine, lay abbots of Cambuskenneth and Dryburgh, were given the task of instructing him in horsemanship and the handling of weapons; while two court musicians, Thomas and Robert Hudson, among their other duties, tried, though without much success, to educate him musically. Dancing lessons, with a master who remains anonymous, also had to be fitted in. Between them these activities must have kept the King a good deal away from the classroom.

There were other more serious distractions. James, like Edward VI, found it hard to combine the rôles of king and schoolboy. His advisers, if such they may be called, had little thought for his real interests. At five, when he ought to have been at work in the schoolroom or playing with his friends, he was sometimes dressed up in the purple and ermine of royalty, and made to preside at meetings of the Council and perform other kingly functions. Thus, almost as soon as he became conscious of anything outside his own immediate world, it was of the strife of rival factions and the plots and intrigues of ruthless men who were prepared to go to almost any lengths to gain power. Several times as a small boy he found himself the centre of a clash of arms; once he was actually kidnapped; and before he was twelve there had been no less than four different regents. All this confusion and uncertainty around him helped to bring about the sense of insecurity which remained with him all his life, and must have been one of the causes of the rather pathetic longing for a friend and confidant which led the adult King so often to make a fool of himself.

His tutors were probably as much at the mercy of circumstances as he was, though Buchanan at least held various public offices and was far from being merely the humble tutor. But, despite the interruptions, they were able to keep the King fairly constantly at his books, with results of which they were proud. By the time he was eight, James had joined the company of royal infant prodigies, and his tutors were putting him through his paces for the benefit of privileged visitors.

One of these was Sir Henry Killigrew, who had seen James as a baby, and now visited him again, as Queen Elizabeth's representative, in 1574, when the King was eight. He was duly impressed with the way James rolled out the graceful compliments proper to such an occasion, and with his command of languages. 'He speaketh the French tongue marvellous well,' he wrote. Buchanan and Young were both in attendance ('rare men', thought Killigrew), and arranged a special display for the ambassador's benefit. James was put to translating a chapter of the Bible, first from Latin into French, then from French into English; and did it 'so well as few men could have added anything to his translation,' thought Killigrew, who had been allowed to choose the chapter himself, to avoid any suspicion that the King had been coached beforehand. Then James was made to dance for Killigrew, 'which he likewise did with very good grace.'

The well-known portrait of James at the age of eight in the National Portrait Gallery shows the King as he must have looked when he received Sir Henry Killigrew; a dapper, elegant little figure, dressed up for the occasion; but also, one cannot help feeling, rather a self-satisfied little prig, who must have thoroughly enjoyed showing off.

Another who was treated to a display of the eight-year-old King's virtuosity was James Melville, a Scottish minister, who visited him at Stirling, and recorded his impressions. To him James seemed 'the sweetest sight in Europe that day for strange and extraordinary gifts of ingine' (that is, quickness of intellect), 'judgement, memory and language'. 'I heard him discourse,' he wrote, 'walking up and down in the old Lady Mar's hand, of knowledge and ignorance, to my great marvel and astonishment.' Once more we see a rather smug little boy, doing his tricks.

From a collection of the King's witticisms and smart sayings, made by the admiring Young at about this time, it appears that James was also, as might be expected, something of a 'smart Alick', who could produce apt quotations from the Bible to meet any situation, and loved puns and jokes depending on the twists and turns of language. His sallies look insufferably tedious in cold print; so would the classroom witticisms of any clever ten-year-old today, if his teacher were so misguided as to record them. But they were the signs of a lively mind, and must have lightened the long hours of concentrated study for both teacher and taught.

By the time he was eighteen this precocious child had finished his formal education, and had assumed the outward semblance of a man. What he was like, how he would have compared with a modern boy in his last year at school, may be judged from the report of another foreign envoy, M. Fontenay, a Frenchman who arrived at the Scottish court in 1584 to treat with James on his mother's behalf. M. Fontenay was a shrewd judge of men. He was impressed, but not so carried away by the brilliance of the young King as to overlook the flaws in his character which adolescence had brought out. James, he wrote,

'is for his years the most remarkable Prince that ever lived. Three qualities of mind he possesses in perfection: he understands clearly, judges wisely, and has a retentive memory. His questions are keen and penetrating, and his replies are sound . . . He is well instructed in languages, science, and affairs of state, better, I dare say, than anyone else in his kingdom.'

But, as M. Fontenay did not fail to observe also, there had evidently been serious omissions in the King's social training.

'He dislikes dancing and music, and the little affectations of courtly life such as amorous discourse or curiosities of dress, and has a special aversion for ear-rings. In speaking and eating, in his dress and in his sports, in his conversation in the presence of women, his manners are crude and uncivil and display a lack of proper instruction.'

It was surely the business of Lady Mar to teach James the elements of good manners; and in her failure we may see perhaps the influence of Buchanan, who had little regard for the opposite sex or for the airs and graces of social intercourse. For one reason or another James as a boy met very few girls of his own age and he grew up with a contempt for women, which did not make his adult relations with them any easier. Someone, we gather, must have taught him to dance. But though at eight he might perform a *pas seul* with a good grace to amuse Sir Henry Killigrew, we have Fontenay's word for it that at eighteen he disliked dancing – a serious deficiency even in a Scottish king. (A partial excuse and explanation of this aversion may probably be found in the fact that, as a result no doubt of rickets in infancy, James had weak legs and a clumsy gait.) Nor did the crude table manners which he had acquired through neglect in early youth, do anything to make him more attractive as a man. These faults, at any rate in their more extreme form, could have been avoided, and reveal a serious lack of proportion in James's early training.

In contrast with this failure, the King's initiation into the art of horsemanship was only too successful. His poor physique was no impediment here, and, as if in compensation for his weak performance in other physical activities, he revealed a special talent for riding. M. Fontenay noted this also:

'He loves the chase above all other pleasures and will hunt for six hours without interruption, galloping over hill and dale with loosened bridle.'

In later life hunting became such an obsession that affairs of state were sometimes held up for days at a time, as the King careered across country with his hounds, while courtiers, officials and foreign ambassadors followed at his heels in impotent frustration.

James's training as a whole in fact was one-sided, and bore the stamp of Buchanan's character. Like his tutor, he grew up with an intellectual bias, and, apart from horsemanship, had little or no taste or talent for the conventional attainments of prince or nobleman. But within the intellectual field his interests were wide and lively. Perhaps the greatest tribute to the influence of Buchanan and Young is that these interests did not die when his formal education ceased: he remained an enthusiastic scholar all his life.

A natural gift for languages, combined with an eye for detail and a good memory enabled him to become a very respectable classical scholar. He was perhaps inclined to pedantry, where his tutor had been the least pedantic of scholars; but he was capable of holding his own in any company, and his learning was acknowledged by impartial contemporaries. As a child he had feared and disliked Buchanan, who was a hard master and thrashed him and boxed his ears as the occasion demanded. To the very end of his life he suffered from nightmares caused by this treatment. But he was well aware that he owed his classical learning – and his un-English pronunciation of Greek and Latin – to Buchanan. When someone complimented him on his Latin,

'All the world knows,' replied James, 'that my master, Mr. George Buchanan, was a great master in that faculty. I follow his pronunciation both of the Latin and Greek, and am sorry that my people of England do not the like; for certainly their pronunciation utterly spoils the grace of these two learned languages.'

His English subjects might have retorted that his pronunciation of English utterly spoiled the grace of that language.

As a Latinist James was in his element when he visited Oxford or Cambridge, and might seem almost to have missed his vocation in not becoming a don. 'If I were not a king, I would be an University man,' he remarked somewhat sadly during a visit to the Bodleian Library at Oxford. When, on the same occasion, as he was listening to the disputations in the Schools, he suddenly took the floor and addressed the assembly long and eloquently in Latin, the dons, it is said, began to fancy that with such a scholar for a king they must be living in Plato's ideal republic.

James earned the respect of the academic world also as a theologian. His infant skill in bandying Biblical quotations formed an excellent foundation. Later, under the guidance of Peter Young, he became well versed in formal theology, and an adept in the rigid dialectic of Calvinism. He had the Bible read every day at meals, and liked to discuss what he heard; even as a boy he shared the fashionable taste for listening to sermons; and in later years was always eager to argue doctrinal points with the eminent ecclesiastics who frequented his court. This very real interest in religion contrasted oddly with an equally real taste for bad language and bawdry, picked up at the same time with equal facility, which evidently afforded him some kind of psychological release.

The love of books which James acquired as a child proved genuine and lasting: he became a bookish man, in the best sense. One of the things he enjoyed most at Oxford was his visit to the Bodleian; and his own library, which had been so carefully built up by Buchanan and Young, was not the empty gesture royal libraries are apt to be. It is quite likely that James in his maturity had read every book he possessed. His wide interests certainly covered most of the subjects represented, including such recherché ones as magic; and some of the volumes in his collection had a lasting influence on him.

It was inevitable that one who read so many books should also turn to writing; and like many adolescents he began experimenting with self-expression in verse. With most boys this is a secret passion, or one shared diffidently with a few intimates. James never had any inhibitions about his writing, and was easily persuaded to take himself seriously as a poet. From the age of fifteen he wrote a good deal of verse. His talent was slight; but helped and encouraged by the members of a small literary coterie, which his position enabled him to form, chief among them Alexander Montgomerie, whom James called his 'master poet', he achieved some technical proficiency. At eighteen he published a volume of verse, which contained also a short prose treatise on the art of poetry (which some think was originally a school exercise), borrowed without acknowledgement from a work by the English poet Gascoigne. Seven years later came another slight collection of verse. After that the inspiration faded, and he turned to prose, which he wrote well, and in which he achieved his ambition of becoming a successful author in his own right. Though James's work as a poet was of negligible quality, we ought to put it down on the credit side that a young king, with so many distractions at his command, thought it worth while to spend so much of his time in literary discussion and composition.

Buchanan naturally took a special personal interest in James's historical studies. When his own *History of Scottish Affairs* was completed, he dedicated it, as we have seen, to the King; and in his introduction mentions that James, then aged sixteen, had already read widely in the subject. 'At this early age,' he writes, 'you have studied the history of almost every nation, and very many of them you have by heart.' That this involved a serious and detailed treatment of the subject may be judged from a casual remark James made

many years later to the Venetian ambassador, that he had studied
the constitution of Venice as a boy with Buchanan.

Yet political theory was the one field of study in which Buchanan
failed to achieve his purpose with James; and, ironically enough, it
was probably the one field other than theology where he would
have most wished to impose his opinions on the King. His own
political convictions were strong, definite and unorthodox. On the
subject of monarchy he held that a king derived his authority, not
direct from God, as many rulers at that time believed, but from his
people, to whose wishes he was therefore subject; and that if he
acted in opposition to the will of the people, he might be called to
account, and even put to death. These revolutionary doctrines were
put forward in a work, *de Iure Regni*, which for a century or more
after its appearance was abhorred by all who believed in the divine
right of kings, and in 1683 was publicly burnt at Oxford. They were
injected into the youthful James with some force by the author in
person. But James, however amenable to Buchanan's teaching in
most other respects, was proof, it seems, against political indoc-
trination. Privately at first, openly as soon as he was old enough to
do so, he reacted strongly against Buchanan's political ideas, which
he rejected in favour of the belief that a king rules by divine right,
and is thus entitled to exercise absolute power. The real opposition
to Buchanan here came from members of James's court and particularly the French influences around him, who had long seized
every opportunity of impressing on James that he was directly
responsible to God and to no one else. It was a flattering conception,
which appealed naturally to an egocentric child, who knew he was
the latest of a line of kings; and Buchanan's insistence on his
heterodox views only served to strengthen James's hostility to them.
By the time he was eighteen, he had come to regard Buchanan's
teaching on monarchy as positively dangerous, and in 1584, when
Buchanan had been dead two years, secured its condemnation in
parliament. Later he told his own son that he was born 'a little god,
destined to sit on his throne and to rule men'. One is tempted to
speculate how the course of events might have been changed, if in
this one matter James had submitted to the guidance of Buchanan,
and had passed on to his successor a more enlightened conception of
monarchy.

We can assume that Buchanan and Young, and no doubt one or
more royal chaplains also, gave time and trouble to the young

King's moral training. Their ambition was assuredly to make him a good man, as well as a good scholar and a good king; and for a time, while in his childhood he was still under their close control, they may have thought they were succeeding. On the whole he was an obedient and submissive child. But the King's adolescence brought increasing disillusion to those who were trying to mould his character. Perhaps they had worked too hard at his moral training, as those responsible for the moral training of princes are always apt to do. By the time he was eighteen it was clear that James was far from being the model prince. In addition to those flaws noted by Fontenay, there were other more undesirable traits, some derived perhaps immediately from his father, some from his wild Stewart ancestors, which circumstances now brought to the surface.

One of these was cunning. James would have been a remarkable boy indeed, if, surrounded as he was by intrigue and double-dealing, he had remained honest and straightforward himself. But in fact he quickly adopted the methods of those around him, and tried to achieve his aims by trickery. He himself referred to it as 'king-craft'. Others, especially abroad, took a less charitable view of such tactics. Queen Elizabeth, with her genius for seeing through the minds of men, called him 'that false Scotch urchin.'

Though he had worked hard as a child under compulsion, by what was perhaps a natural reaction he became idle and self-indulgent as a youth, and was always ready to subordinate his duties to his pleasures. His bad language and coarse manners were notorious, and he no longer created the good impression he had done as a child. Of course he had his good points, some of which have already been noted – his ability, his genuine love of learning, his ambition to succeed by his own efforts as a writer, his daring as a horseman (though he was accounted a coward in other respects), his regard for such worthy people as Lady Mar, Buchanan and Young. Others will emerge in the course of the next chapter. But at this stage in his career his weaknesses were dominant.

They were often encouraged by the company he kept. James chose his own friends, and moral worth was certainly not one of the qualifications for which he looked. Among them were several unscrupulous rascals, who pandered to the King for their own purposes. Perhaps the worst, as well as the most attractive, of these was d'Aubigny, later Duke of Lennox, who arrived at the Scottish court as some sort of envoy from France, in 1579. Of Scottish family but

French upbringing, d'Aubigny was a man of depraved character, but great superficial charm: he was gay and good-looking, witty, elegant and sophisticated. Young James, thirteen years old and unconsciously longing for someone to depend on and admire, had met no one like d'Aubigny among the rude Scots nobility, and was completely carried away. A close friendship developed between them, which undoubtedly had the effect of bringing out homosexual predispositions in James's character, and may thus be regarded as the first of the series of infatuations for which he became notorious.

The story of James I's education and upbringing is in many ways more interesting than that of any other English ruler. So able and zealous were his tutors; so unusual the opportunity they had of moulding him to their liking, unhampered by the interference of parents; so great the effort to give him an education fit for a king; so high the hopes which were placed in the result. Yet the course of events only went to prove that the best education in the world cannot overcome or suppress a man's inborn weaknesses, which have come to him with the genes he derives from his forebears, cannot even counteract the strong influences which play upon him outside the classroom as he grows to manhood; with the additional lesson perhaps that educational pressure applied too strongly defeats its own purpose. In his childhood it seemed at first as if James might become the philosopher king. It was not through lack of effort by his tutors that he came only to be called the British Solomon and the wisest fool in Christendom.

4

A King's Gift

THE BIRTH OF A MALE HEIR IN 1594 PRESENTED JAMES HIMSELF
with the problem of educating a future king–and not merely a
Scottish king. His hopes of being recognized as Elizabeth's successor
in England were now rising rapidly. But he was a superstitious man,
and unfortunately for his peace of mind he had been warned in a
dream that he himself would die prematurely. Suppose he died
before Elizabeth, and never reached the English throne at all? Or
before his son's education was complete? These were disturbing
possibilities, which brought home to the King the urgency of
providing fully for the young Prince Henry's upbringing while he
himself was still alive to make his views known. That Henry should
die before either of them, as actually happened, never occurred to
him for a moment.

James regarded himself as an expert on kingship, about which he
held strong views; and being a practised writer also, he decided
to set down his ideas on the education of princes, as many others
had done, for the use not only of Prince Henry and his preceptors,
but of posterity. Though he did not say so, it doubtless also struck
him as an author that a book on kingship by a king would prove
attractive to the public; and so, as we shall see, it did.

James must have begun drafting the book soon after his son was
born. Four years later he had completed what is perhaps the best
known work by any royal author, certainly the most successful of
James's own writings. He gave it a Greek title in the Renaissance
manner – *Basilikon Doron*, that is, '*A King's Gift*'. Its purpose is set
out more fully in the sub-title, 'His Majesty's Instructions to his
dearest son, Henry the Prince', to whom also it is dedicated. With
the Prince's own copy, presented to him when he was nine in 1603,
the year of James's departure for England, went a message of
fatherly advice:

'Study and profit in it as ye would deserve my blessing. Be diligent and earnest in your studies that at your meeting with me I may praise you for your progress in learning.'

This particular copy was probably of the second edition. The first had appeared before Henry was old enough to know anything about it, in 1598, when he was only four; and it had been a limited edition of only seven copies, issued secretly because the King was afraid what the reactions of the Scottish clergy might be. Some modifications were made before the second edition was given to the public five years later.

Considered merely as a publishing venture, *Basilikon Doron* could not have appeared at a more opportune moment, for it was on the market in London within a few days of Elizabeth's death, when curiosity about James was at its height. Many Englishmen must have read it to find out what manner of man their new sovereign was.

It aroused controversy also, especially on questions of religion. The Papists, as James repeatedly and provocatively calls them, were so incensed that the book was forbidden to Catholics immediately, and has remained on the index to this day. This must have found it many readers. Nor did those of the opposite persuasion, the 'proud Puritans', relish being referred to, among other uncomplimentary phrases, as 'very pests in the Church and commonweal'. But most Englishmen were probably reassured to find the new King steering a middle course through these troubled waters.

Abroad, and especially in France, the book attracted more attention than was given to English books as a rule. It was the first English prose work to be translated immediately after publication into French, German, Dutch and Danish: it appeared also within a few years in Latin, Italian, Spanish, Swedish and Welsh.

Despite all the interest taken in it, there was in a sense nothing unusual about *Basilikon Doron*. It was a type of work which had been popular in western Europe for several hundred years. Other rulers in the past had written and published similar volumes of advice addressed to their sons and heirs. Other writers not of royal blood had set forth their views on the education of princes: James himself had eight standard examples of this kind of work in his own library. It would have been impossible for him to avoid covering much of the same ground as his predecessors in this field, from whom he also borrows freely and often without acknowledgement (as was the common practice at that time), whenever it suits him.

The work is divided into three books, which between them cover the whole conduct of a ruler's life, the first dealing with his duty towards God, the second his public responsibilities, the third his personal behaviour.

Within the framework of this conventional plan James put a good deal of himself into the book. The plain, sonorous style is his. The advice he gives, some of it based on what he calls his 'over-dear bought' experience, some of it (like that on war or sport) ostensibly founded on experience, but in fact purely theoretical, is always very personal. He reveals himself too in his obvious longing for a son more virtuous than himself; and in the almost professional interest he shows in authorship. The emphasis he puts on a king's status as father of his people, owing allegiance direct to God and to no one else, reflects what was his own firm belief. It would be easy to charge James with hypocrisy, because he did not always practise what he preached; but it would also be uncharitable; and most of those who read *Basilikon Doron* today will want to give him credit for a genuinely sincere desire to do the right thing by his son.

Meanwhile Prince Henry was launched upon what was by now a standard form of education. The King had kept up a family tradition which went back several generations by entrusting his welfare to the Earl of Mar at Stirling Castle, where he had been reared himself; though it cost him a quarrel with Anne, his Queen, who naturally wanted to bring up her own son. This was the earl who had succeeded to the title as a boy, and had been one of James's fellow-pupils at Stirling. He was eight years older than the King, and had played a lively part in the struggle for power which went on among the Scottish nobility during the minority of James. The dowager Lady Mar, who had supervised James's own domestic arrangements, was still alive and active, and performed the same service for his son.

But when Henry was six, all feminine influences were withdrawn, and he was handed over to an exclusively male staff. Thus do fathers blindly commit their sons to the kind of régime under which they have suffered themselves. The extrovert Henry, however, seems to have taken more readily than his father to a masculine environment. It is said that he willingly abandoned his toys and devoted all his energies to mastering the manly accomplishments then usual among gentlemen – riding, singing, dancing, leaping, shooting (both with the bow and with fire-arms) and tossing the pike.

When the royal family moved to England Sir Charles Cornwallis, a former ambassador to Spain, became Henry's governor and treasurer of his household. This distinguished man served the Prince faithfully until his premature death at the age of eighteen in 1612, and afterwards wrote two eulogies of him, which are the chief source of our knowledge of his life and fatal illness. In one of these he attributes the Prince's 'unspeakable excellency' to his study of *Basilikon Doron*.

The boy's principal tutor, chosen several years before, was Adam Newton, a Scot who had spent some time in France, to whom James presented one of the seven original copies of *Basilikon Doron*. The obvious intention was that he should make it the basis of his training, and he would have been a foolish and tactless man if he had not done so. Little is known of his personality or his success as a tutor, except by implication. Henry never became a scholar, and his attainments in Greek and Latin have been passed over in silence. But it may be gathered that the King was satisfied with Newton's efforts from the fact that in due course he presented him with some plate and made him Dean of Durham (though he was not in orders), the duties of which office he presumably carried out by proxy. When Henry became Prince of Wales, Newton served as his secretary; and he ended his days a baronet by purchase.

Far more noted, as it happens, was the man who taught Henry French and Italian. This was John Florio, an Italian who spent much of his life in England, and is remembered today for his Italian-English dictionary, *A World of Words*, and above all for his famous translation of Montaigne. In his hey-day he had a high reputation as a teacher of languages, which brought him many private pupils of rank and position, and led to his appointment as instructor to the Prince. There are significantly no anecdotes about Henry's proficiency in modern languages, but if he did not become fluent in French and Italian, it would not have been Florio's fault.

For several years after coming to England Henry is said to have 'plied his book hard', for which Newton may take the credit, for the boy himself, to his father's great disappointment, turned out to be no real lover of books. Not that he lacked intelligence: on the contrary, he had a keen, alert mind; but its bias was practical, with the result that his interests were quite different from those of his father. He is said to have liked history, which was perhaps a consolation to James who, as *Basilikon Doron* makes clear, had hoped for something very different. But his real bent was for the arts of war. This had first shown itself when as a small child he had delighted in playing at soldiers; but it developed more seriously than such childish trends usually do, and with adolescence became his main preoccupation. He did well at subjects useful to soldiers, such as mathematics and cosmography, and presumably neglected the others. These developments may have surprised and distressed the unwarlike King, but he could not disapprove, and even allowed Henry a special instructor in the theory and practice of fortification.

Cornwallis's picture of the young Prince, though it has the shortcomings of all panegyrics, is our best guide to his personality and physical characteristics. He seems to have been different from his father in almost every possible way, not only in the practical bent of his mind, and the love of action and indifference to books and learning, which he showed, but physically also. Whereas James was almost a cripple and incapable of any physical activity but riding, Henry was a straight-limbed, well-proportioned youth, who, like that other Henry whom he would have succeeded numerically if he had lived, took the greatest pleasure in sport, athletics and swimming, as well as in soldierly exercises. But father and son had one trait in common – a tendency to spend too much time on their favourite outdoor pursuits, James on hunting, Henry on military exercises.

The Prince was an excellent horseman. He had ridden every day since he was six, and was fond of equestrian sports like running at the ring and tilting, at which he became so adept, that Cornwallis, with the natural exaggeration of the eulogist, could describe him as 'second to no prince in Christendom.'

On the other hand he openly despised the chase, having perhaps heard too much about it from his father, and once in a rebellious mood observed – with considerable justification, we may think – that the men and horses would have been better employed hunting thieves and rebels.

But he himself was equally intemperate in his fanatical devotion to the military life – with more excuse at his age. When he was sixteen or seventeen he is said to have spent five or six hours a day in armour, practising the use of weapons. He taught himself to endure the privations of war, and, like some keen officers of a much later generation, walked a good deal in order to prepare himself for long marches. Even the Prince's musical tastes had a martial flavour. 'No music,' says Cornwallis, 'was so pleasant in his ears as the sounding of the trumpet, the beating of the drum, the roaring of the cannon.'

He was equally interested in naval affairs, and frequented the dockyards at Chatham, where he spent his time picking the brains of the King's master shipwright, Phineas Pett. James, who hated war and could not stand the sight of a soldier, must have wondered whether he was responsible for all this, with his second-hand advice on a prince's duties in war. But he accepted it, and encouraged Henry's nautical tastes by giving him a yacht, which he sailed assiduously.

The Prince's favourite game was tennis, which was approved in moderation by educational opinion and by James himself. But he was so fond of it that he sometimes played for three or four hours a day, and shocked Cornwallis by stripping to his shirt even in cold weather, which, thought his otherwise admiring governor, was a practice 'rather beseeming an artisan than a prince'. It was as well perhaps that he did not take to football, which would have provoked a sharper reaction, though it had been patronized and even played by some of his rougher Stewart ancestors.

These frenzied activities, however admirable in themselves, must have been rather an embarrassment to the Prince's advisers, who were responsible to the King for his health and education. For us, who know the sequel, they have a hint of tragedy. It seems almost as if this lively boy with his passionate enthusiasms must have felt instinctively that time was short, and that with so many enjoyable things to do, he had only a few years left in which to do them.

The rest of the picture, as sketched by Cornwallis, makes him perhaps a little too good. But he had many of the qualities to be looked for in a ruler. High-spirited though he was, he was no play-boy prince, and did not let his sporting interests interfere with his duties as heir to the throne. On the contrary, he is described as a serious youth, conscientious and businesslike in the conduct of his affairs, with a grave look and measured speech (which had a slight impediment, due, thought Cornwallis, to imitating one of his instructors, but more likely perhaps inherited – his brother Charles had it too). He was just and considerate in his dealings with others, generous to his dependents, and knew how to maintain the dignity of his position without being proud or aloof. With the natural intelligence which he applied so keenly to his military studies went an inquiring mind. He did not take things for granted, preferring, as Cornwallis says, to 'unrip every seam' before accepting what he was told. (An unfavourable critic might have called him argumentative.) Like his father he enjoyed listening to sermons, and was careful of his religious duties. His personal reputation stood high. He had a strong objection to bad language, and in his various houses kept poor-boxes, to receive the forfeits of those who swore in his presence: history does not record how much the poor benefited when his father paid him a visit.

When we recall the shortcomings of James at about the same age – his deceitfulness, his idleness and self-indulgence, his fondness for dissolute company, his uncouth manners and his profanity – two points emerge. There can be no doubt in the first place that Henry was better material than his father. His Danish blood must have brought with it some basic good qualities, despite his mother's frivolity and limited mental range. But special praise must also go to the men who had been in charge of the Prince during the vital years of childhood and adolescence for so successfully bringing out those good qualities. This had been the result of judicious good management on their part. They had not tried to drive their pupil so hard as James himself had been driven; and the fact that Henry seems to have been allowed to follow his own natural bent to a very large extent made him a much more normal boy than his father had been. Perhaps too we may give James himself some credit for this result. If the Prince really studied *Basilikon Doron*, as it seems certain he did, it must have helped.

When, contrary to all expectations, Prince Henry's health began to fail, and a chill caught at tennis eventually proved fatal, it must have seemed to James that *Basilikon Doron* had been written in vain. But there was still 'Baby Charles', who now had to take his brother's place as Prince of Wales and heir to the throne, and of whom James was fonder than he had been of the sometimes self-willed Henry.

It was necessary that he should now be trained to succeed his father; so *Basilikon Doron* was duly passed on to Prince Charles, and James's old Scottish tutor, Peter Young, was called in to inculcate its lessons into the new heir.

Very little is known of the education of Charles, by contrast with that of his father or his elder brother, or even his sister Elizabeth.

He was a quiet, grave child, handicapped by delicate health, and, like his brother, by a slight stammer, which inhibited conversation, and made him seem slow and silent as compared with his quick-witted father. His disabilities were so great that at one stage the possibility of cutting the string under his tongue and putting his legs in irons was even being considered. Nor did he inherit his father's talent; he is said to have learnt more readily by ear than from books, and never became anything of a scholar. Even as a child he was noted for the obstinacy which proved his ruin as king: at the time it was charitably supposed to be a temporary effect of his physical weakness, but the weakness passed as he grew older, while the obstinacy remained. Fortunately his tutor was the kindly Peter Young; and though nothing is known of what took place between them, it must have been with Young's help that Prince Charles outgrew some of the shyness and hesitancy that he suffered from in the presence of his father and by comparison with his abler brother and sister. He emerged a man of strong principles and high moral character; and, except in state-craft, was much more the prince envisaged in *Basilikon Doron* than James himself.

The education of Charles was no more than a pale shadow of the rigorous training to which Renaissance princes and princesses had been subjected, and of which his own father was one of the last products. The education of his sons marked a further dilution of this ideal, though the externals remained much as before.

The elder, Charles (Charles II to be), was given the traditional establishment of Prince of Wales at the age of eight – a nobleman as governor, a learned ecclesiastic as tutor and various lesser personages to instruct him in French, writing and so on. He was fortunate in them all; but though his governor made a strong impact on him, the future Merry Monarch did not take easily to book learning, and it must have been uphill work for his tutor and instructors.

For governor Charles had William Cavendish, Earl of Newcastle, a man of distinguished appearance and high character, whose personal qualities were of a kind to arouse hero-worship in his young ward, for he was reputed to be the most brilliant horseman of his age, and was adept, not only in fencing and other manly sports, but in the arts of music, poetry and the dance. Charles, who spent much time on horseback in his company, became very attached to him. He for his part took his duties so seriously as to set down for Charles's later guidance his conception of how a king should behave, and how a prince should be schooled, or school himself, for his future reponsibilities.

Newcastle's ideal king is a man of action, a man of affairs: and perhaps with some thought of what James I had been, he stresses again and again that book-learning is no essential qualification for kingship.

'I would rather have you study things than words, matter rather than language.'

'I would not have you too studious, for too much contemplation spoils action.'

'Take heed of too much book.'

'The greatest clerks are not the wisest men; and the great troublers of the world, the greatest captains, were not the greatest scholars; neither have I known bookworms great statesmen.'

Much more important, he thinks, are what are now called personal relations. A king should be civil and courteous to all, especially ladies. He should find something nice to say about everyone, and especially those who have come in for criticism by others. But he must also remember his position, and know how to play the king, though without overdoing it. He personally should avoid being too strictly virtuous – this is what Newcastle seems to mean – for 'one may be a good man but a bad king', and he should remember his mortality, yet not have 'a death's head always before him'.

When Charles at length reached the throne, worldly, affable, approachable, certainly not too good, nor obsessed with gloomy thoughts of the life to come, he was not far removed from Newcastle's notion of what a king should be. His weaknesses and faults, harshly judged though they have been by posterity, were not at the time held so strongly against him.

Charles's tutor was a man of equal distinction in his own field, Brian Duppa, Bishop of Chichester, later of Salisbury, finally of Winchester. Like so many famous men, particularly in that age, he was educated at Westminster. Thence he went on to Christ Church, and in due succession a fellowship of All Souls, and other honours, both ecclesiastical and academic.

The soundness of his religious views recommended him to the King as a man to whom the spiritual guidance of his son could be entrusted, and his scholarship was unquestioned; but he had worldly qualifications also. The 'comeliness of his person and gracefulness of his deportment', as Clarendon puts it, equipped him admirably for the courtly life of a royal tutor; and he was, it seems, not so narrowly devoted to pure learning that he could not co-operate with a man of the world like Newcastle, who in fact pays tribute to his breadth of outlook in a letter to Charles:

'Your tutor, Sir (is one), wherein you are most happy, since he hath no pedantry in him; his learning he makes right use of, neither to trouble himself with it or his friends; reads men as well as books; the purity of his wit doth not spoil the serenity of his judgement; and, in a word (he) strives as much discretely to hide the scholar in him, as other men's follies studies to show it; and is a right gentleman, such a one as man should be.'

These qualities were probably the right ones in the circumstances. Duppa had no success in teaching Latin to Charles, who never mastered even the elements. (Clarendon, some years later, advising an obsequious author not to dedicate his work to Charles with a flattering foreword in Latin, remarked that the Prince would be incapable of understanding it.) But Duppa won the respect and affection of his charge, and when many years later he lay dying at Oxford, Charles, being now King, went to see him, and on bended knee asked his blessing.

The personal influence of these two men, his first governor and his first tutor, had been so marked with Charles that one must make an effort to remember that he lost their services when he was only eleven. In 1641 they were both dismissed by the King, Newcastle because he was suspected of complicity in the Army plot of that year, Duppa, as a conciliatory move, because of his Laudian sympathies. Charles must have regretted their going: he did not forget what he owed to them, and after the Restoration they were high in favour.

Newcastle was a difficult man to follow. An anticlimax was almost inevitable, and in fact neither of the rather obscure noblemen who now successively became governor to the Prince was at all suitable: the first, the Marquis of Hertford, was a worthy man but too old, the second, the Earl of Berkshire, a mere time-server. They achieved no success with Charles, who was in any case becoming something of a handful. An anecdote of 1644 brings him to life for a moment. During service at St. Mary's, Oxford, the King, his father, 'hit him on the head with his staff, when he did observe him to laugh, at sermon time, upon the ladies who sat against him'. Boys will be boys.

The new tutor was a better choice. He was John Earle, still remembered today as the author of a minor classic, the collection of character sketches called *Microcosmographie*. He seems to have possessed a certain originality, to judge from Clarendon's description:

'Dr. Earle was a man of great piety and devotion, a most eloquent and powerful preacher, and of a conversation so pleasant and delightful, so very innocent, and so very facetious, that no man's company was more desired and loved. No man was more negligent in his dress and habit and mien, no man more wary and cultivated in his behaviour and discourse.'

Earle stayed with Charles some years, and off and on, as conditions of warfare or exile permitted, he continued to instruct him as best he might. It was a desultory sort of education. The Prince was growing up fast, and even at fifteen was too engrossed with his amours and the fortunes of the royalist cause to pay much attention to his books. He consented, we are told, to read one hour a day with Earle, and in addition received some instruction in mathematics from Thomas Hobbes, the philosopher, whom he nick-named the Bear, one of the numerous Englishmen in exile who had gathered round the royal family during its sojourn abroad. Yet, though Charles probably did not learn much from these excellent men, he was a boy of attractive personality, and was on good terms with both his tutors, as he was with almost everyone he met. 'He kisses and loves all,' wrote Earle soon after he had taken up his duties, 'and when the smart of the rod is past, smiles on his beater.' The rod was probably used a good deal, but it left no permanent mark.

The education of James, Duke of York (the future James II), three years younger than Charles, was even more dislocated. Three Oxford men were his tutors, Brian Duppa himself, and two obscurer figures, Broughton and Croucher. James was stubborn and difficult, and learnt even less than his elder brother, which suggests that it was perhaps a case of trying tutor after tutor. He seems to have had the ability, but may have reacted unfavourably to pressure; for later, in France, when it suited him to do so, he acquired an excellent knowledge of French (whereas Charles had to employ an interpreter, while paying court in Paris, not very enthusiastically, to La Grande Mademoiselle), and he taught himself to play the guitar. But circumstances were against him. Almost all the years when he should have been concentrating peacefully on the processes of learning were passed in the confusion of civil war and foreign exile. His father urged him in 1647 to 'ply his book more and his gun less.' He was fourteen at the time. Who can blame him, if when all around him were plying their guns, he wanted to do so too?

With the last two Stuart kings the Renaissance ideal of a princely education finally died. Newcastle had set before young Charles a limited objective, summed up in simple words:

'Be a brave, noble and just king, and make your name immortal by your acts abroad and your unspotted justice at home.'

To a limited extent it was realized when Charles became King. Thereafter, for nearly two hundred years, no English ruler thought of modelling either himself or his heir to any preconceived pattern.

The education of the two Stuart queens, Mary II and Anne, daughters of James, Duke of York, contrasts dramatically with that of their Tudor counterparts, and in itself illustrates the final abandonment of Renaissance ideals. When they were children it was of course never expected that either, let alone both, would ever succeed to the throne; but it is doubtful if this really made much difference. Neither their own parents, nor Charles II, to whose care they were committed as 'children of the state' after their mother's death, attached much importance to education. Lavish provision was made for their maintenance and well-being; no little princesses were ever reared in happier or more delightful surroundings. But, though every precaution was taken to ensure that they were brought up as Protestants, uninfluenced by their Catholic father, and much attention was given to their religious training, the secular education they received was negligible, consisting as it did of little more than a veneer of ladylike accomplishments. Nothing was done to rouse their minds or sharpen their understanding.

There was a gap of only two years between Mary and Anne, and they were brought up together in the seclusion of Richmond Palace, along with the six daughters of their lady governess, Lady Frances Villiers, and other girl companions. Their first and most influential tutor, Dr. Henry Compton, Bishop of London, had been chosen for his fiercely militant Protestantism, which owed much of its quality to the fact that he had been a soldier before taking orders. He was naturally not congenial to the Duke of York, who said that he 'talked more like a colonel than a bishop'; and he fell foul of

James as soon as he succeeded to the throne. But he made himself very agreeable to the princesses, in whom he implanted his own unshakable Anglican faith. 'The more I see of those fooleries,' wrote Anne, when she was fifteen, during a visit to Catholic Brussels, 'and the more I hear of that religion, the more I dislike it.' To this opinion she adhered steadfastly, even when her Catholic father was on the throne, and every effort was being made to win her over to Rome. Her sister Mary, even as a child, was equally decisive in her rejection of Catholicism, and likewise, during her residence in Holland, of Calvinism. Bishop Compton had performed his task well.

Two other tutors, Dr. Edward Lake and Dr. Doughty, were employed to second the bishop's efforts. Dr. Lake particularly was a kindly and devoted man, of no high intelligence but dedicated to his task. When, after seven years service, he took leave of Mary at the time of her marriage, he begged her to remember one thing especially–that he had never taught her anything not in accordance with the doctrines of the Church of England; so great was the importance he attached to this part of his charge, so anxious also was he to ensure, with a view to preferment, that others did not forget how he had fulfilled it.

The princesses' other teachers and instructors were of an inferior grade, and no one, unless perhaps Lady Villiers, paid much attention to what they taught. The French tutor was Peter de Laine, thanks to whom the princesses learnt to speak and write the language with an erratic fluency, which equipped them for social contact with foreigners, but for little else other than the reading of contemporary French fiction. Neither princess learnt any other foreign language as a child; but after her marriage to William of Orange Mary managed to pick up some rather halting Dutch during her eleven-year sojourn in Holland.

Much, perhaps most, of the princesses' time was spent in acquiring the elegant arts of the drawing-room. They were taught to dance by another Frenchman, the elderly M. Gorey, and were taught well, Mary, as in all things, taking the lead. Samuel Pepys, a good judge of feminine talents, noted in his diary how he had watched her 'dance most finely, so as almost to ravish one–her ears were so good'. Both girls were musical, though not to a degree which would have been remarked in anyone but a princess. They learnt to sing charmingly, and to play those still fashionable instruments the lute, the viol and the harpsichord; and were coached in voice production by the actress Mrs. Betterton (who was rewarded with a pension of £100 when Anne came to the throne). Scope for the exercise of all these graceful gifts was provided when, in 1774 (Mary being twelve and Anne ten), a full-scale masque, in which the princesses and their friends played leading rôles, was specially composed and produced for them by order of the King himself.

Most remarkable of all the professors of polite accomplishments in attendance on the two princesses were Richard Gibson and his wife, who taught drawing and painting; remarkable, not so much for their own artistic talents, though Richard Gibson had, and still has, some fame as a miniaturist, as because they were both dwarfs, 3 feet 10 inches tall. Richard Gibson had long been in the service of the Stuart family, for he had started his career in the household of Charles I (which did not prevent him from enjoying the patronage of Cromwell during the Commonwealth); and when Mary went to Holland, he went with her. Miniature-painting remained one of her chief leisure occupations, both as Princess of Orange and as queen.

It was thus mainly with trivialities, delightful trivialities no doubt, that the princesses were busied during their working hours as children. The situation was not one in which strength of character or firmness of purpose were likely to develop; and in fact both girls, motherless and starved for affection as they were, passed through a silly stage during their early teens, the effects of which lasted long.

In Mary's case it took the form of a schoolgirl 'crush', a romantic infatuation for Frances Apsley (daughter of her father's receiver-general, who was nine years older than she was. Sustained by a complicated apparatus of go-betweens and secret notes, partings, imagined misunderstandings and artificial quarrels, pledges and reconciliations, this make-believe romance lasted much longer than such affairs usually do. A good deal of Mary's side of the fantastic correspondence which passed between the two girls has survived, revealing the tangles of misdirected emotion in which the younger at least was caught up. One sample, the last sentence–if it is possible to have sentences where there is no punctuation–of one of three letters received by Frances Apsley in a single day, will be sufficient.

'you are loved,' wrote Mary, 'more then can be exprest by your ever obedient wife vere afectionate friand humbel sarvent to kis the ground where one you go to be your dog in a string your fish in a net your bird in a cage your humbel trout Mary Clorine.'

It seems that Frances Apsley, who was a young woman in her twenties when this affair was at its height, did nothing to help Mary adjust her emotions.

Anne for her part, after figuring for a while as Mary's rival for the affections of Frances Apsley, was beginning her long association with Sarah Jennings, the future Duchess of Marlborough. It was not a passionate attachment, like Mary's, but it went deep and lasted long; and meanwhile the influence of the domineering, strong-minded Sarah, who boasted that she never read a book, and played cards all the time, even on Sundays, was disturbing to an otherwise docile child like Anne. It was she who, when Lady Villiers died of smallpox, helped to turn Anne against her new governess, Lady Clarendon (who was her aunt) with the remark that 'she looked like a mad woman and talked like a scholar'.

These things were quite beyond the range of the martial Bishop of London, who may not even have been aware of them. Though Lady Villiers disapproved, she did not intervene; in fact it would have been very difficult for her to do so, while Dr. Lake and Mr. Gibson even connived to the extent of carrying notes and acting as go-betweens for Mary. For both girls adolescence was thus a period of abnormal emotional stress. But, though the psychological effects lasted far into adult life, both in the end shook themselves clear; Mary with the slow fading of passion after seventeen years, Anne not till she had the strength of mind as a woman of forty-seven to dismiss the Duchess of Marlborough. It is worth remembering that both became devoted to their husbands.

Meanwhile, as time went on, and Charles II remained without legitimate children, while his brother's sons died in infancy, it was becoming increasingly likely that Mary at least would succeed to the throne. Yet little or nothing was done to introduce her and her sister to history, 'the school of princes' (as Hannah More later called it), or to make them acquainted with world geography or with the current political and international situation. Living in their own narrow world of dreams and petty day-to-day affairs, they remained for many years wholly ignorant of what was going on outside. It is true that both of them, particularly Anne, were handicapped by weak eyesight, and on that account would have been incapable of a rigorous bookish education; and neither in any case had the intellect or the resolution to undertake such exacting work. But the fact was the educational climate had changed, and it was no longer felt desirable that ladies of royal birth should be equipped to hold their own intellectually with men. Blue-stocking princesses, like royal infant prodigies, were no longer admired.

5

Problem Prince

ENGLAND HAD ALREADY HAD ONE FOREIGN KING IN WILLIAM OF
Orange, Dutch born and bred, though of partly Stuart stock. But,
whatever we may think of his policies or his personality, he had at
least had an education worthy of a king. He was a brilliant linguist,
completely at home in English, Dutch, French and German, with a
working knowledge of Spanish, Italian and Latin. While still no
more than a child he had been put through a very exacting course
at the university of Leyden, and the most distinguished professors
had been employed to instruct him, with characteristic Dutch
thoroughness, in the subjects judged appropriate to a prince – not
only foreign languages, but theology and history, mathematics and
philosophy (though of course at the time it was not envisaged that
he would succeed to the English throne). As well as being intellectually the ablest, he was certainly the best educated member of the
house of Stuart since his great-grandfather, James I.

But when, on the death of Queen Anne, the succession passed to
the Elector of Hanover, the new king, George I, another of James I's
great-grandsons, was not merely a foreigner, but wholly incapable
at fifty-four of adapting himself either to English ways or to the
English language, and quite uneducated in any real sense. His
schooling, such as it was, had been narrow and provincial. He had
learnt Latin, though he was certainly no scholar: later he was to
find it unexpectedly useful. French, the polite language of the petty
German courts, he wrote and spoke more readily than his native
tongue. For the rest, his education had been purely military; he was
on active service with his father when no more than fifteen, and
there can have been little time for culture. He grew up without
intellectual interests, and was indifferent to all the arts save music.

George I's arrival among his new, notoriously monoglot subjects

G   97

resulted in some linguistic embarrassment in court and government circles. Those who had any French made haste to brush it up. None of his English ministers knew German: some of them, thanks to their classical education and insular upbringing, even had no French, and were reduced to conversing with George in an inadequate dog Latin. Walpole himself was one of these: he controlled the King, he said, 'by bad Latin and good punch'. Meanwhile the King, at loggerheads with his heir, like every Hanoverian ruler, was reluctant to employ the Prince of Wales, who understood English, as an interpreter, and was too lazy and too prejudiced to learn any English himself apart from swear-words. In the end he gave up attending meetings of the cabinet, thereby incidentally introducing a new principle into English governmental procedure.

The education of George I's son, George Augustus (later George II) had followed much the same pattern. As a child he was bullied or ignored by his father, alternately petted and scolded by his mother. He was eleven when his mother's notorious liaison with Königsmarck, resulting in her divorce and imprisonment, put an end to such home life as he had enjoyed and he and his sister were committed to the care of their grandparents, the Elector Ernest Augustus and his wife Sophia. For the right boy this might have opened up new horizons, for Sophia was a woman of rare talents, fluent and well read in six languages and a patroness of scholars. But George Augustus was unresponsive to the cultured aura of his grandmother (though his sister, who became the mother of Frederick the Great, drew much from it). His only intellectual asset was a good memory: he enjoyed history as a boy because he found it easy to remember dates, and later became an expert in the genealogies of the royal and noble families of Europe, and acquired a comprehensive acquaintance with the uniforms, badges and accoutrements of every regiment in every army.[1]

Like his father, he learnt Latin and French, but had to pick up his English as best he could, when the need arose: he became proud of his command of the language, but it remained at times almost unintelligibly Germanic. Apart from this his education was wholly military. He was in uniform from an early age, and under the strict supervision of a military governor was thoroughly grounded in

---

[1] This not very useful gift kept cropping up among his descendants. Queen Victoria's father, the Duke of Kent, and her son, the Duke of Connaught, both had an encyclopedic knowledge of such matters.

drill and the science of war. Naturally he longed to go on active service; but for many years his father would not allow this, and he remained a parade-ground soldier. But eventually, at the age of twenty-three, he was allowed to serve under Marlborough, and was present at the battle of Oudenarde, where he won the respect of his future English subjects by his courage. His prowess at Dettingen on a later occasion has become almost legendary.

Slow progress was made in the anglicizing of this Germanic royal family. George I had been wholly Hanoverian. George II too, though he spoke English after a fashion, and took his duties as King of England seriously, was never anything but a German. He even educated his eldest son Frederick (who died as Prince of Wales) in Hanover, with the result that, when that unsatisfactory young man arrived in England, he was as German as ever his father had been.

But the first sign of a change came when George's third son, William (later Duke of Cumberland, the notorious 'Butcher'), was brought up in England; though the initiative came from his mother the Princess of Wales, who had some intellectual interests and patronized scientists and poets, rather than from George himself. The boy's governor was the diplomatist, Stephen Poyntz; his tutors the astronomer Halley and a talented Welshman named Jenkin Thomas Phillips, a professional teacher of languages, and later royal historiographer, who followed ancient precedent in composing a grammar and various other manuals for his pupil, and took the greatest care over his instruction.

Ironically enough, however, it was Frederick, the next Prince of Wales, with his strong German accent, who eventually broke the sequence of German kings by having his son George educated in England, where he had been born, with the deliberate purpose of making him an Englishman rather than a German. In a political testament which he wrote for his son, Frederick recommended him to make people understand that he was 'not only an Englishman born and bred', but an Englishman 'by inclination'. George did not forget the advice: in his first speech from the throne he used words now famous. 'Born and educated in this country,' he said, 'I glory in the name of Britain'; and if it was 'Britain' he wrote when drafting his speech, rather than the more frequently quoted 'Briton', it makes very little difference. All his active life he remained to his subjects a typical Englishman.

Frederick himself was a poor specimen of a man. Probably he was mentally arrested, certainly of no great intelligence, though, as we shall see, he showed some good sense in the educational arrangements he made for his children. Like every other Hanoverian Prince of Wales, he was at odds with his father the King, who described him as 'the greatest ass, and the greatest liar, and the greatest canaille, and the greatest beast in the whole world'. Even his mother had a low opinion of him. Circumstances were all against his living a normal, balanced adult life, and in his thirties he could still behave like a naughty schoolboy. Even as a married man and a father he derived pleasure from such pranks as breaking other people's windows at night; and half the pleasure probably came from the thought of how angry his father would be.[1]

It would have been surprising if the son of such a man had been a normal boy. Fortunately for Prince George, his mother, who had been Princess Augusta of Saxe-Coburg, was a woman of more conventional stamp. She was not beautiful, she was not intelligent, and had been chosen as bride for the Prince of Wales, according to George II, because most of the other eligible Protestant princesses had madness in their families. 'I did not think ingrafting my half-witted coxcomb upon a madwoman would mend the breed,' he said. But she made a good wife and mother within her limitations, though it cannot be said that the union was successful in mending the breed, which afterwards produced many peculiar characters.

With the birth of sons, of whom the eldest, George, was born in 1738, and the next, Edward, his childhood companion, in 1739, Frederick, Prince of Wales, so far laid aside his irresponsibility as to make sensible plans for their upbringing and education. Following the traditional method of rearing princes by dual control, he entrusted the boys to the care of a governor and a tutor.

The tutor, or preceptor, as he was now fashionably called, appointed when George was seven to look after all the royal children as they became old enough, was the Rev. Dr. Francis Ayscough, a worthy, solemn man, afterwards Dean of Bristol. As he was also Clerk of the Closet to the Prince of Wales, he soon had to be relieved of some of his tutorial duties by the appointment of a sub-preceptor; and for this subordinate office the choice fell upon a man of considerably greater parts than Ayscough himself. This was George

[1] It is fair to remember that Frederick was not unique among royal persons in this trait. Practical jokes, often rather cruel ones, were common practice in the royal families of Europe for generations after this. Edward VII himself was famous as a practical joker.

Lewis Scott, a very able mathematician and a Fellow of the Royal Society whose appointment must have owed something at least to the fact that he had been born in Hanover, where his father held a diplomatic post, and was named after George I. His personal qualities endeared him to his pupils, who could probably make little contact with Ayscough. He was tall and massive, 'very sociable and facetious', according to Fanny Burney, and according to another contemporary witness 'amiable, honourable, temperate, and one of the sweetest dispositions I ever knew'. A few years later Francis North, first Earl of Guilford, known to history as father of a future Prime Minister, became governor of the young Princes.

This was the establishment with which the future George III began what was to turn out a very disjointed and partial education. Frederick, Prince of Wales, it need hardly be said, had no plans for bringing up his son as the perfect prince. Such notions were very far from the thoughts of any of the house of Brunswick, though it is worth remembering that just about this time in Prussia another Frederick, soon to be called the Great (who was also a grandson of George I), had visions of becoming a philosopher king in the Platonic manner, and was busy writing his *Antimachiavel* and exchanging a correspondence with Voltaire.

The curriculum provided was very ordinary, somewhat broader but less demanding than the exclusively classical course then and for long afterwards normal at the public schools: it included Latin (but not Greek), history and mathematics. In addition the little Princes could scarcely avoid learning the native German of their parents and the French which was commonly used in polite German society.

A memorandum under the heading 'The Hours for the two Eldest Princes', drawn up by the Prince of Wales in 1750 for the benefit of Francis North, is interesting both as evidence of their daily routine and because it shows that their father was alive to his duties as a parent. The programme, though not comparable with those to which Tudor royal children were subjected, is sufficiently exacting. Having risen at seven, the Princes, now aged thirteen and twelve, begin work at eight o'clock on a morning session which lasts four and a half hours, divided between four separate masters: first Mr. Scott, presumably teaching mathematics, for one hour; then Dr. Ayscough, concentrating probably on Latin and history, for two hours; after that for an hour Mr. Fung, who may have taught music; and finally, for half an hour, Ruperti, who can only have been the fencing instructor, during whose lesson Mr. Fung is instructed to remain, perhaps with the implication that Ruperti needed someone to keep order for him. At half past twelve the two small Princes, by now sufficiently fidgety and inattentive, are allowed out to play.

One of their favourite games, as may be learnt from the contemporary Memoirs of Lady Hervey, was baseball or rounders, played indoors during winter, in which all present, even foreigners, were expected to join. Lady Hervey has an anecdote of an elegant French marquis, who, expecting some sophisticated entertainment on visiting the home of the Prince of Wales, found to his horror that he had to choose between playing rounders and listening to a reading from Addison. It has been said, though probably without foundation in fact, that baseball was introduced into the U.S.A. by someone who had learnt it from the youthful George and his brothers and sisters. How pleasant it would be if we could be sure that the Americans owed their national game to an English king whom they still tend to look upon with detestation. But the truth probably is that rounders or baseball, like football, had long been a popular English game, and like football made its way to America in the natural course of events with English colonists.

Play-time was interrupted at three o'clock by dinner. Three times a week at 4.30 came Mr. Desnoyer, the dancing master; then Mr. Fung again from 5 till 6.30, and Mr. Scott from 6.30 to 8, after which came supper, followed by bed between 9 and 10. On the face of it this seems a very long day's work for boys of that age, or indeed of any age: seven and a half hours of instruction (or eight on the days when Mr. Desnoyer came), six days a week, as compared with an average of five and a half hours, five days a week, in grammar schools today. On the other hand there was no homework additional to this, and probably more interruption of the routine than is normal in school.

One such interruption may have been for amateur theatricals, which the Prince of Wales seems to have strongly favoured. At any rate he not only allowed his family to spend a lot of time acting, but even employed one of the best known actors of the day, James Quin, to produce the plays and coach the royal children and their friends[1] who took part in them. For a few years the productions of

---

[1] Among them was the future Prime Minister, son of the Prince's governor. He was a few years older than Prince George, and already at Eton.

this juvenile company were ambitious indeed, and included Addison's *Cato*, with Prince George as Portius, in 1749; Rowe's now forgotten *Tragedy of Lady Jane Grey*, and Arne's *Masque of Alfred*, in which 'Rule Britannia' was first sung. It was in the prologue to *Cato* (which some think was written by the Prince of Wales, though it may be wondered whether he had the talent to compose these polished rhymed couplets–Lord Bute seems a more likely author) that Prince George's claim to be an Englishman, despite his German parents, was first publicly stressed in a reference to him as 'A boy in England born, in England bred'.

Acting was a field in which Prince George excelled, for he had a good memory and good speech. To these youthful stage appearances and the careful tutelage of Quin he owed both a lifelong interest in drama and the clarity of diction which was a feature of his public utterances in later life. When, after his first speech from the throne, there was favourable comment on his fine delivery, Quin was tremendously proud of him: 'Ay,' he said, 'it was I who taught the boy to speak.'

In view of what happened later one may doubt whether George did so well in the work of the classroom. But in these early stages there is no hint of trouble. Ayscough had formed a very favourable impression of all his royal pupils at the outset–four of them were old enough to have come under his care:

'I thank God,' he wrote in a letter to a friend, 'I have one great encouragement to quicken me in my duty, which is, the good disposition of the children entrusted to me . . . And I must say of all the children–for they are all committed to my care– that they are as comfortable and as capable of receiving instruction as any I have ever yet met.'

But whether the Princes continued so 'conformable' as they grew older is not so certain. Edward soon had a reputation for general naughtiness, and his future career, cut short by a fatal chill at twenty-eight, was by no means a model of propriety. George, as we shall see, became a problem child. It is said that he could not even read till he was eleven. The situation seems to be summed up pictorially in a painting by Richard Wilson at the National Portrait Gallery, which, in its original form (see Plate 5), showed the majestic gowned figure of Dr. Ayscough dominating two overdressed little urchins, squirming upon a sofa. One senses a gulf between teacher and taught.

Problem Prince

This period of comparative stability in the educational routine of Prince George came to an end in 1751 with the premature death of his father, the Prince of Wales, who succumbed to a chill contracted while playing tennis, the second Prince of Wales in English history to do so. One of the first results was the dismissal of North and Dr. Ayscough by the Whig ministry of the Pelhams, then in power, who, in view of the fact that the King was already sixty-seven, wanted to make sure that the new heir apparent, who might well succeed while still a minor, was effectively under their control.

To the young Prince, thirteen years of age, the upheaval was meaningless and disturbing. The change from North to Simon, Lord Harcourt, maliciously described by Horace Walpole as a 'civil, sheepish peer', more in need of a governor himself than fit to be governor of others, may have meant little to him. It is possible too that he parted with Dr. Ayscough without regret, though he can scarcely have welcomed his successor, Dr. Thomas Hayter, Bishop of Norwich, a good scholar but too politically minded to be a good tutor. But when it was suggested that George Scott should go too, the young Prince had a tantrum and threatened to burn his books. Supported by his mother, he was allowed to have his way, and Scott remained in uneasy partnership with the new preceptor. A sub-governor was also added to the Prince's staff in the person of Andrew Stone, an able civil servant, secretary to the Duke of Newcastle.

The new quattuorvirate did not function long without friction, and it was friction generated by political rather than educational causes. A period of mutual bickering presently ended with governor and preceptor lined up in partnership against their two subordinates, both of whom were found, so it was alleged, to be men of dangerous character. Scott, the mathematician and scientist, was charged with being an atheist and with using violence and insulting language. Stone was said to be a Jacobite in disguise, who had drunk the health of the Pretender, at that time the most deadly smear of all. Both of them were accused of instilling Tory principles into the two young Princes and of teaching them to admire Bolingbroke, whose *Idea of a Patriot King*, laying down that a monarch, 'instead of putting himself at the head of one party in order to govern his people' should 'put himself at the head of his people in order to govern . . . all parties', was anathema to all good Whigs. The motive behind this raising of bogeys was of course to get rid of Scott and

Stone, and to obtain complete control of the Prince of Wales, even to the exclusion of his own mother's influence. She for her part naturally resisted these manœuvres, the more so when her own secretary, Cresset, was accused of complicity with the two alleged villains.

The King was away in Hanover when the trouble flared up. On his return he ordered an inquiry, which, however, could find little evidence to support the accusations of Harcourt and Hayter. The little Princes, who, it must be remembered, were only thirteen and fourteen at the time, might have been reading books of which the Whigs disapproved, even perhaps Jacobite books, though it did not appear that any designing person had induced them to do so. One of them – and assuredly it was the lively Edward – might have asked awkward questions, such as why was a Tory not as good as a Whig. But nothing more. Having succeeded in creating a scare of a kind with which we are only too familiar nowadays, Harcourt and Hayter resigned. Although the Prince of Wales had never liked Hayter, whom he found too dry and pedantic, as well as too strict, he gave him as a parting gift a portrait of himself in ivory. The new governor and preceptor were the Earl of Waldegrave and Dr. John Thomas, Bishop of Peterborough, neither of whom seems to have made much impact on the situation.

All this was exceedingly bad for the Prince, who, as adolescence took hold of him, was becoming more and more difficult. The indolence and apathy of the mentally retarded seemed to blanket all progress. He was asleep all day, as one of his tutors put it. Even before his father's death this had been apparent: in a letter to his son, Frederick, Prince of Wales, had written of 'that nonchalance you have, of not caring enough to please'. In the modern catch-phrase, he couldn't have cared less. Even his mother was conscious of his faults, though like all mothers she made the most of his good points. He was certainly intelligent, she said, though not quick, and had 'a tendency to seriousness'; but later admitted that he was backward and childish for his age, and cared for nobody except his brother Edward. As for his grandfather the King, his exasperation boiled over so violently on one occasion at Hampton Court that he was provoked into chastising the irritating boy – an incident which remained so vivid in George's memory that as a grown man he could not bear even to think of living at Hampton Court.

The only person who could make any impression on George at

this awkward time was George Scott, in whose support the boy had at any rate woken up sufficiently to threaten rebellion. Scott's account of the Prince seems biased in his favour, when set against the judgements even of his own parents; but, as we shall see, it brings out remarkably well the undistinguished virtues which George eventually revealed, when his troublesome youth was past.

'He is,' he said, 'a lad of very good principles, good natured and extremely honest; he has no heroic strain, but loves peace, and has no turn for extravagance; modest, and has no tendency to vice, and has as yet very virtuous principles; has the greatest temptation to gallant with the ladies, who lay themselves out in the most shameful manner to draw him, but to no purpose. He says if he were not what he is they would not mind him.'

This supposed indifference to the opposite sex did not last long – it could not have lasted long in the scion of so strongly sexed a family as the Hanoverians. Already Prince Edward, more amorous than his brother according to Scott, had at fifteen been caught philandering with a milkmaid, who locked him in the dairy till his mother came home. George was a little slower to respond; but at seventeen he too had gone the same way, and was filled with romantic imaginings about the daughter of a Quaker linen-draper named Hannah Lightfoot, whose roving eye caught his as he passed by her house. The attraction in this case became commonly known, and there were rumours that the girl was Prince George's mistress or even his wife; but, though either or both of these tales might have been true about almost any other male member of the House of Brunswick in a similar situation, it is most unlikely that they were true of Prince George. But his mother had for several years been aware of the danger of such possibilities, and when he was sixteen was afraid for him to mix with other young people, owing, as she said, to the 'universal profligacy'. As his younger brother, the Duke of Gloucester, said later, 'No boys were ever brought up in a greater ignorance of evil than the King and myself. We retained all our native innocence.' The high principles and blameless moral character which George retained throughout his life have often been attributed to his mother's strictness at this time. But none of his brothers, who were subjected to the same control, was conspicuously virtuous – and strictness in any case often has the opposite effect to that intended. It must rather be put down as a strange biological phenomenon that, while his grandfather, father, uncle, brother and sons were all notorious for their sexual irregularities, he alone during a long life was untouched by scandal.

Meanwhile the uphill educational struggle was continuing. Scott's final verdict is unknown. But when George was eighteen, his other tutor, unable to penetrate below the surface, reported unfavourably: the Prince, he wrote, was 'averse from work, indifferent to pleasure, usually in a state of total inaction, and for practical purposes still in the nursery.' His governor, the Earl of Waldegrave, described by himself as a man of the world, and by George in later years as 'a depraved, worthless man,' also reported somewhat cryptically in terms which seem to reflect his own suspicious nature: 'I found his Royal Highness,' he said, 'uncommonly full of princely prejudices contracted in the nursery, and improved by Bedchamber women and Pages of the Back Stairs'. This was in the year of his coming of age as heir apparent, when he was given a household and establishment of his own, with an income of £50,000 a year.

But, unknown perhaps even to the sympathetic Scott, Prince George had at last found the anchorage for which he craved. The strange story of his devoted and almost dog-like attachment to the Earl of Bute was revealed in full detail in 1939 with the publication of the letters – some 340 of them – which he addressed to Bute during the years following 1756.

This elegant and attractive Scottish nobleman had been for some years on very friendly terms with Frederick, Prince of Wales, and his wife, at whose home he was constantly to be seen. There were obvious reasons why he should cultivate the favour of the heir apparent. But when he continued his visits even after the death of the Prince of Wales, the scandal-mongers were ready with their own explanations. Once again they were probably wrong. The Princess, mother of eight children, was far from attractive. Bute himself was happily married, and had a family of his own. What continued to draw him to Leicester House, the Princess's residence, was almost certainly no illicit passion for the mother, but the close friendship which had grown up between him and the son.

It is easy to imagine how a backward and difficult boy, harassed by the attentions of mainly unsympathetic governors and tutors, must have welcomed someone to whom he could turn for sympathy and encouragement. Obviously his own father had been no help – fathers seldom are in crises like this; and in any case the need only became pressing after his father was dead. At the time when their friendship suddenly ripened, Bute was forty-two years old to George's seventeen. He was handsome, well dressed, witty, and a man of the world: he must have seemed the very quintessence of sophistication to the slow-witted and awkward Prince. Hero-worship followed inevitably; and Bute for his part, though very little of his side of the correspondence survives to prove it, must have come to feel a strong affection for the boy who seemed so ready to respond to his sympathy. Certainly he gave the Prince fatherly advice, and helped him with his study and his reading. By the time George was eighteen he had usurped in effect if not in name the functions of both governor and preceptor. One of the first things George, Prince of Wales, did on coming of age was to request the appointment of Lord Bute as Groom of the Stole, that is, administrative head of his establishment. The King had scarcely heard of Bute. The Whigs feared and suspected him. But the request was supported by the Dowager Princess, and the King, eventually and with an ill grace, gave his consent. With this office went a seat in the cabinet.

Bute's political rôle from this point has been a matter of intense controversy, which it would be out of place to recapitulate here. It is no longer believed by historians that he used his influence to indoctrinate George with the reactionary views of Bolingbroke, as was at one time the fashionable theory; and the idea that Bute was the young King's evil genius, who tempted him to act unconstitutionally, has been abandoned. But he undoubtedly achieved a position of dominance behind the scenes, which led logically to his appointment as Prime Minister in 1761.

Our concern here, however, is with the personal relations between Bute and his protégé, brought out into the open with the publication of George's letters. These show that for a period of six years George, even as king (for he succeeded in 1760) subjected himself almost abjectly to the will of Bute. Whatever Bute advised he would do. Whatever Bute approved was right during these years of dependence. Judging from George's replies, it seems that in the early stages Bute must have been making vigorous efforts to get the Prince to realize and remedy the defects in his character. Evidently he had criticized the indifference, the childishness and the indolence which others had commented on without effect. Coming from Bute, the criticism struck home. In a letter of 1756 (dated, whether carelessly or ignorantly, June 31st) George responds with a plethora of good resolutions:

'I have had the pleasure of your friendship during the space of a year,' he writes, 'by which I have reap'd great advantage, but not the improvement I should if I had follow'd your advice; but you shall find me make such a progress in this summer, that shall give you hopes, that with the continuation of your advice, I may turn out as you wish ...

I will take upon me the man in everything, and will not show that indefference [*sic*] which I have as yet too often done ...

... I will throw off that indolence which if I don't soon get the better of will be my ruin ...

I am young and unexperienc'd and want advice. I trust in your friendship which will assist me in all difficulties ...'

There were times when George was hurt and offended by Bute's home-truths, and seemed to sulk, as he must often have sulked under the criticism of his official tutors. But such moods did not last. In September, 1758, a reprimand from Bute, which seems to have touched on the Prince's 'incomprehensible indolence, inattention and heedlessness', reduced him to silence. Next day he wrote to explain and apologize:

'My Dearest Friend ... I am confident that anyone who did not know me so well as you do my Dearest Friend, would have looked on [my silence] as sullenness or indifference, both of these are very different from what I felt.

I am deeply afflicted at the many things you told me then and for some days pass'd. They have set me in a most dreadful light before my own eyes. I now see plainly that I have been my greatest enemy; for had I always acted according to your advice, I should now have been the direct opposite from what I am; nothing but the true love you bear me, could have led you to remain with me so long, or to speak to me in the manner you have of late.'

When his susceptible fancy became so closely caught up with the charming fifteen-year-old Lady Sarah Lennox that he even thought of marrying, he poured out his passion to Bute:

'I am daily grown unhappy, sleep has left me ... I protest before God I hever had any improper thought with regard to her ... I mince nothing to you ... I surrender my fortune into your hands ... if I must either lose my friend or my love, I will give up the latter ...'

Bute very sensibly pointed out how inappropriate such a marriage would be for the Prince of Wales: 'Think, Sir,' he wrote, 'who you are, what is your birth right, what you wish to be'; at which, without more ado, George abandoned the idea. A few weeks later he was writing to say how he and his mother had been searching through the New Berlin Almanack for eligible princesses; and within less than two years he was happily married to the one whose qualifications seemed most suitable, the plain but worthy Princess Charlotte of Mecklenburg-Strelitz, who was his wife for fifty-seven years.

Such subservience to the will of another even in an affair of the heart was unhealthy. It must no doubt be explained as homosexual in essence, though not overtly so, despite contemporary gossip. Yet it must be acknowledged that it did Prince George a lot of good, as his own mother noted with gratitude. Though very little is known of Bute's side of the affair, it is obvious that he must have handled the situation very judiciously. It would have been easy to play on the feelings of a boy so emotionally under-developed as George, and to accentuate his dependence by doing so. But, reading between the lines of George's letters, one sees Bute as a steadying influence. As the correspondence proceeds, 'My Dearest Friend' gradually gives way to 'My D Friend'; practical and political problems take the place of personal ones; and, as the infatuation fades at last into normal friendship, the King is seen to be a man, standing unsupported.

At the time of his emancipation, George III was a very personable youth, fair and of fresh complexion, with fine teeth and blue eyes. Outsiders can scarcely have imagined the internal stresses and strains to which he had been subjected. One of his wife's ladies-in-waiting, who saw him in the best possible light, gave this description of the young King:

'He had extremely solid sense and more knowledge than most Princes, he was perfectly good natured, a most dutiful Son, a fond Husband, an affectionate Brother and a firm friend.'

This was substantially true, though his affection for some of his brothers was marred by disapproval of their amorous exploits; and during a long life, and in fact till the insanity which had perhaps always underlain the instability of his youth, finally prevailed, this man of wholly German blood maintained and enhanced a reputation for English middle-class respectability. This is not the place to touch on the political ups and downs of his sixty-year-long reign, or the fluctuations of his own popularity. The general picture he increasingly conveyed was of a typical English country gentleman; bluff and hearty, amiable, God-fearing, strictly virtuous (the only man in four generations of Hanoverians to be so). It was not for nothing that he was called Farmer George, for he was genuinely interested in agriculture, and liked to think himself a practical farmer. He loved outdoor sports. His personal tastes were simple: he got up early, lit his own fire and drank no more than a cup of tea for breakfast. He ate very little, and took a great deal of exercise in the interests of his health. Like many country gentlemen of the day, he had cultured tastes also. Though not in any sense a scholarly man, he liked reading, built up a large library and was very well informed. Naturally he could speak both French and German. He was a lover of music, especially opera, and his own youthful successes on the amateur stage had left him with a strong interest in drama. He was a generous patron of art, and particularly of painting. He enjoyed dancing at small informal gatherings. But court balls, banquets and state ceremonial in general he cut down to a minimum. Neither he nor his wife liked such things: they were happiest in their own domestic circle, surrounded by their ever increasing progeny.

Looking back from this solid and worthy man to the problem child of earlier years, it is difficult to imagine how the one can have been transformed into the other. But so it was – and so it fortunately is with many problem children. Often in such cases the change is due to one man or woman, who by understanding and sympathy, by simply being there as a prop to lean on, can achieve something quite beyond the child's own parents. In the case of George III there can be no question who filled that rôle.

6

A Flock of Black Sheep

No ENGLISH KING HAD TO CONSIDER THE PROBLEM OF EDU-
cating princes (or princesses) on such a scale as George III. Thirteen
of his fifteen offspring, seven boys and six girls, reached maturity;
and of these, twelve were born within a space of sixteen years, so
that for a time all were being educated simultaneously. The royal
establishment at Kew, where the children mainly lived, must at this
time have resembled a school—a school, however, in which the
teachers outnumbered the taught. Fortunately nature so spaced the
almost annual births according to sex, that it was possible to organ-
ize the boys in three groups, each with a set of tutors, while the girls
were spread out at intervals in a way which kept a staff of governesses
and other instructors busy for many years.[1]

Despite his admiration for Eton and his love of English institu-
tions, George III did not send any of his sons to that school. All of
them were committed to the care of governors and tutors in the
traditional way during the early stages of their education; and five
of the seven were then sent abroad to Hanover to complete the
process. Only the two who actually succeeded to the English throne
were wholly educated in the English way. In the case of the Prince
of Wales this was done advisedly. But it was pure chance, or perhaps
his own breezy nature, which led to Prince William's being trained
as a naval officer; although in the event, when he became King, it
proved to have been a happy chance.

All the boys were naturally intelligent, most of them more so than
either of their parents, and they had no difficulty with the normal
classical curriculum of the day, to which they were subjected.
Shelley was very wide of the mark, when he described them as 'the

---

[1] There was a gap of six years between the last two princesses, which should have been
filled by the princes Octavius and Alfred, who died in infancy.

5   PRINCE GEORGE FREDERICK (George III) AND HIS BROTHER EDWARD, with their tutor, Dr. Ayscough, *c.* 1745: by Richard Wilson

6 GEORGE III's CHILDREN IN 1779: from Benjamin West's portrait of Queen Charlotte

dregs of their dull race', for they were well above the Hanoverian average, though they may not have looked it after reaching middle age.

During the period when all were simultaneously at Kew, that is, from about 1778 to 1780, the boys were quartered in three separate houses around Kew Green with their tutors: the Prince of Wales (George IV) and Prince Frederick in one house, Princes William and Edward in another, Princes Ernest, Augustus and Adolphus in a third. When the King and Queen were also in residence at Kew Palace, their favourite house, the daily routine for the Princes and Princesses began with family breakfast; after which the older boys dispersed to their respective houses for work, while the girls, and any who were still too young for lessons, joined the governesses and nurses. In play-time during fine weather the public liked to watch from a distance while the children were at their games – the boys busy with their model farm (for their father was bringing them up to share one of his interests – or so he fondly hoped), all the older children, girls as well as boys, playing stump-cricket, or even foot-ball or hockey. When the whole family went out together, the King driving the Queen, the two eldest Princes on horseback, the rest of the children following in a procession of carriages, it must have presented an idyllic picture to the good citizens, doffing their hats or curtseying on the side-walks, as the cavalcade passed. What man could be happier in his family, they must have thought, than the worthy father of all these good-looking children; for indeed in their youth they were all handsome – none of the boys yet showed signs of the extraordinary grossness which overtook most of them later, while several of the girls were beautiful. It was true that at this stage the King enjoyed his family. He liked to have them round him, and was keenly interested in the details of their upbringing. The problems which were to confront him in a few years' time, which revealed a harsh and uncompromising side to his character, and may have hastened the breakdown of his own unstable psychology, were as yet only dimly to be seen on the horizon.

There was a gap of a year between the Prince of Wales, born in 1762, and Prince Frederick, later Duke of York. When they were old enough to begin their serious schooling, in 1771, the King made the customary appointments. The Earl of Holdernesse, described by Horace Walpole as a 'solemn phantom', became joint governor of the two boys: he was a man to whom George perhaps thought he owed something, having dismissed him many years before from the post of Secretary of State to make way for Bute. For tutor the King's choice fell on William Markham, Bishop of Chester, an able scholar, who had been headmaster of Westminster, his own old school, and Dean of Christ Church, Oxford, his own old college, and later became Archbishop of York. Markham was a tall, portly man of magnificent presence, who looked every inch the headmaster. But it was said of him by Jeremy Bentham, one of his old boys, that at Westminster 'his business was rather in courting the great than in attending to the school'; and evidently he had courted the great to good purpose. His assistant was Dr. Cyril Jackson, a man of outstanding ability, who had been one of Markham's own favourite pupils at Westminster, and had performed the unusual feat of winning scholarships at both Oxford and Cambridge, rejecting the latter in favour of the former. Later he too became Dean of Christ Church.

When Markham asked the King 'How would your Majesty wish to have the Princes treated?' 'Like the sons of any private English gentleman,' was the reply. 'If they deserve it, let them be flogged; do as you used to do at Westminster.' Markham evidently took the King at his word. The standard of discipline he maintained is said to have resembled that of a public school, and it is not likely that young George and Frederick had much opportunity of kicking over the traces with the ex-headmaster, who certainly grounded them very well in Greek and Latin. In addition to the classics, they learnt modern languages from a Swiss tutor, M. de Sulzas; and such diverse accomplishments as drawing, elocution and practical husbandry from other instructors.

A few years later there was friction between Markham and Lord Holdernesse, who complained to the King that his colleague had turned the royal boys against him and was making his task impossible. It seems unlikely that this can have been true, though it is easy to believe that these two lively boys may not have shown sufficient respect for the 'solemn phantom'. But the King, who had experienced similar strife as a boy among his own educational staff, and perhaps detected faults on both sides, thought it best to change both governor and tutors. Accordingly in 1776 Lord Bruce took the place of Lord Holdernesse, himself to give way soon afterwards to the Duke of Montague; while Markham was superseded by Richard Hurd, Bishop of Worcester. This may have been change for the better. Hurd was a very human character, highly popular with the royal family, who nicknamed him 'The Beauty of Holiness.' When as a mark of his esteem the King wanted to make him Archbishop of Canterbury, he declined on the grounds that he was unequal to the task. He was an excellent judge of boys, and evidently had some talent for the kind of epigrammatic school report which tends to cause friction with parents. It was he who said of the Prince of Wales at fifteen that he would become 'either the most polished gentleman, or the most accomplished blackguard in Europe—possibly both'.

Bishop Hurd's assistant was Mr. Arnold—a name which catches the attention. Was he a relation of the great headmaster of Rugby, as yet unborn? The answer seems to be, No.

As a small boy the Prince of Wales is said to have been timid, and on his fifth birthday the King gave him twenty-one brass cannon of one pound calibre in an attempt to arouse some martial feelings in him. But by the time he was seven, he seems to have been already at war with his father, and it was a war which continued off and on for almost another forty years. Even if the King was not conscious of taking a dislike to his son at such an early age, the Prince thought he had done so, which had the same psychological effects. 'He hates me,' he exclaimed in his early twenties. 'He always did from seven years old.' The resulting strife, fierce even by the standard of Hanoverian feuds between fathers and sons, warped the lives of both of them. By the time Prince George was twelve the King was complaining to Holdernesse of his evading application, his duplicity, his bad habit of not speaking the truth—all of them natural reactions to parental pressure.

Yet this was only one side of the Prince's character, if unfortunately the one of which his father was most conscious, and the one which his father's reactions tended to accentuate. Other people found him a charming boy. With the fair hair and blue eyes of his race, he was handsome and knew it; he talked easily, smiled readily and had a nice sense of humour, which ran particularly to mimicry.

That he had also some of the other propensities of his race was also revealed when, at the age of sixteen, he had his first affair, falling violently in love with one of his sisters' governesses, named Mary Hamilton, who was six years older than himself. She was the first of a life-long series of women, all notoriously older than their lover, who from time to time engaged his affection. It may be that

Miss Hamilton did not take it as seriously as he did; but it was all most romantic–billets doux and trinkets were exchanged, and during the few months that it lasted, the ardent lover was protesting his eternal devotion.

What he looked like at this time we may learn from the best, or the worst, of all authorities, himself. Writing to Miss Hamilton with an amusing blend of vanity and self-conscious mock modesty, he draws a self-portrait, clearly the fruit of much pondering before the mirror:

'He is now approaching the bloom of youth, he is rather above the common size, his limbs well-proportioned, and upon the whole well made, tho' too great a penchant to grow fat, the features of his Countenance are strong and manly, tho' they carry with them too much of an air of hauteur, his forehead well shaped, his eyes tho' none of the best, and tho' grey are yet passable, tolerable good eyebrows and eyelashes, un petit nez retroussé cependant assez aimé, a good mouth tho' rather large, with fine teeth, a tolerable good chin, but the whole of the countenance is too round. I forgot to add very uggly [sic] ears . . .'

This must have both charmed and amused Miss Hamilton, who will not have failed to notice the one spelling mistake, the erratic punctuation and the nicely calculated phrase in French.

With this went a character sketch in the same style, which, with our knowledge of the adult man, we can recognize as substantially true, as far as it went:

'His sentiment and thoughts are open and generous, above doing anything that is mean (too susceptible, even to believing people his friends, and placing too much confidence in them . . .) grateful and friendly to excess where he finds a *real friend* . . . rather too familiar to his inferiors but will not suffer himself to be browbeaten or treated with Haughtiness by his superiors. Now for his vices, or rather let us call them weaknesses–too subject to give loose or vent to his passions of every kind, too subject to be in a passion . . . he is rather too fond of Wine and Women.'

One of the weaknesses Prince George does not mention is inconstancy. A few weeks after this he is writing to say that he has fallen deeply in love with someone else, this time an actress named Mary Robinson, only four years older than himself. All is over for Mary Hamilton. 'Adieu, Adieu, Adieu,' the letter ends. 'TOUJOURS CHÈRE. Oh! Mrs. Robinson.'

It was Oh! Mrs. Robinson indeed. The lady was fascinating and had plenty of more mature lovers, as well as a husband, but no doubt it was something to have attracted the heir to the throne, though he was only seventeen. She encouraged the Prince, who bombarded her with letters for a whole year, which, when the affair reached its natural termination, his father had to buy back for no less than £5,000, remarking as he did so that it was a shameful scrape, and that he personally had 'never been engaged in such a transaction'; which was only partly true, though in his case there had been no love-letters to be redeemed.

This incident did nothing to ease relations between father and son. But it left very pleasant memories with Mrs. Robinson, who, looking back many years later through the mists of time, drew this idealized picture of the youthful Prince, as she recalled him:

'The graces of his person, the irresistible sweetness of his smile, the tenderness of his melodious and manly voice, will be remembered by me till every vision of this changing scene shall be forgotten.'

Meanwhile Prince George's education had been proceeding, and though it is easy to imagine that he may have found difficulty in giving his mind to Latin and Greek, which lacked the practical uses of French, he eventually became quite a good classical scholar, and, like so many of his contemporaries, picked up the knack of quoting aptly from Greek or Latin authors. He is said to have been particularly fond of Tacitus, a writer who has much to say of special significance for princes. Many years later Dr. Burney, the celebrated musician, when dining with the Prince, was agreeably surprised to find that he could quote Homer in Greek and discuss Greek literature with understanding.

He had a good command of French, German and Italian, acquired without much effort from M. de Sulzas and other native speakers, of whom over many years there was always a selection in attendance on the royal children. In a sense it was a trilingual court. For the Queen, English was very much an acquired language; and though she acquired it very well, she was most at home in French and German; while the King, proud as he was to regard English as his native tongue, nevertheless spoke the languages current among his German relations with ease. His sons were all taught French and German, and learnt them the more readily, though with varying degrees of proficiency, through hearing them so often spoken.

It has often been said, following Thackeray, that the Prince of Wales grew up partially illiterate in his own language, which he could not spell, and which he wrote in a 'lax, maudlin, slip-slop' way. This is a gross exaggeration. His private epistolary style was indeed very personal to him. There is a letter to his mother which begins like this:

'What a kind, oh! what a kind kind very kind dear letter I have been favoured with from you; never no never never can I find words sufficiently strong or powerful to express to you the full tide of all my gratitude . . .'

But, as he said himself, he preferred to pour out his thoughts in their own 'misshapen and crude state' when writing intimately, and there is something to be said for so doing. When the occasion demanded it, he was quite capable of writing, or speaking, English in the formal periodic manner of his age.

Again, it is often forgotten that amid all the other preoccupations of his life, some of them far from reputable, whether as Prince of Wales, Regent or King, George continued to read and interest himself in English literature. It is difficult to know how much credit to give his tutors for this: someone must have aroused his interest in the beginning. But this is a problem which arises with all educated men of the period. They were reared exclusively on the classics; no attention was paid either to the English language (except as a medium of translation) or to English literature at school; and yet on the whole they were more competent in both than their modern counterparts, who have been taught English, in most cases with little or no Greek and Latin, from infancy. This was true of the Prince of Wales. He retained for life a taste for reading modern English literature, surely acquired as a boy. Byron was his favourite poet–though it would be far from the truth to say that he was Byron's favourite prince; and he was on very friendly terms with Scott, whom he honoured with a baronetcy on becoming King. Among other novelists he had a great admiration for Jane Austen, read all her novels repeatedly and kept a set of them in each of his houses.

When he was eighteen the Prince came of age as heir apparent. This was the moment when a wise father would have relaxed some of the restraints under which the hot-blooded and precocious youth had long been chafing. It was not politic to let the heir to the throne cool his ardour on the battlefield or sow his wild oats on the continent. But Prince George should certainly now have been allowed in some way to 'dash into the wide world' –his own phrase–to have his own establishment and manage his own affairs. But the King was not a wise father –and of course it is very difficult to be a wise father, when it involves allowing your son to do so many things of which you disapprove, in the hope that he will come right in the end; and especially when he is only eighteen. He compromised fatally. The Prince was given a small allowance and horses for his own use; but he was required to live in his father's house, not in one of his own, still under the supervision of a governor and a sub-governor (whose task must have been extraordinarily difficult), while the King kept a firm hold on the purse-strings. 'It is ever better,' he said in a letter to Lord North, 'that Persons should feel their situations will by degrees improve, and particularly Young persons.' No doubt such a rule may work when father and son are congenial, and the son has the feel of controlling his own destiny. But it had the worst possible effect on Prince George. This period of semi-tutelage became one long rampage. The Prince did everything possible to annoy his father, throwing himself into a life of reckless self-indulgence with all the zest of which a Hanoverian was capable, and building up a mountain of debt. When he was still a boy one of his tutors had said that he could not be taught to understand the value of money; and if his father had thought that he would learn it by having to manage on a small allowance, he had misjudged him completely. The King's reaction to this behaviour was naturally savage; the Prince responded to his harsh comments with still greater follies; and a situation of complete deadlock between father and son was established.

Amid this unhappy discord the Prince's formal education came to an end. It would be too much to say that it had been a complete success. His tutors and instructors had done their work well in the circumstances, and in his adolescence particularly George must have been a difficult pupil to manage. He had learnt five languages and cultivated a taste for literature, modern as well as ancient: he had acquired a considerable knowledge of music, and had learnt to play the 'cello with moderate skill. Somehow he had laid the foundations of what later became an expert appreciation of art. This was no small achievement. But no one had been able to mould his character, to control his growing flamboyance, or direct his wilfulness and egotism into productive channels; and his father's ill judged attempts to do so only made things worse. It was of course an age of flamboyance, and it was natural that the Prince of Wales should set the pace and take the lead; and in fact he did this very well. His taste, though extravagant, was sound. The houses he built, the pictures, the furniture and the silver he purchased so lavishly, set a standard which gave the period of the Regency a unique artistic quality which is still admired. But the heedless way he spent money at a time when poverty was widespread, and the scandals of his private life (which might not have occurred if his marriage had not been so disastrously inadequate) tended as time went on to obscure his good points. His natural kindliness, and the almost fatherly devotion with which, as Regent and King, he looked after the interests of his sisters, who adored him, were not appreciated by the public, who saw only the seamy side.

The popular impression of the Prince Regent as a middle-aged man was in fact summed up in the famous words for which Leigh Hunt went to prison in 1812 – 'a violator of his word, a libertine over head and ears in debt and disgrace, a despiser of domestic ties, the companion of gamblers and demireps, a man who has just closed half a century without one single claim on the gratitude of his country or the respect of posterity.'

Some of these things were partly true. After another century and a half we can see that he had positive virtues too.

Prince Frederick, later created Duke of York, was only a year younger than his brother, the Prince of Wales, and built to the same pattern. He too was a tall, fair, nice-looking boy, a lively talker and an amusing companion, the sort of boy whom everybody finds attractive (and he too in later years grew grossly corpulent). Like his elder brother, Frederick was physically strong and good at games; but he was less able, and though he had no difficulty with the classical curriculum to which he was subjected by the worthy bishops of Chester and Worcester, it made no permanent impression. He grew up without intellectual interests. In some ways he was a typical public-schoolboy, though he never went to school.

As the King's second son, Prince Frederick was almost automatically destined for the army, and it was a career for which he was well suited, both physically and temperamentally. In 1780, when he was seventeen, he was sent overseas to Hanover, accompanied by Colonel Greville as supervisor, to learn his trade as a soldier. He was away till 1787, and during this period of freedom from parental control he acquired not only some knowledge and experience of the military art, but a considerable taste for the lusts of the flesh also; and it was the latter which came the more easily to him. He was popular wherever he went, and received far more attention in Germany as an English prince than he ever did at home as Duke of York. Frederick the Great himself gave a state ball and a dinner in his honour when he visited Berlin, and he attended the manœuvres of the Prussian army as a distinguished guest. This kind of treatment before he had mastered the duties of a junior officer must have interfered with his military education, besides giving him an exaggerated view of his own merits. Perhaps it was not surprising that, when Lord Cornwallis was sent to report officially on the Prince's progress in military science, he found little to praise but his charm and good nature:

'The Royal Person whom I saw,' he wrote, 'does not give much hopes, further than a great deal of good nature and a very good heart. His military ideas are those of a wild boy of the Guards . . . One cannot help loving him . . . There is no chance of any good coming but by his being kept abroad, and of the English being kept from him.'

But he continued to make progress in other less desirable fields, aided and abetted perhaps by some of the English in Hanover, whose company Lord Cornwallis thought so detrimental. When at last he returned to England, the dashing young officer his parents now saw was very different from the boy who had left with their blessing seven years before; and the change was not altogether welcome to his father, especially when the Prince came immediately under the influence of his elder brother, then in full rebellion, whose lead he was only too willing to follow.

However, he too had his good qualities, and as the years passed, he calmed down sufficiently to enjoy a moderately distinguished military career. Though unsuccessful as a general in the field–his methods are even satirized in a familiar nursery rhyme–he managed the British army efficiently and progressively, when he became commander-in-chief. It was unfortunate that his career was interrupted for a time, when he thought it proper to resign, after an inquiry had revealed that his mistress had been trafficking in army commissions, though he himself had done nothing discreditable. But he lived it down, and when in due course he was reappointed to his old post, he showed himself once more a good public servant.

A Flock of Black Sheep

It is always difficult for a prince to enjoy a successful professional career. But Frederick, Duke of York, must be given credit for doing so; though whether he would have reached the highest rank on his own merits, if he had not been a prince, is quite another matter.

The two eldest boys were scarcely afloat educationally, when the King had to launch his second couple, Prince William, later Duke of Clarence, and Prince Edward, Duke of Kent. As it happened, these were boys of some consequence historically, the one destined to be King William IV, the other father of Queen Victoria; but who could have guessed it then?

They were born in 1765 and 1767 respectively, and the two-year gap may have made it difficult to teach them together; but they lived together in the same house, with the same pair of tutors. The senior of these was Dr. John Fisher, later Bishop of Salisbury, who had a long and close connection with the royal family, which led to his being known as the King's Fisher. More than thirty years later he became tutor to George IV's daughter, Charlotte. It is not easy to appreciate why the Georges, father and son, thought so well of him, for he seems to have been a pompous, self-important man in later life, and surely showed symptoms of it in youth. Probably, like Dr. Markham, he knew how to court the great. But he had other qualities also, as we shall see later. The royal children, who were quick to notice the pomposity, called him the great U.P.

The lively and irrepressible Prince William was destined for the 'glorious profession' of the navy, as his father called it, and was sent to sea as a midshipman when he was thirteen, having been grounded in the classics by Dr. Fisher. Some time before he was due to leave, the King, like any father sending his son to boarding school, wrote anxiously to inquire 'what clothes, necessaries and books he ought to take', promising also to have him instructed in any subject the naval authorities thought desirable—he had already made a start with geometry. When the Prince joined his ship in 1779, the King wrote that he had despatched for his use 'an hair-trunk, two chests and two cots done up in one mat'. 'I flatter myself,' added the proud father, 'you will be pleased with the appearance of the boy, who neither wants resolution nor cheerfulness.'

One of the objects of sending him to sea was to teach Prince William to stand on his own legs, though perhaps he did not need much teaching. He was to be received 'without the smallest marks of parade', and to be given no privileges, said the King. 'The young man,' he explained, 'goes as a sailor, and as such . . . no marks of distinction are to be shown unto him; that would destroy my whole plan.'

Yet at the same time, with a curious inconsistency, the King expected Prince William to continue his classical studies at sea, which must at once have put him in a different category from the other midshipmen. For this purpose he was to be provided with 'a small place made with light sufficient' for study, a privilege indeed on board ship; and was accompanied by his tutor, the Rev. Henry Majendie, who was created an honorary midshipman for the occasion. This sounds more ludicrous than it perhaps turned out. Majendie, whose father was also a tutor in the royal employ, and had taught Queen Charlotte English, as well as helping with the two eldest boys, was still quite young. The corpulence and imperturbable gravity of expression for which he was noted, when in years to come, as Bishop successively of Chester and Bangor, he reaped the reward of service to the royal family, were not yet evident, and he probably fitted in quite well among the junior officers. In any case young William does not seem to have been much inhibited by the presence of a tutor in the background. Announcing that he wished to be known, not as Prince William Henry (which was how he was described on the ship's books), but as plain William Guelph, he was soon playing practical jokes and getting into scrapes ashore with the best of them.

His independent and outspoken manner sometimes led to friction. But William was handy with his fists, and had no objection to resolving differences of opinion in what was then the good old-fashioned way. It was after one such bout, with a Lieutenant Moodie of the Marines, in which he had been the winner, that he gave a foretaste of the jovial tactlessness for which he was famous all his life. 'You are a brave fellow,' he said to his defeated opponent, 'though you are a marine.'

He was present at the battle of Cape St. Vincent when still only fourteen, and during the next few years saw plenty of active service, which he thoroughly enjoyed. It was good for him to be away from his father. But when he came home on leave, they were in immediate collision, and the King must have been sadly disillusioned with his 'young sailor'. The first time the fault lay with those deplorable elder brothers, who took it upon themselves to initiate the boy, still only fifteen or so, into the delights of dissipation. He was only too willing; but when one night he was taken up by the watch for brawling, King George quickly cut short his leave and sent him back to sea. The next time he became entangled with a sixteen-year-old girl, and again had to return to his ship precipitately. Of what went on in foreign ports the King mercifully knew nothing.

Meanwhile Prince William was understandably not making very much progress with his naval studies–and even less, one imagines, with his classical education, which at some stage must have been tacitly abandoned. 'William was ever violent when controlled,' the King wrote back resignedly, on receiving a somewhat unfavourable report from Sir Samuel Hood (later Lord Hood), commanding the squadron in which the Prince was at that time serving aboard H.M.S. *Barfleur*. 'I had hoped by this time he would have been conscious of his own levity.' But by now he should have realized that it was vain to hope for such a transformation in any son of his.

Yet, like the rest of them William grew up, and in due course became a reasonably competent officer. One of his instructors at this time was Nelson, already in his early twenties a captain. The two had something in common, and Nelson, who was always rather biased in favour of royalty, reported perhaps too optimistically on Prince William's talents. Whether because of this or because of his birth, he was promoted rapidly, and reached the rank of captain at twenty-three. But his natural impulsiveness and independence of character led him into several minor acts of insubordination; and when finally he was so irresponsible as to sail home from the West Indies without orders, it became clear that he could no longer be actively employed. In short, though he received further promotion from time to time, he was shelved professionally. This was a sad blow, for he was taking his naval career seriously. Aggrieved and unemployed, he joined his two elder brothers in opposition to the King, and for a time caused what trouble he could.

Years later, when he actually became king, it proved an advantage to him to have been a naval officer. He was often blunt and tactless – the direct methods of the quarter-deck were not always appropriate to some of the delicate situations with which he had to deal. But his accessibility and bluff, hearty manner appealed to a people who, during the Napoleonic wars, had come to love a sailor, and, though he never mastered the functions of a constitutional monarch, he was generally a popular king.

When Prince William went to sea, the young Prince Edward, later created Duke of Kent, who was twelve years old at the time, faced the concentrated attentions of governor and tutor, and enjoyed the combined services of a housekeeper, a porter, three maids and two pages in the house which the two boys had previously shared on Kew Green. His household expenses amounted, we are told, to £2,000 a year, his drink bill to £200; which, considering that the purchasing power of money was then about twice what it is now, seems to indicate that the great U.P. and his colleague did themselves pretty well.

Prince Edward was probably not daunted by this isolation, for at an early age he had shown himself a boy of forceful character, already in miniature rebellion against his father. The great U.P. himself used in his old age to relate an anecdote illustrating the boy's determined nature and an aversion from telling lies which seems to put him in the same class with George Washington at about the same age. Annoyed in some way by his father, young Prince Edward revenged himself by smashing a valuable clock much prized by the King. When the shattered remains were discovered, no one at first suspected the Prince of doing such a thing; but on a casual question being put to him, the following dialogue ensued:

Prince: I did it.
Questioner: But your Royal Highness did it by accident?
Prince: No. I did it intentionally.
Questioner: But your Royal Highness regrets what you have done?
Prince: No, not at all.

And that was that. The Prince, it need hardly be said, was punished severely, and, as we gather from Dr. Fisher, it was not the only time. He was by no means the favourite son of his parents. His own perversity and their attempts to crush it only widened the breach. Yet his brothers and sisters thought well of him.

At that time there was no possible career for a prince but in the services: he must either be a soldier, or a sailor, or nothing, but preferably a soldier. So in 1785, when he was seventeen, Prince Edward was packed off to Luneburg in Hanover to complete his education and be trained as an officer. His governor for the occasion was a certain Baron Wangenheim, no doubt a native of Hanover, whose function was to control both the Prince and his finances. It was not a good choice. Wangenheim was too strict in handling the boy, and scarcely honest in the way he managed his money. Presently Prince Edward was referring to his governor as 'a mercenary tyrant', and accusing him of 'open robbery' in appropriating to his own uses the Prince's personal allowance of £1,000 a year, out of which he allowed him only a guinea and a half a week. The King had certainly not intended this, but probably Prince Edward's complaints never reached him, for Wangenheim took counter-measures. As the Prince wrote later:

'My letters were interrupted; several never reached the King; he was displeased at my apparently undutiful silence; false representations were made to him respecting my conduct; I was described to him as recklessly extravagant: I had the means of being so, undoubtedly, on a guinea and a half a week.'

The Prince for the moment was powerless; but he was not the kind of young man to submit tamely to such tyranny, and when in due course he was transferred to Geneva and the same treatment continued despite a nominally increased allowance, he finally left Wangenheim to his own devices and went home. The King was naturally incensed by this second display of insubordination on the part of one of his sons. He refused to see the Prince, who inevitably asserted himself by joining his three brothers already in opposition.

But presently the situation was resolved when the King, despite his anger, allowed the young man's military career to proceed. The details of this are not to the point here. But it is interesting to see the family character, with its faults and its virtues, emerging in yet another variation. Prince Edward was as hopeless with money as any of the brothers, and what with his father's parsimony and Wangenheim's dishonesty, he grew up in a chronic state of insolvency which never left him.

Yet in matters other than the spending of money he was dependable and efficient, and in some respects, as for example in anything connected with military uniforms or decorations, even meticulous. An anecdote, which he recorded himself, tells how as a young cadet in Hanover he had somehow been overlooked on the dismissal of the parade, and remained at his post for four hours, till his commanding officer, warned by someone who had seen the boy still standing there, came back to release him. Here in embryo perhaps was the sense of duty which his daughter so notably displayed: she too stuck to her post. Like all the men of his family, Prince Edward was a brave soldier, and as a military commander he showed good administrative capacity; but, unlike his brothers in one respect, he was such a stern and heartless disciplinarian that he had to be relieved of his post as Governor of Gibraltar to forestall a mutiny.

This was probably the reflex of the harsh discipline to which he himself had been subjected as a boy; and it seemed to sit oddly on a man who in ordinary relationships was amiable and kind.

While the four older boys were busily employed sowing their first crops of wild oats, a third instalment of princes, three in number, was making its way forward. This trio consisted of the Princes Ernest, Augustus and Adolphus, the future Dukes of Cumberland, Sussex and Cambridge, who had been born in rapid succession in the years 1771, 1773 and 1774, and thus formed a conveniently homogeneous group. They were committed to the care of tutors not otherwise distinguished, the Rev. G. Cookson, later a canon of Windsor, and Dr. Hughes, who between them maintained a high standard of discipline and work.

Compared with their elder brothers these three boys were easy to handle. As commonly happens with the younger members of a family, their father put less pressure on them. The urge to be top dog, natural in fathers, had long been under strain and was noticeably weakening; and in any case the King must have been considerably preoccupied with the goings-on of the other boys. Not that these young ones never annoyed him: they would have been less than boys, and he more than a man, if they had failed to do so. The story is told, for example, how Prince Augustus got a rise out of his father when he was seven by wearing the election colours of a candidate disapproved by the King, and was locked up and sent supperless to bed for his pains. But relations between King George and the three junior Princes were comparatively normal and healthy. The King was particularly fond of the youngest of all, Prince Adolphus, who was unique among the seven boys in never rebelling seriously against paternal authority.

Educationally these three were treated as a unit, and after the usual grounding, they were all sent in 1786 to the University of Göttingen, to have a German superstructure erected upon the English foundations laid by Cookson and Hughes. Since they were only fifteen, thirteen and twelve at the time, it does not seem that they can have really followed a university course. The set-up was more like that of a small boarding school on foreign soil, in which the teaching was shared between the boys' own tutors and members of the university staff; and the impression of a school was heightened when in 1790 all three boys caught measles. Each Prince was accompanied by a governor, a preceptor and a gentleman, who between them, with odds of three to one in their favour, must have easily stifled any tendency to revolt. All twelve seem to have lived together, with a generous allowance from the King.

Some insight into the working of this establishment may be derived from one of the King's letters to the Bishop of Worcester, who had tutored Princes George and Frederick, and would have been particularly interested in this German experiment:

'My accounts from Göttingen of the little colony I have sent there is very favourable. All three seem highly delighted and pleased with those that have the instruction of them. But what pleases me most is the satisfaction they express at the course of theology they have begun with Professor Less. Professor Heyne gives them lessons in the classics, and has an assistant for the rougher work. They learn history, geography, moral philosophy, mathematics and experimental philosophy, so that their time is fully employed. I think Adolphus at present seems the favourite of all, which from his lovely manners is natural, but the good sense of Augustus will in the end prove conspicuous.'

Reading between the lines here we may suspect some inadequate grounding in classics, which called for 'rough work' from junior staff, before the pupils were ready to confront Professor Heyne himself (who was paid, like his fellow professors, at the rate of £400 a year for this special service). And did they really enjoy the theology lessons most?

The subsequent careers of these three Princes present still further variations on the same theme. Prince Ernest was something of an enigma. Whereas the other six looked, as has been said, like comfortable merchants, he resembled an elegant cavalry officer. This was in fact quite appropriate, for it had been the King's plan from the outset that he should become in due course commander-in-chief of the Hanoverian army, with which object he was specially coached in military subjects by General Malortie. During his early service with the Hanoverians he proved a conspicuously good soldier and was severely wounded. There were other contrasts between him and his brothers. While they never tried to conceal the irregularities of their private lives, his remained sinisterly obscure. The scandal-mongers even hinted at incest; and the suicide of his valet after attempting to murder him raised questions as to possible motives which were openly canvassed in the hostile press. While the others were great talkers, he was a silent man, and what he did say

7 ALBERT EDWARD, PRINCE OF WALES (Edward VII), with his tutor,
Mr. Gibbs, *c*. 1853

8   PRINCE ALBERT VICTOR AND PRINCE GEORGE (George V), aged 13 and
12, as naval cadets, 1877

was direct and forthright, though often obscene. He was perhaps the most intelligent of the seven too: his mind was clear and incisive. His greatest achievement came late in life. When at sixty-six he succeeded to the throne of Hanover, he ruled that country with unexpected success for fourteen years to the great satisfaction of his subjects, who were glad to have a king amongst them after being governed by absentee monarchs for several generations. He even took the unprecedented step of introducing a liberal constitution; and when he died at the age of eighty he was hailed by a grateful people as Father of his Country.

Prince Augustus, Duke of Sussex, was the only son of George III – the only Hanoverian prince perhaps–to be in any way a scholar. This arose partly no doubt because in early life he suffered from asthma, which both debarred him from military service, and led to his wintering in Italy, where (in addition to making an injudicious morganatic marriage) he was exposed to cultural influences not to be found in England. But seeds had been sown in Göttingen, where he had come in contact with real learning, particularly in the person of Heyne, who was a noted classical scholar. An interest in Hebrew, which he continued to read with a private tutor all his life, possibly dated from this time. He was well read also in a general way; and, like many independent-minded people, he had the habit of making critical notes in the margins of his books, often with the sketch of a hand to direct attention to the passage under comment. These often vividly reveal his cast of mind, as when the pointing hand appears against the Athanasian creed in a prayer book, with the comment, 'I don't believe a word of it.' He was a bibliophile also from quite an early age, and amassed a splendid library, which included the finest collection of Bibles in the world–he had over 5,000 different varieties. Like several of his brothers, he had rather a flair for music, which his residence in Italy as a young man–he first went there when he was nineteen–encouraged him to develop. He took lessons in singing, practised assiduously, and looked back on his youthful triumphs as a singer with pride. 'I had the most wonderful voice that ever was heard,' he said with naïve egotism to someone who mentioned it, 'Three octaves; and I do understand music. I practised eight hours a day in Italy. One may boast of a voice, as it is a gift of nature.' A more valuable and lasting reminder of Italy was the collection of manuscripts of Italian operas, which he brought back to add to his library.

Prince Adolphus, Duke of Cambridge, known to the family as Dolly, also had some pretensions to learning. The King, who was perhaps prejudiced, thought him the most promising of the Göttingen trio. Even during a period of service in the Hanoverian army (in the course of which he was wounded), he continued his education on his own initiative, and at twenty-six was getting up early to work and taking four lessons a day in science and other subjects with private tutors. One of them was probably Mr. Tatler, who had been with him at Göttingen, and continued to attend him with great devotion. When he was stationed at Oldenburg the only thing that made life tolerable in an otherwise boring town was the local library. He was an excellent linguist, but was chiefly remarkable for the sometimes almost unintelligible speed with which he spoke not only French and German but English – the result not of nervousness but of a very quick intelligence. He was at ease socially, enjoyed conversation and shared the family talent for music. When, at the age of forty-two, he was appointed viceroy of Hanover, the good qualities which he had always possessed found full scope, and he retained the post for twenty-one years, until in 1837 Hanover became a kingdom, and his brother, the Duke of Cumberland, succeeded to the throne. In his later years he became somewhat eccentric, and was noted for his habit of repeating things three times (referred to by Horace Walpole as 'triptology') – a peculiarity which was almost as fertile of anecdotes as Dr. Spooner's amiable weakness.

When George III looked back on the education of his flock of black sheep, those seven sons, whose gallivanting so notably caught the public attention, he must sometimes have wondered what he had accomplished and whether he could have done more. These boys had started life with some very strongly marked inherited characteristics, which probably no training or education could have eliminated entirely. 'Mud from a muddy spring,' Shelley called them – and it would have been impossible to refine away the mud derived from so strongly tainted a source. They were all built on a massive scale physically; most were over six feet tall, and all but one grew corpulent. Their personal characters were made to match. Their exuberance and exaggerated tastes were part of a sort of inborn megalomania. They lived large: their eating, their drinking, their public behaviour, their gambling, the reckless speed with which they drove or rode – all betokened an exaggerated outlook on life; and all these things involved spending money on such a monstrous scale, that its real value was completely smothered. This was one of the things which, during their lifetime, got them into the greatest ill odour because of its repercussions on the exchequer. It was the Duke of Wellington who referred to the royal dukes as 'the damnedest millstone about the neck of any Government that can be imagined.' They were – most of them – headstrong and self-willed, and as young men, the more they were disciplined and restrained the worse they became; and they retained these adolescent traits well into adult life. Few fathers can have had such a difficult brood. Sexually also they were generously endowed, and in an age when scandals in society were almost normal, they had such a reputation for amorous intrigue, that today they are chiefly remembered for their mistresses and their morganatic marriages. Yet – and this too was a family trait – in all this preoccupation with the opposite sex it was the craving for domestic bliss rather than glamour which led them on, and most of them achieved it for a time with their middle-aged mistresses.

None of these things could have been changed by education. But among the seven not all were equally guilty of the charges which collectively have been levelled against them; and none of the seven was wholly bad. They all had something attractive about them. They were liked by most of those who knew them personally, and in varying degrees admired and adored by their sisters. Apart from the Duke of Cumberland, they were animated conversationalists and enjoyed good talk and the company of intelligent people. Their own ability was quite considerable; and all of them in the course of their education had developed a variety of talents which were entirely praiseworthy.

All of them, in the fashion of their day, had a smattering of classical learning, and some had a little more. They were all at home in at least two foreign languages. They were fond of making speeches, in the House of Lords and elsewhere, and did so at least as well as the average contemporary in public life. Several of them had literary and scientific interests, and they had a naturally good though far from austere taste in art. They were most of them naturally musical also, and, in an age when a pleasant singing voice was a drawing-room asset, those of them who could sing frequently entertained their friends by doing so. Their other social accomplishments were in keeping; and they could all play the part of the prince in something like the Renaissance manner, when the occasion demanded.

Of course, by contrast, their shortcomings were on a massive scale. The Victorians of the next generation, looking back at them, were horrified, and good Prince Albert, planning the education of the future Edward VII, said that the great object must be to make him as unlike as possible to any of his great-uncles. But we, who are separated from them by 150 years, can take a more balanced view, and, without losing sight of their vices, give these Brobdingnagian brothers credit for their virtues.

The education of the six Princesses in itself produced fewer difficulties; though even they, as grown up young women, seem to have run true to stock, if any weight is to be given to the circumstantial rumours of illicit liaisons, secret marriages and, in two or three cases, even illegitimate children, which broke from time to time in later years, and which affected at least four of the six. But nothing of this kind emerged to spoil the happy atmosphere of early days in nursery or schoolroom.

The eldest of the six, Charlotte, the Princess Royal, later Queen of Würtemberg, was born in 1766: she had been preceded by three brothers, and was followed immediately by a fourth. The Princesses Augusta and Elizabeth followed in 1768 and 1770: then, after an interval of six years, during which the birth of three more boys brought the male total up to seven, came Princesses Mary and Sophia in quick succession, with Princess Amelia as a distant afterthought in 1783, twenty-one years after her eldest brother, the Prince of Wales. This, with the two Princes Octavius and Alfred, who died in infancy, completed a remarkable performance by the Queen.

Alike in looks and in behaviour the girls seemed to be models of what princesses should be. 'Never in tale or fable were six sister princesses more lovely,' wrote Fanny Burney, who had a post in the Queen's entourage; and though her uncritical admiration of the royal family may have led her into some exaggeration here, it is certainly true that they were six very nice-looking and attractive girls. As to their personal charm, their wit, their humour, their liveliness and friendly, open manner all witnesses are agreed. They seem to have presented few problems to their governesses, whose recorded comments are seldom anything but favourable.

The education and training of the Princesses was controlled personally by the Queen, who, until her attention was distracted by her husband's malady, of which the first signs began to appear in 1788, kept a very close eye on what was going on. It was a strict régime. The Princesses themselves, as they grew older, thought it too strict. But accounts of life at court make it clear that there was plenty of freedom as well, and the girls did not lack opportunity for amusement. In fact, with so many boisterous brothers about, the play was often rough. The Princesses are said to have played cricket, hockey and sometimes even football with the boys, and some of them, especially Princess Augusta, a good cricketer, passed through a tomboy phase. Like their brothers, they often found the regular family routine irksome. All of them disliked the ritual of strolling on the terrace at Windsor *en famille* under the public gaze, which was known to them as 'terracing'. With the particular exception of Princess Augusta, they were not nearly so fond of trips on the royal yacht as their father liked to think, and they would gladly have avoided being ducked by the bathing women at Weymouth, if they had been able. But there were balls and dances and parties, country visits and plenty of indoor fun to make up for this; and in general life outside the schoolroom, seen through the eyes of the ladies in waiting, the governesses and the admiring visitors whose accounts have survived, was rosy indeed.

Their actual education, conventional enough for girls of high birth in the period, cannot but strike one as empty. It had no objective but the idle life of courts and drawing rooms. These girls were condemned by social custom from the outset to doing nothing; and even if they married (which only three of them did) they would still be doing nothing. With this aim in view, they were instructed in trivialities. Virtually their only solid achievements were in foreign languages, which they learnt well; but languages are only a means to an end, and they scarcely, if at all, attained the end, of intelligent intercourse with foreigners and the reading of foreign literature. When we consider how the Tudor princesses threw themselves into the study of Cicero and Demosthenes, or wrestled eagerly with problems of theology, whereas their Hanoverian counterparts busied themselves with nothing more solid than netting purses or embroidering cushion-covers, the contrast becomes painful. Even one of their own governesses had doubts about the value of what the Princesses were being taught, but comforted herself with the thought that possible alternatives might have been worse.

'If they had been great geniuses,' she wrote, 'or had revealed much taste for study, it would be a pity to see them occupied with needles and paint-brushes. But those things are better occupations than gaming, novels and intrigues.'

Unfortunately the novels, and in some cases the intrigues, followed in due course, though not the gaming. But there was of course no likelihood or possibility of the Princesses' being educated in any other way: it was all dictated by the fashion of the day, in accordance with which Queen Charlotte herself had been reared.

Even a programme of trivialities called for a considerable staff. At its head for thirty years was the governess, Lady Charlotte Finch. This really admirable lady had been appointed on the birth of the Prince of Wales in 1762 to manage the royal nurses, and retired in 1792, having in the interval supervised the early training of the entire family, boys as well as girls, who nicknamed her 'Cha' and loved her all their lives. Obviously she must have had personal qualities uniquely suited to her task; but she was a woman of more than average distinction in other ways too. She had 'brains, breeding and culture', as has been said, and, according to the percipient Horace Walpole, was 'the cleverest girl in the world', and spoke 'the purest Tuscan, like any Florentine'. How Lady Cha managed to combine her arduous duties with marriage and with the lively social and intellectual life which she enjoyed is not easily explained.

Among the sub-governesses the doyenne was Miss Martha Caroline Goldsworthy, known even to the King as Gooly, another lady of birth and breeding, whose brother, General Goldsworthy, was for many years one of the King's equerries. She too devoted the best years of her life to the royal children. With her immediate colleague, Miss Jane Gomm, she was always to hand, if not always on duty—watching over her charges at meals, supervising their lessons, superintending their afternoon preparation, teaching them manners and deportment—which were the functions laid down by the Queen herself as proper to a sub-governess. Of the two, Miss Goldsworthy was preferred by the children, who had known her all their lives. Miss Gomm had come on the scene rather later, and one suspects may have possessed some of the less amiable traits often associated with the profession of governess. 'She is very sensible and well informed,' wrote Fanny Burney, who had evidently been put in her place, 'but her manner is not pleasing to strangers.' Both ladies were fierce champions of the proprieties—they have been described as 'twin dragons of decorum'—and it was their business to be so. When the already mortally ill Princess Amelia had a romantic love affair with one of her father's equerries, it was Miss Gomm who discovered it, and reported it through Miss Goldsworthy to the Queen. Princess Amelia never forgave the twin dragons for this. But their standing with the rest of the family was not affected, and when they retired and went to live together in Berkeley Square, their welfare continued to be a matter of interest to princes and princesses alike, from the Regent downwards.

There must have been a great contrast between these formidable ladies—formidable even in their youth, one imagines—and Mary Hamilton, the Scottish girl to whom the sixteen-year-old Prince of Wales temporarily lost his heart. Hammy, as they called her, can scarcely have been more than twenty when she joined the royal household. Her vivacity and love of boisterous games endeared her to the children, especially the tomboy Princess Augusta, and it may have been during some game of cricket, or even football, that she caught young George's fancy. Not that she was by any means a hoyden: her letters disclose a warm, affectionate, intensely feminine person, devoted to the Princesses, and particularly to her own special charges, Elizabeth and the 'sweet engaging child', Sophia, whom in one letter she brings vividly to life 'playing about like Butterflies in the sun, and culling wild flowers on the Grass whilst I am watching them.'

One particular Swiss family, the Montmollins, supplied no less than three of the royal sub-governesses. One of them, Charlotte Salomé Montmollin, known to the children as La Mont, who had formerly been a governess at the Russian court, established herself, as governesses will, as a sort of family institution. She taught French of course, but also needlework, purse-netting, bead-work, and, strange to say, ancient history, which the intelligent Princess Sophia, appreciating perhaps some solid employment for her mind, found particularly enjoyable. When La Mont got married, the succession descended almost as if by right to her cousins, Julie and Marianne, who became royal governesses in their turn. Both had a talent for the work, and soon won the affection and regard of their pupils. When in her turn Marianne married a French pastor, whom she had met as court chaplain, and went to live in Bristol, she kept up friendly relations with the royal family and the Queen and Princesses used sometimes to visit her. Many years later, when Princess Sophia in her old age lost the sight of both eyes through cataract, one of her daughters became the Princess's companion.

There was a swarm of other governeses and tutors, whose periods of service and respective duties it would be tedious to enumerate in full, even if it were possible. They included some curious personalities. The Rev. Charles de la Guiffardière, whose duty was to teach French and read aloud to the Princesses, and who enjoyed flirting foolishly with his pupils, to whom he was known as Mr. Turbulent, seems almost like a character from fiction. Another curiosity was Mr. Webb, one of the music masters, who had such an enormous nose that it occupied the whole of the centre of his face: the little Princesses were warned not to stare at him, when he first appeared, hiding his face behind a large bunch of flowers. Mr. Desnoyer, elderly but elegant, who taught the Princesses how to manage their hoops and trains, had been dancing master to the royal family for two generations. These people must have formed a little community of their own. Another of the French teachers, close friend and colleague of La Mont, at whose wedding she was one of the bridesmaids, was Mademoiselle Suzanne Moula; and when she in turn married an Englishman, Captain Cooper of the East India Company, it was the Rev. Charles de la Guiffardière who performed the ceremony. Suzanne Moula in her turn had a sister Marianne, and it was she who was concerned at the triviality of the Princesses' education. Religious instruction was given under the personal eye of the Queen, by Mr. Schräder, the German chaplain. Miss Planta taught English, despite her Swiss name; and Sir George Bolton, unexpectedly for a man of his rank, taught Geography. Art was entrusted to a team of four: Biachio Rebecca taught figure-drawing, Mr. Cooper landscape-drawing in chalk, Miss Black painting in crayons, and M. Rustan, a Fleming, specialized in drawing heads, hands and feet on a large scale in black chalk, earning himself thereby the nickname of Count Smudge.

All these people, and probably many more in various permutations and combinations, were presumably under the direction of Lady Charlotte Finch, who begins to appear as something between a headmistress and a manageress, and, if it was she who taught some of the Princesses Italian, a teacher as well. It would have been both surprising and sad if, with all this teaching talent at their disposal, the six Princesses had not grown up into highly accomplished young women. This they certainly were; and if their accomplishments were all rather lightweight and trivial, it was the fault, not of the girls themselves or of their teachers, but of the convention in which they were brought up.

Their gifts varied considerably. Though all of necessity knew foreign languages, the ablest linguist among them was Princess Sophia, who, after going blind, employed four readers for an hour apiece every day to read to her in English, French, German and Italian. They were all taught music; but their aptitude for it ranged all the way from a complete absence of talent or even liking in the Princess Royal to the charming virtuosity of Princess Augusta's talent as harpsichordist, singer and composer. Princess Elizabeth, known to her sisters as the Muse, was the artist of the family and exercised her skill in a variety of mediums—crayon, pastel, water-colour, charcoal, mezzotint, gouache, lacquer. Princess Mary, the most beautiful of them all, showed no interest in art, played no instrument, but relied entirely on her looks and her exquisite manners. Princess Charlotte, the Princess Royal, who married the Hereditary Prince of Würtemberg, wrote the most beautiful hand and the most correct English among the sisterhood. Princess Amelia, whose education suffered through constant illness and who died at twenty-seven, showed no more than promise. All the Princesses were clever with their fingers, and the royal apartments must have been well provided with chair-covers, curtains, screens, table-cloths and other products of their industrious but empty leisure.

The instruction which brought out all this talent had been admirably done. The Princesses had been beautifully trained too in every social accomplishment; their manners and deportment left nothing to be desired; they were at ease in the narrow world which surrounded them. It could be said that, as girls and young women, they were happy too, living as they did in a cheerful, lively crowd, moving from house to house, to London or the seaside, with all their governesses and maids. In many ways they must have been very like one of those large families which became common among the middle class in Victoria's reign.

Yet as they grew older they were dissatisfied. The boys could kick over the traces and annoy their father with impunity, and he could do nothing to restrain their extravagances and their amours. The girls were kept well within bounds under the strict control of their admirable mother. Inevitably, as they reached the age when in the normal course of events they should have married, these high-spirited young women rebelled; and it was a much subtler rebellion than that of the boys. There was no open defiance, no quarrelling or theatrical displays of independence. They simply fell in love with the wrong people – with equerries or officers, excellent men but commoners, even perhaps in one case with a page; and, though the real truth of it can never be known, it seems likely that at least three of them were secretly married, and several are thought to have had children. In their favour it must be said that these affairs seem all to have been genuine romances. They were not vicious or promiscuous girls: it was simply that in every case hot blood had triumphed over sober sense.

All this could probably have been avoided, if as girls they had been allowed to meet eligible young men, who would almost inevitably have been German princes. But both King and Queen were loath to let their daughters go, and little was done to help them make suitable marriages. The Princess Royal escaped, when she was thirty-one, from what she called the cloister by making a childless marriage with the Hereditary Prince of Würtemberg, a corpulent middle-aged man, whose first wife had vanished in mysterious circumstances. Princess Mary wasted her good looks on Silly Billy, Duke of Gloucester; and Princess Elizabeth made up for the indiscretions of her youth by marrying the uncouth Landgrave of Hesse-Homburg when she was forty-seven. But the others – outwardly at least – remained spinsters all their lives, and, except in the case of Princess Amelia, they were long lives.

It is a sad note on which to end the story of these once beautiful Princesses. Not one of the six had achieved a normal, happy marriage. None of them had legitimate children. And yet, in their middle age, when the ardours of youth had died down, and even in old age, while health allowed, the five survivors were not unhappy, for thanks to the manner of their upbringing they had resources at their command which filled their leisure with gentle activity.

7

Problem Princess

IT IS EXTRAORDINARY THAT GEORGE III'S NUMEROUS AND HIGHLY sexed family should have produced so few legitimate offspring. As far as the succession was concerned it did not matter that the six girls between them bore no children in lawful wedlock; but a very serious situation would have arisen if none of the seven boys had done so either. There was therefore considerable relief and expectation when, in 1795, the Prince of Wales consented to marry. The lady selected, Princess Caroline of Brunswick-Wolfenbüttel, who turned out to be vulgar, eccentric and unclean, was not his choice: in fact a very brief acquaintance with her was sufficient to arouse feelings of revulsion in him. But, sustained it is said by brandy, he went through with the business under heavy pressure in the interests of the dynasty, and having done his duty by begetting a child, thereafter lived apart from his wife. The offspring of this sordid union, born the following year, 1796, was Princess Charlotte Augusta, whose life was destined to be both stormy and short.

With only her father and her grandfather between her and the throne, Princess Charlotte became dynastically the most important infant in the kingdom. She was also for the same reason a bone of contention in the royal family. Her parents had separated even before she was born, and throughout her life there was constant warfare between them about the daughter in whom, despite their own personal shortcomings, they both took a strong parental interest. There was strife too between her father and her grandfather: there had always been strife between these two, but it was now exacerbated since the King (in his lucid moments) had no faith in his son's competence to take charge of the future heir presumptive, and wanted to do so himself. Meanwhile the Queen, whose antipathy to the Princess of Wales was almost as strong as that of the Prince himself, was understandably anxious to remove the baby Princess from the possibility of contact with her mother.

These disagreements turned mainly on the question where and with whom Princess Charlotte should live. She was at first housed by the Prince of Wales in Carlton House, or the adjoining Warwick House, where during her infancy she lived with her governesses, who were allowed to take her from time to time to visit her mother. But neither the King nor the Queen thought this a satisfactory arrangement. The former had no objection to Princess Charlotte's seeing her mother occasionally, but considered that the Prince of Wales was neglecting his daughter; as indeed he probably was, for, though he was undoubtedly fond of her, his own urgent affairs usually came before everything else. The Queen wanted as strongly as ever to get the child away from what she regarded, rightly enough, as her mother's undesirable influence. Negotiations between the various contending parties were far from smooth; but it was eventually agreed that the Princess should live with her father when he was in town, and with her grandparents at Windsor when he was away; and that she should be allowed to see her mother only at weekly intervals. Naturally Princess Caroline was dissatisfied with this: she kept up a constant agitation to be allowed what she very properly regarded as her rights as a mother, and at the same time did all she could to make her company more attractive to the Princess than that of her father or aged grandmother and middle-aged aunts. This was not difficult as Princess Charlotte grew older and became conscious of her environment. Apart from the natural affinity between mother and daughter, Princess Caroline's free and easy ways and unconventional friends must have seemed a pleasant change to the Princess after the stiff régime at Windsor – 'this prison', 'this den,' as she called it – or her father's intermittent and unpredictable displays of interest.

While her elders were disputing in this way for possession of her person, the infant Princess spent her days in seclusion with a succession of governesses, sub-governesses, and, as soon as she was old enough to benefit from their services, of other teachers. For the first nine years of her life, till 1805, she was under the placid direction of the dowager Lady Elgin, assisted as sub-governess by a Miss Hayman, whose description of her written in 1797, when she was in her second year, shows that even at that age Charlotte had a Hanoverian temper: 'She is the merriest little thing I ever saw – pepper-hot, too: if

contradicted she kicks her little feet about in a great rage, but the cry ends in a laugh before you well know which it is.'
Others of the family failings, and some of its good qualities too, emerged in the next few years.

In 1805, as the result of a fresh agreement between the King and the Prince of Wales, who at least had an antipathy to Princess Caroline in common, a drastic overhaul of Charlotte's establishment took place. Lady Elgin, too placid perhaps, or too old, was relieved of her post. In a final report she wrote that the little Princess, then eight or nine, was

'free from all fault whatever, both in character and disposition; that her mind was perfectly pure and innocent, and that her progress in learning had been uncommonly great';

a judgement, which, as events soon proved, was at best disingenuous, at worst deliberately calculated to deceive.

In her place came Sophia Lady de Clifford, described not without malice by a contemporary as 'a good-natured, commonplace person'. Her instructions – never to let the Princess out of her sight, and to keep her away from her mother – were really impossible of fulfilment; but somehow she succeeded in giving qualified satisfaction to the Prince of Wales, without antagonizing his daughter, for the next seven years. In the end, however, the Prince was so rude to her that she resigned, to be succeeded as governess by the more complaisant Duchess of Leeds.

Shortly afterwards Miss Cornelia Knight, a lady well versed in the domestic and personal affairs of royalty, who had been lady companion to the Queen for a number of years, was appointed (against the Queen's wishes) to a similar position with Princess Charlotte. Miss Knight was very conscious of her exalted status as lady companion: when a newspaper referred to her as sub-governess, she wrote insisting on a correction (in spite of which she is still sometimes described as a sub-governess). But though she may have seemed rather a superior person to lesser breeds, such as teachers of French and music, not to mention sub-governesses, or even sub-preceptors, she devoted herself to the Princess's interests, and did her best to preserve for her a sense of direction through the tangled thickets of plots and plans which surrounded her. Princess Charlotte's own tribute speaks for itself: Miss Knight, she said, was 'an excellent valuable person, straightforward, open and honourable', 'clear-sighted and firm, accomplished and talented'. She was eventually dismissed for her loyalty to the Princess, whose refusal to marry Prince William of Orange she supported.

There were two sub-governesses at this time, Mrs. Campbell, comfortable, kind-hearted, lovable; and Mrs. Udney, known to the Princess as Mrs. Nibs, who seems to have been everything a sub-governess should not be, and was on the worst possible terms with her pupil, whom she even chastised physically. 'Mrs. Udney really is beyond anything I ever knew,' wrote Charlotte, aged fifteen, in one of those confidential letters to her friend, Mercer Elphinstone, which are so revealing of her innermost feelings. '*Contempt* is not *sufficient* for her, for I now *dislike* and I am *disgusted* with her.' But we may be sure the fault did not lie entirely with Mrs. Udney, who had to do with an extremely difficult child.

Other instructors appeared from time to time, hoping no doubt to find the Princess in a recipient mood. They were not always lucky. She refused to take lessons at all from Mr. Küper, who was engaged to teach her German, on the grounds that he was a spy – and indeed it was true that tale-bearers and eaves-droppers, acting for one or other of her parents, were everywhere in her establishment. French she learnt, and learnt quite well, from Mr. Sterkey, minister of the Swiss church, 'a man of good manners for his station, and of a pliant disposition, ready to do anything not actually wicked,' says Miss Knight mysteriously in her Memoirs – what could he have done, which fell just short of being wicked, we wonder. There were drawing masters, too, whose lessons she enjoyed. But the musicians were perhaps the most welcome of all, for Princess Charlotte had some of the Hanoverian talent, and learnt to sing and play various instruments agreeably, if perhaps no more. Miss Miles, the chief music mistress, and Miss Lindly, who taught singing, are shadowy figures, and seem to have made little personal impact. But there was excitement in learning to play the newly fashionable guitar, first from a Venetian called Ventura, who also sang prettily, then from Vaccari, a 'scientific professor of music', and an excellent violinist, formerly a member of the King of Spain's personal band, who taught Princess Charlotte the wild Spanish manner of playing, which suited her temperament. She enjoyed it particularly when a violinist and 'cellist from the King's band came sometimes in the evening to make up a small ensemble. Her efforts to learn the harp were not so successful, and her harp-master, Dizzi, proved rather trying.

'I must make bitter complaints of him,' she wrote when she was fifteen, 'as he is much too *minucieux for a beginner*, & for me to make any progress, & is always full of complaints at my oreille qui n'est point trop bonne or of my want of patience, & that I do not practise; till he quite puts me out of humor with his air doucereux & his petit voix intéressant & ses manières si sentimental, besides wh. he always takes everything I say à coeur & frets himself yellow . . .'
How vividly from this one may visualize, not merely the irritating Dizzi, but the lively, precocious Princess herself, with her slapdash impatience and her fluent, inaccurate French.

But the most important decision reached by the King and Prince of Wales in 1805 was to put the main part of the Princess's education into the hands of male tutors. There was ancient precedent for this, going back to Tudor times; and it was no doubt felt that a princess who, it seemed, would almost inevitably become queen one day, should have a background of solid learning rather than the ornamental kind of education at that time customary for ladies of birth and breeding. In this situation King and Prince—though perhaps it was more particularly the King's choice—had recourse to old Dr. Fisher, Bishop of Exeter,[1] the King's Fisher, who many years before had taught the Dukes of Clarence and Kent, and remained high in royal favour. This prelate was now summoned to attend the Princess three or four times a week, 'to do the Important', as it was said, while others were left to perform the more hum-drum duties.

Whatever he may have been in youth, Dr. Fisher was now a pompous man of strong Tory prejudices and somewhat narrow views, who had an exaggerated idea of his own consequence, and was chiefly concerned as tutor, so some people said, to arm his pupil against what were to him the roots of all evil, Popery and Whiggery. He had a hot temper, and, according to some accounts, bad manners also; but he probably kept these shortcomings out of sight in his dealings with the royal family, though they led to terrible disputes with Lady de Clifford, and would have done the same with the Duchess of Leeds, if she had not been so easy-going. How he appeared at this time to a prejudiced observer may be seen from a retrospective view of the bishop written in later life by Lord Albemarle, who as a boy at Westminster had been one of Princess Charlotte's girlhood friends, and saw something of Fisher at close quarters:

[1] He was translated to Salisbury in 1807.

'A dull, solemn-looking man with a severe expression of countenance, to which a projecting under-lip contributed not a little. He
was a good classical scholar, but had no more knowledge of mankind than was to be acquired in the quadrangle of a college, where
he had passed most of his life. He was precise in dress and formal
in manner. In language he was a thorough pedant, seeming to
consider the force of words to be in proportion to the number of
syllables they contained.'

Princess Charlotte's own very schoolgirlish attitude to 'his
Reverendship', as she called him, comes out amusingly from time to
time in her letters. Though outwardly very respectful, and careful
'*never* to give him cause for complaint or uneasiness', her real
feelings were very different. When he lectured her, it was 'tiresome
and odious': lunch with him and his family was not merely a bore,
but, surprisingly, 'a bitter pill': the bishop himself became in
mangled Latin a '*lucis natura*'; as for his sermons, 'I never heard so
weak a voice and so bad a delivery'.

Quite obviously this solemn pedant, some fifty-seven years of age
at the time of his appointment, was not the ideal tutor for the
bouncing, self-willed, obstinate girl, which Charlotte was now
becoming. Yet he certainly took his duties very seriously, as will
shortly be seen; and a less critical account refers appreciatively, in a
phrase of such polysyllabic pedantry that the bishop himself might
have composed it, to 'the peculiarly felicitous manner in which he
conveyed instruction.'

But Princess Charlotte had strong likes as well as dislikes, and
not all the 'black-coated gentlemen' (her phrase for tutors) were
equally antipathetic. Her new sub-preceptor, the Rev. George Nott,
earned her wholesome respect, and, in time, affection, chiefly, we
may guess, because she could feel that he was completely on her
side, when, as she was to find more and more, so many were against
her. For this we must give Nott all due credit, for the management
of a difficult adolescent girl cannot have come easily to this able
classical and Italian scholar, whose chief interest was in sixteenth-
century literature.

His first impressions of her were most unfavourable. He was
horrified by the faults which Lady Elgin had so smoothly ignored –
her inattentiveness and laziness, her moodiness and bad temper, her
atrocious spelling, her abominable handwriting. He was irritated by
her habit of sending little notes excusing herself from doing the

work he had set, and shocked by her mendacity. One of the first exercises she did for him in 1805 was a six-page composition, in part illegible, which contained over fifty spelling mistakes – mistakes, said Dr. Nott, which 'a common servant would have blushed to have committed'. He too could write notes, and did so with considerable force on this occasion:

'Where, may I ask your Royal Highness, is this to end, or when are we to have the satisfaction of seeing your mind animated with a becoming pride and a generous resolution to improve? More than three months have passed, during which the most unremitting exertions have been employed by those about you, and what is the progress you have made? Let the enclosed paper speak. I shall only add that ignorance is disgraceful in proportion to the rank of the person in whom it is found, and that negligence, when the means of improvement are in your power, is criminal in the sight of the Almighty'.

Princess Charlotte was one of those children who are filled with penitence and contrition after every fall from grace, and then go on to commit the same offence again. Every time she had been irritable or bad-tempered, she grovelled abjectly. When she told lies, and Dr. Nott threatened to punish her, she would write imploring forgiveness and promising never to offend again:

'O, my God, my God, enable me to do my duty in this world and in the world to come . . . Never shall another lie come out of me.'

Finally, when the strain of these repeated emotional exchanges caused Dr. Nott to have a nervous breakdown, she became genuinely upset at what she had done, and tried to make amends:

'I solemnly *declare* that I owe everything to the Rev. Dr. Nott,' she wrote in May, 1806, when she was just ten. 'I must entreat the Almighty God . . . to forgive me my former sins and to implore the forgiveness of Mr. Nott. I here solemnly declare that from this time forward I give myself entirely to make him happy, & a child under pupilage will do my utmost to regain my benefactor's friendship.'

Dr. Nott's absence, for which she was responsible, intensified Charlotte's emotional dependence on him, and, when he resumed his duties, she told him that he had never been out of her thoughts during his illness. Referring to herself henceforward as his 'dutiful daughter by adoption', she now sought every opportunity of proving her devotion. She even drew up a will, half seriously, half in play, leaving all her books to Dr. Nott, directing that he should be responsible for distributing her money to the poor and expressing the hope that the King would make him a bishop. But, characteristically, she could also use her regard for Dr. Nott as an excuse for leaving work undone: protesting that she disliked Latin more than anything else in the world, she said she was afraid to write to him in that language, because her blunders would give him pain. Meanwhile there was no sign of any genuine improvement.

But this stormy and one-sided idyll came to an end in 1809, when someone complained to the Prince of Wales that Dr. Nott was using his position to influence the Princess unduly, and that he had encouraged her to speak disrespectfully of her father and of Mrs. Udney, the sub-governess. She needed little encouragement to speak disrespectfully of either of these, especially Mrs. Udney, as her letters show. But the charge was taken seriously; and though Nott indignantly denied it and was strongly supported by the bishop, he was suspended. Though nothing is known for certain, it seems likely that the accusations originated with Mrs. Udney, who had been reported by Nott, strange as it may appear, for giving Princess Charlotte an improper cartoon of Lady Hamilton and a translation of Ovid's *Metamorphoses* in defiance of instructions that all books read by the Princess had to be approved by the bishop. Nott was never reinstated; but the incident was not held against him, and he went on to a successful ecclesiastical and literary career.

Princess Charlotte mourned his loss in language which recalls her grandfather's letters to Lord Bute:

'If we never meet again, keep for me your regard and affection . . . I shall ever remember your kindness & good advice . . . I trust you will be able to give a good account of me . . . What you have taught me I shall never forget . . . Once more retain for me your affection, for if I should have the affliction of losing my parent, I shall ever look upon you as my protector, guardian and second parent . . .'
Dr. Nott himself may have been glad to escape.

He was succeeded as sub-preceptor by Dr. Short, whom Miss Cornelia Knight from her lofty standpoint describes as 'a good sort of Devonshire man, with some classical knowledge, very little taste, an honest heart, but over-cautious temper, fearful of offending'. What lay behind this judgement remains tantalizingly obscure; but there is no doubt that a tutor, in the circumstances which confronted Dr. Short, needed to tread delicately.

Dr. Short appears to have concentrated mainly on teaching

English, which was certainly an urgent necessity; and though, as may be seen from the Princess's correspondence, he failed to curb the exuberance of her language, he evidently found favour with his pupil, who calls him briefly 'the good doctor', and he remained on with her after her marriage as chaplain.

The Princess's daily life meanwhile was dull enough; how dull may be judged from the fact that this most unscholarly girl came to regard the visits of her tutors and teachers, and the resulting pre-paration and book-work, as a relief from boredom. 'Studdy . . .is now my greatest resource, as it passes away hours of ennui,' she wrote in 1812. Probably she did not study very deeply, and a good deal of her working time was given to music and drawing, which she enjoyed most. Yet, considering her temperament and circumstances, she managed to learn a good deal. In her early teens she had a fluent if inaccurate command of three foreign languages; and anyone who reads her correspondence of the same period must be struck by the racy flamboyance of her English style, which, with all its under-linings and exclamations, seems to reflect her own unrestrained character. Reading too, as she says herself, was one of her passions – 'I read a great deal both serious and light,' she wrote – and references in her letters to what she is reading show that her taste was fairly eclectic, ranging from the philosophical works of Diderot on the one hand to the *Life and Campaigns of Sir John Moore* on the other, from *Sense and Sensibility* to Mrs. Edgeworth's latest romance, from Byron (whom every romantic young girl at that time was reading) to *The Sicilian Mysteries*.

Yet, though she had long felt herself neglected and ill-used by her own family, there had always been considerable public interest in the Princess, both as a future queen of England, and because of the constant disputes which surrounded her, and of which she was thought to be the innocent victim, as indeed she was. Even when she was quite a small child there had been a strong feeling among serious-minded people that she was not being educated as well as she ought to have been in the circumstances; and this led to a situation unprecedented in the history of royal education.

One of the best known and most highly respected women of the day was Hannah More, in early life blue-stocking friend of Johnson, Garrick and others of their circle, later famous for her voluminous writings on religious and educational subjects, and for her practical philanthropy. She was now sixty (with another twenty-eight years before her). She had already written a treatise on the education of girls, of which she had had ample experience while conducting schools for young ladies with her four sisters. In 1805, the year of upheaval in Princess Charlotte's education, it was suggested to her by a clerical friend that she could be of service to the royal family, if she gave her views on how a future queen ought to be educated. Somewhat presumptuously we may think, since her advice had not been asked by the royal family, she at once adopted the idea, and within the year produced and published a two-volume work with the title *Hints towards forming the Character of a Young Princess*. The book appeared anonymously, but its authorship was soon known; it became immediately popular and went into six editions.

This was of course not the first work of its kind written for a young princess. Ludovicus Vives, writing 300 years before for Mary Tudor, had set a precedent in this country, and there were probably others. But it was the first written by a woman for the guidance of a woman. Hannah More herself believed she was following in the footsteps of Fénelon, whose *Télémaque*, a work of fiction utterly different in every respect from her treatise, had been intended to influence the character of Louis XIV's grandson and heir, the Duke of Burgundy; apparently it had been successful, and Hannah More hoped for a similar success with Princess Charlotte.

The work was tactfully dedicated to Bishop Fisher, whose appointment as royal preceptor had not yet been announced when Hannah More undertook her task, and who, far from resenting it as a gratuitous attempt to teach him his business, said he had learnt more of his duties from it than from any other reading. Copies were sent also to the King and Queen, and to the Prince and Princess of Wales; and here too it was well received, at any rate by the Queen, who summoned Hannah More to visit her at Weymouth, where, together with the Princess's governess, they talked over the problems of her upbringing.

There was some expectation, when the book came out, that Hannah More herself might be appointed royal governess; but she did not take the suggestion very seriously.

'Am I fit for the situation?' she asked. 'I understand there is to be a governess, a sub-governess and an assistant governess. I have not the rank for the first, or qualification for the second, and I am too old for the third.'

In fact Dr. Fisher used her *Hints* as a kind of textbook for his lessons with the Princess. Not surprisingly perhaps, Charlotte herself found this insufferably tedious.

'The Bishop of Salisbury is here,' she wrote, 'and reads with me an hour or 2 every day from Mrs. Hannah More's Hints for forming the character of a Pss. This, I believe, is what makes me find the hours so long. I am *not quite good* enough for that yet.'

Perhaps she ought to have said 'not old enough'–she was sixteen at the time. But it would have been better if the bishop had taught to a syllabus based on Hannah More's recommendations, instead of introducing the book itself direct to his pupil. Though an excellent, if tendentious, guide for royal tutors, it is no more suitable for a young princess's personal use than a Ministry of Education handbook would be for use in the classroom.

The emphasis of the book is practical, the first part dealing largely with curriculum, the second with the ideal ruler's character and the 'art of reigning'. There are some surprising, yet wholly logical, recommendations about curriculum: science is to be excluded as superfluous for royalty, the classical languages as unnecessary for a woman, even the arts because no ruler has time to master them. On the other hand, stress should be laid on modern languages for their practical usefulness, English (especially reading and conversation), and above all history–'History, which is the amusement of other men, is the school of princes'; the whole founded upon religion. As for the prince, he–or she–should cultivate wisdom rather than learning, judgement rather than knowledge, humility, discretion, consideration for others, punctilious efficiency.

These are high ideals. Most of them had been expressed before; but several centuries had passed since they had last been set out so cogently, and they had perhaps never been explicitly applied to a woman. It was not surprising that they attracted attention among those who were concerned for the Princess's future.

How Charlotte herself reacted to the practical application of Hannah More's principles in her own case–if indeed a serious attempt was made to apply them–it is not easy to say. At first they made no visible impression at all. During her adolescence she became, if anything, even more troublesome than she had been before. Her father was constantly irritated and annoyed by her lack of dignity and control– even more so, perhaps, because he remembered how undisciplined he himself had been at the same age. He was touchy too about the impression she made in public, and when she went out preferred her to be accompanied by some of his own sisters. Even then there was a danger of her attracting attention by unseemly conduct, as happened in 1812, when, attending the opening of Parliament with some of her aunts, she 'talked and laughed much, and turned her back often on papa'.

Though in the more flattering contemporary accounts emphasis is laid on her fine features, her noble expression, her fair complexion, her sweet and flexible voice, it must be added that she was also somewhat plump and awkward, that she enjoyed her food and drink rather too obviously, and that her laugh was loud and her chatter irrepressible.

But she was attractive in a voluptuous way also; and family history was soon repeating itself, when at exactly the same age as her father she began exchanging clandestine notes with a lover. The favoured young man, a Captain Hesse, reputed to be a bastard of the Duke of York, and thus Charlotte's own cousin, even took to riding by her carriage, as she drove with her governess in the park. The Prince Regent was incensed, more particularly perhaps because his wife was actively encouraging the affair – on one occasion she actually locked the two young people up together in a bedroom – and he reacted sharply with a complete ban on meetings between mother and daughter. But the best long-term solution seemed to lie in matrimony; and the Prince accordingly determined to marry his daughter off as soon as a suitable bridegroom could be discovered. The most eligible politically seemed to be Prince William of Orange, who was accordingly brought over to pay official court to Princess Charlotte. She for her part, perhaps seeing in matrimony a chance of escape from frustration, proved surprisingly amenable at first, and an engagement was announced. But, diverted momentarily by the superior charms of a young Prussian prince, whom political match-makers dangled before her, she quickly lost interest in William, whom she referred to as 'that nasty, ugly, spider-legged little Duchman [*sic*]'; and when a list of wedding guests which did not include her mother's name arrived from her father, her temper flared up, she crossed out her own name and sent it back. Though the engagement broken in this dramatic way was patched up again after some violent exchanges between father and daughter, it did not last, and the unfortunate Prince William (whose feelings were not much consulted in the matter) retired from the field.

The Bishop of Salisbury meanwhile must have been finding it

even more difficult than before to interest his pupil in Hannah More's views on the dangers of flattery, the defects of heathen philosophy or the arts of moral calculation. But Charlotte's affairs had reached their grand climacteric. Even before Prince William had faded from the scene, she had met and fallen in love with Prince Leopold of Saxe-Coburg, and he with her. Two years later they were married. These happy events were accompanied by a complete change in her character. The garrulous hoyden, who had caused so much embarrassment in earlier years was transformed almost over-night—or so at any rate some of those who wrote in praise of the Princess after her death would have us believe—into a sweet, gentle girl of irreproachable behaviour; and if the metamorphosis was not really quite so sudden and dramatic as this, it was remarkable enough to excite general comment.

Admirers of Hannah More put it down to the *Hints*; and indeed the Princess is known to have read the work several times for herself during the last years of her life, and, with growing appreciation of the rôle she believed she would have to play as queen, was at last taking Hannah More's advice seriously. But, though some credit must go to Hannah More, and some too to Bishop Fisher, it is much more likely that the changes wrought in the Princess's character were the result of a truly happy marriage and the prospect of motherhood.

But at this moment, when everything seemed set fair for the future, tragedy struck; and before anyone was well aware of the possibility, Princess Charlotte died in childbed in November, 1817.

The English people, who had come to love her as their future queen, were hard hit by this unexpected calamity. National grief was universal, and everywhere people were in tears when they heard the news. They were lamenting, not merely the death of a popular Princess, but the parlous state in which their royal family now stood. The house of Hanover, though the old King, now eighty-nine and quite mad, was still on the throne, and all his sons still alive, was left without a single eligible representative in the younger generation.

8

'I Will Be Good'

THE HANOVERIAN SUCCESSION CONTINUED TO DEPEND PRE-
cariously on the lives of the elderly royal dukes for two years after
the death of Princess Charlotte, while the three of them who were
still unmarried, the Dukes of Clarence, Kent and Cambridge,
hastily took wives appropriate to their station, in the hope of begetting legitimate children.

For some years the uncertainty remained. Four children were
born, two of whom died almost at once. The old King, George III,
and two of the senior royal dukes were also removed from the scene
by death. Out of this fluid situation it gradually emerged that the
Duke of Kent's daughter, Victoria, born in 1819 just eight months
before her father's death, would certainly, if she survived, be queen
one day. Finally, the accession of William IV in 1830 confirmed her
position as heir presumptive; and for the second time within a
generation the future of the English throne rested with a young
princess.

Princess Victoria was brought up under the eye of her mother at
Kensington Palace, where various elderly members of the royal
family had suites. It was at first a very secluded life. The Duchess of
Kent, a princess of Saxe-Coburg, widow of Prince Charles of Leinin-
gen, sister of the late Princess Charlotte's husband, Prince Leopold,
could not at that time even speak English. She had few friends and
acquaintances in England, and felt a stranger in a strange land.
For some reason the English royal family treated her rather coldly,
and for company she had only her own relations and members of
her household. But her brother Leopold, who became King of the
Belgians in 1831, was fortunately at that time still living in England.
He was a man of sound practical wisdom: his advice, much of it
derived from his own very able adviser, Baron Stockmar, was

always good, and in the next few years both the Duchess and her daughter came to rely on him at every moment of decision. He was the first of several dominant figures, who, partially and for a time, fulfilled the Princess's unconscious longing for a father.

The Duchess was at first afraid that George IV or his ministers would take away her daughter to be educated elsewhere. This did not happen; but the resistance she put up, when ten years later William IV wanted the heir presumptive to live at court for a time each year, shows how jealously she guarded her rights as a mother. In a narrow, homely way she felt herself well capable of bringing up a future queen, and was not prepared to surrender the responsibility.

So Princess Victoria remained at Kensington Palace; and for better or worse spent her earliest years under somewhat Spartan conditions, hedged in and restricted by what must have seemed irksome controls, and plagued by petty economies. One of her chief memories of childhood was that they had mutton every day. On Prince Leopold's advice it was not explained to her till she was twelve that she would one day be queen, and we have her own word for it that she never suspected the truth. But, in the chancy situation which still remained, she was watched over with particular care and more closely guarded than otherwise would have been the case. When she went out for a walk in Kensington Gardens, a footman in livery dogged her footsteps at a discreet distance. When she went up or down stairs, someone always had to hold her hand. She slept in the same room as her mother, and in fact actually continued to do so till she became queen at the age of eighteen. She was not allowed to talk to anyone except in the presence of her mother or her governess, though in any case there were not many people to talk to.

These rather pettifogging precautions made a deep impression. Looking back on this period of her life many years later, 'I was extremely crushed and kept under,' she wrote, 'and hardly dared say a word.' To her much older half-sister, who shared the restrictions without any compensating advantages in prospect, these were 'years of imprisonment', when, as it seemed to her, she had been 'deprived of all intercourse', and there was 'not one cheerful thought' to relieve her dismal existence. But memory must surely have darkened the picture somewhat, for the glimpses we get of the Princess at this age – playing with her dog, picking flowers, riding on her donkey, visiting her elderly aunts – do not suggest an unhappy childhood; and one has only to turn the opening pages of her diary to see what a full and interesting life she was leading only a few years later.

When she was five Princess Victoria came under the direction of the Baroness Lehzen, a governess whose name became a household word, and who later, in her brief hour of hubris, before nemesis overtook her, wielded a power in some respect comparable with that of the Prime Minister. Lehzen, as Princess Victoria always called her, was the daughter of a Hanoverian pastor and was created a baroness of Hanover by George IV in 1827 in recognition of her services. She had originally been brought to England by the Duke of Kent to look after his wife's daughter by her former husband. She was thus a part of Princess Victoria's world from the very start; and even before she became her governess must have been, next to her mother, perhaps even before her mother, the strongest influence in her life. Lehzen was a woman of narrow horizons and provincial outlook, unimpressive in appearance, unmarried, harsh of speech, yellow of complexion, perpetually chewing caraway seeds as a remedy for flatulence – the very epitome, it would seem, of all the most unattractive peculiarities of German governesses. Yet her love for Princess Victoria was profound and unassailable; and Victoria for her part found in Lehzen something which no one else could give. As soon as the Princess became articulate for posterity in the pages of her diary, phrases like 'my precious Lehzen', 'my dearest kindest Lehzen', 'my most dearly beloved angelic Lehzen', 'that most dear Being', characterize every reference to the faithful governess. Nor in years to come, when the glow of girlish heroine-worship had faded, did she forget all that Lehzen had once been to her. 'She had devoted her life to me, from my fifth to my eighteenth year, with the most wonderful self-abnegation, never even taking one day's leave,' wrote the Queen in 1870, on hearing of the death of Lehzen. '. . . She was an admirable governess, and I adored her, though I also feared her.'

No other children were brought in to share the Princess Victoria's lessons, and so absorb some of the concentrated attentions of Lehzen. This was certainly a mistake, for the intimate daily association of governess and pupil, as they worked together in isolation, inevitably tended to make the one too possessive and the other too dependent, and set up a situation which was not resolved without distress to both, when the Princess at length outgrew her need for Lehzen's continual presence. Even in these early stages Lehzen showed signs of wanting to claim a monopoly in Victoria. Sometimes she presumed to know better than the Duchess of Kent herself what was best for the Princess. Since she was scarcely parted from her charge for a moment, except at night, it may have been true that she did know more about her in some ways than her own mother. But she certainly went too far, when she began interfering in matters which were not strictly her business, such as the Duchess's refusal to allow her daughter to go to court, or her plans for a regency. In these two instances she may have been right, and the Duchess wrong. But there were follies to come, of which these were no more than a foretaste.

For the moment, however, life in the schoolroom at Kensington Palace must have been uneventful but agreeable for both teacher and taught. There is no indication that Lehzen's rule was harsh, though it may have been strict. The educational foundations she laid were by no means German, despite the predominantly German character of the Duchess of Kent's household. The little Princess was grounded in the popular picture-books of Mrs. Trimmer, which strike the cautionary, didactic note then the fashion in children's books:

'As for Sugar Plums and the rest of those foolish things,' wrote Mrs. Trimmer severely, in her *Easy Introduction to the Knowledge of Nature*, 'they answer no purpose in the world but to make people disrelish what is wholesome; and when they have lost all their teeth by indulging themselves with them, it will be too late to resolve against eating any more . . .'

Let us hope the future Queen, laboriously spelling her way through Mrs. Trimmer's arid prose, took note of this and other perils which beset her: at any rate she had beautiful teeth.

According to Lehzen herself, she was by no means a model pupil: she had 'never seen such a passionate and naughty child' as the Princess, she remarked on one occasion in 1838; but went on to add that, even to escape punishment, she would never tell a lie. This aversion from mendacity had been much admired in her father at about the same age, and was evidently an inherited characteristic. Both father and daughter grew up to be singularly direct and straightforward in all their dealings.

Though Lehzen herself was far from religious and later on even disapproved of the Queen's reading religious books with her husband, she implanted in her pupil a strong consciousness of right and wrong, and it was impressed upon her from an early age that she had a duty. Sometimes it seems that the Princess Victoria, like the children in her school-books, must have been rather a prig. But the famous anecdote which above all gives this impression, telling how, when Lehzen revealed to her at the age of twelve that she would one day be queen, she answered solemnly, 'I will be good', is misleading. She was referring, not to moral goodness, but to doing her lessons, as her complete reply makes clear. 'I am nearer than I thought,' was what she really said, 'I see now why you always wanted me to work well at my lessons. I will be good.' But even this is perhaps a rather solemn reaction for a twelve-year-old.

Lehzen did not long hold the monopoly in the Princess's education, though she held it long enough to establish herself firmly as the central figure around whom other teachers and instructors revolved. In 1837 the Very Rev. George Davys, Dean of Chester, was appointed tutor to the Princess. His function was to teach her Latin, and to direct her general reading, for which purpose he attended intermittently for an hour or two a day. Princess Victoria never had any very strong feelings for Dr. Davys, though she liked him and respected him, and years afterwards, in gratitude for what he had done for her, she made him a bishop. He for his part seems to have been rather lacking in imagination and too closely bound by the conventions of the day. He had no original ideas about how a future queen should be educated, and might have derived much benefit from reading Hannah More. The Princess, industrious and conscientious by nature, was not a difficult pupil, despite what Lehzen had said. 'I *love* to be *employed*; I *hate* to be *idle*,' she wrote when she was fifteen, with characteristic emphasis and economy of words. The Dean certainly faced none of the problems which had confronted Princess Charlotte's preceptors. Yet she was not in the academic sense a good pupil. Latin was either beyond her capacity, or, more probably, she did not give it adequate time and attention. Certainly she disliked it; and though she did prose exercises for the Dean, she rebelled against writing verses – who can blame her? – and after horrifying him with her false quantities was apparently allowed to have her way. Among the authors she read were first Eutropius, then Caesar, later selections from Vergil, Ovid and Horace: an unambitious programme, but more than most girls ever attempted at the beginning of the nineteenth century; yet even this, as she rather sadly confessed to Lord Melbourne some years later, had benefited her little, since she could not even translate or understand a Latin quotation.

We have several times touched on the influence of Latin in developing a command of English. Queen Victoria was one of those, who, like Sir Winston Churchill, with no memories of Cicero to help, could use the language with truly Elizabethan vigour, especially at moments when national prestige was at stake. This was largely a matter of character; yet, perhaps unknowingly, Dr. Davys may have played some part in forming the Queen's English. When her eldest daughter was about to marry Prince Frederick William of Prussia, and the Germans had what she thought was the effrontery to suggest that the Princess should come to Berlin for the wedding, rather than Prince Frederick William to London,

'The Queen *never* could consent to it,' she wrote . . . 'and the assumption of its being *too much* for a Prince Royal of Prussia to come over to marry the *Princess Royal of Great Britain* in England is too absurd to say the least. Whatever may be the usual practice of Prussian princes, it is not *every* day that one marries the eldest daughter of the Queen of England.'

That last sentence is in the great tradition. Yet one is bound to add that in careless moments the Queen's English style could be untidy, ungrammatical and undignified.

The Princess Victoria's reading under the Dean's direction seems, unlike her study of Latin authors, to have been quite formidably substantial, though it was also unsystematic. It included the Bible of course, with such commentaries as the Bishop of Chester's *Exposition of the Gospel of St. Matthew* (which at sixteen the Princess described as 'just the sort . . . I like'), massive philosophical or historical authors like Clarendon and Hume, English classics such as the Spectator, Boswell's *Life of Johnson* and *Paradise Lost*. Her reading undoubtedly interested her, and there are pages in her journal devoted to comments on books and plays. Even at fifteen she understood the special importance of history for a future sovereign:

'Reading history is one of my greatest delights . . .' she wrote to her Uncle Leopold in 1834, 'I am very fond of making tables of the Kings and Queens, as I go on, and have lately finished one of the English Sovereigns and their consorts, as, of course, the history of my own country is one of my first duties.'

But how unsophisticated her literary taste was as compared with that of Princess Charlotte may be judged from the fact that she was eighteen before she sampled her first novel, *The Bride of Lammermoor*. There is no sign that she read any of the great books of the day, or any contemporary poets – Wordsworth, Coleridge, Byron, Shelley – though as Queen she heard about some of them from her well-read Prime Minister, Lord Melbourne.

Modern languages had never presented any difficulties to members of her family. She grew up speaking German as easily as English, yet her clear and bell-like English utterance was wholly without accent. German was the language she and her husband most often spoke to one another in private, for it was of course his native tongue. Lehzen naturally spoke both French and German, and the Princess doubtless had plenty of opportunity of using them in the nursery and the schoolroom, as well as hearing them spoken around her. By the time she was thirteen formal teaching in French was in the hands of a certain M. Grandineau, while Lehzen spent her periods of instruction reading, mostly French, but sometimes German, and on occasion English literature, with the Princess. No concessions were made to girlish taste: at fifteen Racine ('which I delight in', said the Princess); at sixteen Sully's Memoirs, a gift from her uncle Leopold; at seventeen the Letters of Mme de Sévigné in ten volumes (read while dressing), Raumer's *Königinnen* and Corneille; at eighteen, just before becoming queen, *Les Mémoires de l'Impératrice Joséphine*. These are no more than samples of the mostly very weighty works she tackled with her governess. Sometimes Lehzen would read aloud, sometimes the Princess: sometimes Lehzen would dictate. To save time the Princess would often read or be read to when dressing or having her hair done (as Hannah More had recommended for Princess Charlotte). These lessons with Lehzen must have been very solemn, and it is not likely that humour often broke in. Princess Victoria at this age, like most intelligent adolescent schoolgirls, was receptive rather than critical, enjoyed what she was supposed to enjoy and accepted what she was told. There was no longer any rebelliousness, if there ever had been. How successful her moral training had been, how deeply implanted her sense of duty, is revealed in the good resolution which she committed to her diary on her eighteenth birthday.

'I shall from this day take the *firm* resolution to study with renewed assiduity, to keep my attention always well fixed on whatever I am about, and to strive to become every day less trifling and more fit for what, if Heaven wills it, I'm some day to be.'

Lehzen had long since ceased to hold the official post of lady governess, which in 1830 passed to the Duchess of Northumberland; but it was a change of name rather than function. The Duchess seems to have done little more than attend the Princess when she appeared in public, and chaperone her lessons with Dr. Davys; while Lehzen, holding no office, remained the controlling power. This anomalous state of affairs continued even after Victoria became queen. 'My *dear* Lehzen will ALWAYS remain with me as my friend, but will take no situation about me, and I think she is right,' wrote the Queen on the day of her accession in 1837. At that moment Lehzen must have felt herself securely established behind the very throne.

The other instructors who attended at Kensington Palace found Princess Victoria a ready pupil. Her art master was Mr. Richard Westall, R.A., an elderly protégé of the Duchess of Kent; and though it cannot be said she ever became an accomplished artist, she was certainly an enthusiastic one – it was a hobby she later shared with her husband. Quantities of her drawings and sketches survive, including numbers of portraits done from memory. Penmanship she learnt from Mr. Thomas Steward, the writing master at Westminster School; and dancing from Mme Bourdin. Here again special talent was revealed. She became a beautiful dancer, her lightness and grace enhanced by her tiny figure. She passionately loved dancing, until the death of her husband cast a pall of gloom over her life – strange to say, he did not like it, though he did it well – and the pleasure returned briefly thirty years later, when, as an old lady of seventy, she was seen to be dancing with all the verve and airiness of fifty years before. Again there comes to mind the inevitable comparison with Queen Elizabeth I, so different in character yet so like in queenly qualities, who also in old age delighted the spectators with her dancing.

But one of her chief delights was music. Like so many of her family, male and female, she learnt to play several instruments and sang charmingly. Her piano teacher was Mrs. Anderson, a pupil of Mendelssohn, who was a brilliant musican herself and wife of the Master of the Queen's Music: her connection with the royal family continued for many years, and she taught all the Queen's children. Another of Princess Victoria's music teachers was Mr. J. B. Sale, organist first of St. Margaret's, Westminster, later of the Chapel Royal. But most admired of all was Luigi Lablache, the operatic singer, a magnificent bass, who was engaged to give the Princess a series of lessons in 1836. For him she had an admiration and an affection which in a less open and straightforward personality might have become an emotional entanglement, though Lablache was in his thirties at the time, and the father of eight children. Already a great lover of opera, Princess Victoria had heard Lablache the year before. 'I am to learn to sing next year . . .' she confided to her diary, '. . . and I hope to learn of Lablache. What a delightful master he would be to learn of!' And so it turned out: his lessons were inspiring, he was a most understanding teacher and personally he was charming. Soon Princess Victoria, and her mother, were looking forward to these weekly operatic sessions, in which they both took part, as one of their chief pleasures. All this is very evident from Princess Victoria's diary, in which, though other teachers are usually dismissed with a brief allusion, she notes in detail everything she sang with Lablache, as well as commenting on his looks and personality. 'Il mio buono e caro maestro,' she calls him, for the language in which they sang was of course Italian, though they conversed in French. She sketched him from memory also, revealing incidentally that he was a very fat man; and when the course of lessons was over summed up her feelings:

'I like Lablache very much, he is such a nice, good-natured, good-humoured man, and a very patient and excellent master; he is so merry too. En profile he has a very fine countenance, I think, an aquiline nose, dark arched eye-brows, and fine long eyelashes, and a very clever expression. He has a profusion of hair, which is very grey, and strangely mixed with some few black locks here and there . . . I liked my lessons extremely. I only wish I had one every *day* instead of one every *week* . . .'

Victoria's delight in opera remained, till, like most of her other pleasures, it was smothered by Prince Albert's death. While he lived, their conflicting musical tastes were a source of amicable disagreement, on which they finally agreed to differ, she remaining faithful to the Italians, he to the Germans. It is strange to think that Queen Victoria actually had no liking for Handel's *Messiah*, which for us has such Victorian associations.

After her recognition as heir presumptive Princess Victoria's life became fuller and more public, and in consequence, for a lively and sociable girl, more enjoyable. There were house parties, dances and dinners; visits to the theatre, or the opera, or the races; progresses arranged, somewhat against the King's inclination, by the Duchess, simply, in modern terms, to give her daughter publicity. All this gave a sparkle to life, and her diary leaves no doubt that the Princess found it, to use a favourite expression of hers, very amusing. Her comments on people and events become more numerous and more copious. The underlinings and the capital letters, which remained such a feature of her adult literary style, are sprinkled more generously about. Everything is suffused with a sort of golden glow.

But this busy social life interfered very much with her formal education, which had to take second place when anything more interesting or important presented itself, and from the age of thirteen onwards became desultory indeed. Even the normal day's routine—and paradoxically there were not many normal days—made few demands on the Princess, as compared with those of an ordinary school time-table. Here is the programme for a single day in May, 1836, when the Princess was sixteen, built up from information given in her diary:

9.0	Breakfast.
10.30–11.30	Walk with Lehzen in the garden.
11.45–12.30	Tutor: New Testament and Clarendon.
12.30–1.30	Writing master.
	Played and sang.
2.15–3.0	Tutor: Paley's *Evidences*.
3.0–4.0	Music mistress.
4.45–5.30	Walk with Lehzen in the garden.
	Wrote diary.
7.0	Dinner.
10.30	To bed.

This is the equivalent of only half a day's real work—three and and a half hours in all; though the walks with Lehzen may well have been in some degree instructional. On many days there was not even this.

By the time she was eighteen and queen, the effects of this haphazard kind of instruction were seen. The Queen became conscious of her ignorance, and did not like to be left alone long with well-educated people, in case the gaps in her knowledge should be revealed. Probably they were less obvious than she supposed; but those who knew her well were aware of them. Her uncle the Duke of Cumberland, King of Hanover, declared in his outspoken and brutal way that 'from her retired and bad education' she was 'more

ignorant than any girl of her age almost in the world'. Like most of
the Duke's pronouncements, this was too emphatic, though not
without some foundation in fact. Yet, let this be said in her favour –
however defective she might be in book-learning (and her reading
list shows that even in this respect she was not as bad as he thought),
she had acquired something which no amount of study could have
given her, and which was more important to a queen than learning.
Princess Lieven, the wife of the Russian ambassador, noted how
perfectly she fitted the part, when she emerged as queen in 1838:

'She possesses a composure, an air of command, and of dignity,
which with her childlike face, her tiny figure, and her pretty smile,
create one of the most extraordinary impressions that it is possible
to imagine.'

It was this same queenly air which aroused the admiration of all
those who saw her at her coronation. 'You did it beautifully – every
part of it, with so much taste,' said Lord Melbourne, who, however-
was not unacquainted with the art of judicious flattery.

But the Queen's inexperience, like her ignorance, was very real.
Despite her easy and natural assumption of regal dignity, she
really knew very little of the art of reigning, which Hannah More
had said was the profession of princes; and those closest to her at
this time realized that she had a great deal to learn, and would
need help and guidance, if she was to perform her task successfully.
Neither her mother, nor Lehzen, nor any of those who had played
a part in her education could have been of any assistance here –
their own horizons were too restricted. But providentially three men
who had the necessary understanding and experience were at hand
to give her the support she needed – her uncle Leopold, King of
the Belgians, who as a sovereign himself knew the pitfalls; his
confidential adviser, Baron Stockmar, who had an unrivalled
theoretical knowledge of state-craft; and the Queen's own Prime
Minister, Lord Melbourne. At this critical stage in her career
Queen Victoria owed more than can be easily expressed to these
three kindly and sympathetic men.

Princess Victoria had always admired and trusted her uncle
Leopold, who was the first father-figure of her infancy. She had
grown up to regard him as the protector of her family, as indeed
he was in a quite literal sense, for he provided financial support for
his sister, the Duchess of Kent, when she was left in financial
difficulties at the death of her improvident husband. Even when he

himself had ceased to live in England, and was fully occupied with a kingdom of his own, he still found time to study the interests of his English niece, to whom he wrote constantly. He was a very competent ruler himself, and one of his weaknesses—an amiable one—was that he never forgot it; which was perhaps why he came to be nicknamed the Nestor of Europe, after the Homeric character so called, who was not so much wise, as fond of airing his wisdom. Believing that he had reduced the rules of sovereignty to a science, and that he was qualified to advise beginners in the art, he had set down his views in a pamphlet entitled 'Directions and Advices'. This was meant primarily for his nephew Ferdinand, who was about to embark on an uncertain future by marrying the Queen of Portugal. But a copy was also sent to the sixteen-year-old Princess Victoria, who read it aloud to Lehzen, and was much impressed: 'most cleverly and beautifully done,' she thought. But at this stage of her impressionable adolescence everything her uncle Leopold did was cleverly and beautifully done: he was her ideal of what a king should be.

'He is *so* clever, *so* mild, and *so* prudent,' she wrote ecstatically in 1836, when she was seventeen; '*he* alone can give me good advice on *every* thing. His advice is perfect. He is indeed il mio secondo padre, or rather "solo padre".'

One is tempted to wonder—irrelevantly—what would have happened if Princess Charlotte had survived to become queen and if the partnership had been, not Victoria and Albert, but Charlotte and Leopold.

In his dealings with his niece King Leopold himself relied strongly on his own confidential adviser, the celebrated Baron Stockmar, whose long back-stage rôle in English history began when his master sent him to England to advise Princess Victoria in person. Stockmar was a native of Coburg (though of Swedish extraction), who had started his career as physician to Prince Leopold, as he then was, but quickly graduated to the position of counsellor, when Leopold ascended the Belgian throne; and thus he remained for the rest of his life, a sort of professional right-hand man, who played an intimate part in the affairs of both the Belgian and the English royal families.

Stockmar had a high opinion of the Princess's natural ability; and it was on his recommendation, after his opinion had been confirmed by an independent witness, that the Duchess of Kent reluctantly abandoned her plans for a regency. With the Princess personally he was a great success. Combining, as he did, charm with wisdom, kindliness with common sense, he was all that she admired. 'My good and honest friend,' she called him in her diary, when she had had time to sum him up:

'He is one of those few people who talk plain honest truth, don't flatter, give wholesome necessary advice, and strive to do good and smooth all dissensions. He is Uncle Leopold's greatest and most confidential attached and disinterested friend, and I hope he is the same to me, at least, I feel so towards him.'

As the King's life drew to a close, Stockmar was much in the Princess's company. What advice he gave can only be conjectured, but there is no doubt he was doing his best to prepare her for the fateful moment. On the day of her accession and subsequent days, interviews with Stockmar alternated with the audiences she was necessarily giving to the great officers of state, and with meetings of the Privy Council. The Queen's journal does not disclose what passed at these private talks, but Stockmar was obviously acting as prompter; and with his help behind the scenes the Queen played her part brilliantly. But again her own contribution must not be overlooked. Though she perhaps leant on Stockmar in private, nothing can detract from the personal triumph which she enjoyed: even in these earliest days she seemed to have a natural gift for saying and doing the right thing.

For some weeks she continued to rely on Stockmar, and at one point he seemed to become so necessary to her that she invited him to become her private secretary. Very sensibly he declined, on the grounds that the Queen's secretary must not be a foreigner, to the relief of those who feared the prospect of a power behind the throne. Stockmar himself appreciated the undesirability of this as much as they did; especially if, as he feared might happen, the power was a female one. He did not think much of Lord Melbourne; but, in default of anyone better, he advised the Queen, on taking leave of her for the last time, to rely on the Prime Minister.

It was wise advice again. Despite Stockmar's unfavourable opinion, Melbourne soon showed that he was well capable of guiding the Queen through the complicated maze of royal duties and functions which confronted her. He was fifty-eight years old to the Queen's eighteen; and once more inevitably something of the relationship of father and daughter entered into the partnership.

She succumbed at once to his personal attraction: his frank and unaffected way of talking, his good looks, his twinkling eyes and merry laughter, his deep, musical voice–all appealed to her. With his experience of affairs, his knowledge of men and books, he seemed to her to sum up in himself all worldly wisdom. Whatever subject came under discussion, he was always ready to instruct and inform the Queen, yet without seeming to do so. His literary and historical judgements, as reported in the Queen's diary, may at times appear superficial and prejudiced–and so no doubt they were; but he was extremely well versed in the political history of England, and none could have initiated the Queen into the arts of government more dexterously than he. Of course Melbourne had his faults– indolence, snobbishness, a narrow outlook were three of them– but they were not of a kind to affect his relations with the Queen. Very quickly a bond of mutual confidence and liking was estab- lished between them. They met almost daily. He handled her with consummate skill; at all times considerate, respectful, deferential, never for a moment forgetting that she was the Queen and he her servant, and yet paternal, protective, and, if need be, critical. The Queen loved it. 'I am so fond of Lord Melbourne,' she wrote unaffectedly in her diary, 'and he *has been* and *is such a kind friend* to me.'

This dependence on a Prime Minister, who was also a party politician, was bound to create a difficult situation, when the Whig ascendancy ended at last, and Melbourne went out of office. But no one for the moment was concerned with such possibilities–the Whigs seemed almost a permanent fixture; while the Queen under Melbourne's tutelage made rapid progress in the art of reigning.

Meanwhile Lehzen was still lurking in the background, unob- served perhaps in the midst of all the comings and goings around the new Queen, but still dominant in her influence on Victoria. We remember how on the day of her accession the Queen had written that Lehzen would ALWAYS (in capital letters) remain with her as a friend. In fact, Lehzen, who had no official status (unless she might be described perhaps as lady in attendance), soon drifted almost imperceptibly into the rôle of private secretary and con- troller of the royal household. All the Queen's domestic affairs were soon in the hands of this no longer humble ex-governess; she appointed the staff and chose the ladies and gentlemen about the court (the fact that they were all Whigs had repercussions later);

she allocated their duties, and, when necessary, dispensed with their services. So all-powerful did she become in this department, that it seemed almost, as has been said, as if the country were being governed by a triumvirate–the Queen, the Prime Minister and Lehzen. The Queen's mother, the Duchess of Kent, who had hoped to see herself wielding some power for a brief spell as regent, and might reasonably have played some part in her daughter's domestic affairs, lived at the Palace, without functions and seemingly quite content.

But events were soon moving far beyond the control of the Baroness Lehzen. Having seen his niece safely seated on the throne, King Leopold, with his faithful henchman at his side, was now turning his attention to the problem of finding a husband for Queen Victoria: she would not be able to exist, he said, without a happy home life. It was not a difficult problem (provided the parties most intimately concerned were willing), for the possibility of a union between Victoria and her cousin Prince Albert of Saxe-Coburg-Gotha had long been in the minds of both families. Fortunately Prince Albert was in every respect a most eligible young man: there was not a prince in Europe to equal him in looks, character, intellect or education. It was only necessary to throw the two young people together in the rather obvious and deliberate way then normal among royalty, in the hope that they would fall in love, or at any rate appreciate the desirability of marriage. For our purpose it is sufficient to recall that the ensuing love-match, so artificially induced, turned out to be one of the most lasting and perfect ever enjoyed by royal lovers; and remained without flaw till its sudden dissolution with the death of Prince Albert in 1861.

To the immature and inexperienced Queen marriage made one great difference–it freed her from the necessity of dependence on others. She no longer felt the unconscious or half-conscious need for the father-figure on whom to lean, for at her side was now one who was capable of sustaining her whatever difficulties might lie ahead. So the kindly men to whom she had owed so much now stepped down into second place, though they were never forgotten.

With King Leopold, her dear uncle, she retained the friendliest relations; but even the wisdom of Nestor seemed less indispensable now. As for Stockmar, he remained on for many years as friend and counsellor, a familiar figure at Windsor or Balmoral; and in this case it was as much for Albert as for Victoria, for he had been the

Prince's mentor in boyhood and still retained his affection and regard. But even his usefulness began to fade, and the moment came when tact, combined with ill health and advancing years, led to his withdrawing to his native Coburg. When a friend expressed surprise at his going, 'Have you not learnt,' he asked, 'that in the case of Royalties, so soon as one is neither useful nor amusing, one's only course is to disappear?' Though the slightly cynical note here suggests that he felt he was no longer wanted, in fact both Queen and Prince were sorry to see him go, and kept in touch with an affectionate exchange of letters. Stockmar died at the age of seventy-five, two years after the Prince himself.

The Queen's inevitable separation from Lord Melbourne came in 1841, when the Whig government finally lost the confidence of the House and a dissolution could no longer be postponed. The final parting between them was almost like a parting between lovers. 'It is very, very sad,' sighed the Queen in her last letter to Melbourne as Prime Minister. 'We do, and shall, miss you dreadfully': while Lord Melbourne, in the course of his final interview with the Queen, confessed, with tears in his eyes, 'I have seen you daily, and I liked it better every day.' But it was probably just as well, both on political and on personal grounds, that the breach took place when it did. Already the Queen, through her liking for Melbourne and her dislike of the Tory leader, Peel, was closely identified with the Whigs; and if the situation had developed any further, her popularity and even her throne might have been in danger; while her complete personal reliance on Melbourne would surely in the end have set up some barrier between her and her husband. Melbourne in his wisdom perhaps saw the danger. His last advice to the Queen was that she should trust her husband's judgement in all things; and, as she had always done, but now for the last time, she took his advice. Looking back some years later, when these events were only a memory, the Queen realized that she had been rather silly.

'My unbounded affection and admiration for Lord Melbourne,' she wrote somewhat incoherently in her journal, 'which I said to Albert I hardly knew from what it arose, excepting the fact that I clung to someone and having very warm feelings. Albert thinks I worked myself up to what really became quite foolish.'
Foolish perhaps, but not unnatural in a fatherless, eighteen-year-old girl, placed suddenly on the lonely pinnacle of sovereignty.

There remained only Lehzen, more deeply entrenched than

anyone else in the Queen's affections. There is no doubt that from
the start she resented the presence of Prince Albert, and from her
vantage point as controller of the household tried to restrict his
influence. Of course she was fighting a losing battle, but she was not
easily dislodged. The Prince, irritated by her petty machinations to
the point of calling her, in letters to Stockmar, the 'house dragon
spitting fire' and 'the yellow lady' (in allusion to her jaundice),
quickly resolved that she must go. But Albert himself had to move
cautiously. When in a moment of exasperation he told her to leave
the Palace, Lehzen replied that he had no power to turn her out of
the Queen's house; and not even Albert at this stage dared go to the
Queen and denounce Lehzen for her insolence. Stockmar did his
best to help by telling the Baroness to her face that she would
never be forgiven if she came between the Queen and her husband;
and Lehzen did not strengthen her own position by dabbling in
politics. Gradually the Queen was brought to realize that the
situation was impossible. At last in 1841 she consented to set out on a
round of visits with her husband but without Lehzen. It was the
first time she had ever been separated from her governess since she
was five, and, as she said herself, it made her feel a little low. But
Prince Albert's way of putting it was that the moon was on the
wane; and next year, accepting defeat, Lehzen retired to her native
Hanover, while everyone at court breathed more freely. Once more
the Queen was brought to realize her own foolishness, when Prince
Albert disclosed to her the details of the undignified guerrilla warfare which he had been compelled to wage with the dragon. 'I
blame myself for my blindness,' she wrote. 'I shudder to think what
my beloved Albert had to go through . . . it makes my blood boil
to think of it.'

But now Albert was supreme. All the props on which Victoria
had depended in her girlhood were down, and she leaned happily
henceforward on her remarkable husband. It is difficult to realize
that he was still only in his early twenties, when he took upon himself quite deliberately to draw out his wife's powers and make good
the deficiencies of her education. To Englishmen, who are self-
conscious about assuming superiority, such a plan, conceived by
one so young, seems heavy with priggishness; and perhaps if Albert
had been an English prince he would not have thought of it. But
here, as in much else he did, Prince Albert's German thoroughness
and seriousness of purpose come out.

He himself was for a prince exceptionally well educated. He had been soundly tutored at home and at the court of his uncle Leopold; he had taken his studies at the University of Bonn very seriously indeed; and he had derived every benefit from a period in Italy under the tutelage of Stockmar. He now tried to pass on to Victoria some of his knowledge and wisdom. She was a willing pupil. Their hours of study and discussion together were hours of bliss for both. Like many other Victorian husbands and wives, they liked reading works of solid learning aloud to one another – histories, memoirs, sermons. They took lessons in art, and painted and drew together. They shared the pleasure which both found in music, singing, playing, listening to concerts and recitals – Prince Albert was a good organist, and like Henry VIII had some small talent as a composer. Until she met him, Victoria found no pleasure in the country – it was one of those gaps in her make-up which were waiting to be filled; and Prince Albert, who had all the German's romantic passion for wild and beautiful scenery, set himself to fill it. The results of his tutelage here took concrete shape in those country houses at Osborne and Balmoral, which he and the Queen loved so intensely. It is strange to think that the royal love for the Scottish Highlands, which now persists as strongly as ever in the third and fourth generations, originated in this way with a German prince's romantic longing for the mountains and forests of his native land.

The Queen acknowledged and rejoiced in her transformation. The whole weight and value of her debt to Albert is conveyed in those simple words addressed to him and so often quoted – 'It is you who have entirely formed me'. Forty years after his death she had not forgotten.

9

A Prince Under Pressure

IT IS NOT OFTEN THAT WELL-INTENTIONED PARENTS ARE SO misguided as Queen Victoria and Prince Albert were in the way they handled their eldest son's education. The upbringing of this unfortunate boy, the future King Edward VII, is remarkable in the history of royal education, both for the intensity with which it was pursued, and for its failure to produce the results hoped for – and, perhaps one might add also, for its failure to extinguish the natural good qualities of the victim.

The master mind behind this vast educational project was that of Prince Albert, who threw his full weight into it; but the Queen identified herself completely with everything he did; and, unlike most sons of stern fathers, the Prince of Wales could never take refuge from paternal pressures with his mother. These two young parents, still no more than twenty-two years old when their eldest son was born in 1841, took parenthood very seriously indeed. They already had a daughter, the Princess Royal, born the year before. But their son, as heir to the imperial throne, became the focus of their anxieties. The way he was brought up, as Prince Albert said, was 'a *public matter* not unconnected with the present and prospective welfare of the state'.

The British public saw it this way too. There was intense interest in the plans being made for the education of the young Prince Albert Edward (as he was then called). In 1843, when he was two, an anonymous pamphlet with the title 'Who should educate the Prince of Wales?' attracted a good deal of attention, including that of Prince Albert himself, who read it with care. Conscious of their youth and inexperience, the royal parents sought advice from every possible source at their command, and did not resent gratuitous suggestions. But they naturally turned first to the faithful Baron

Stockmar, whose ready store of wisdom was always at their disposal. He responded with a memorandum, the first of a sheaf of such documents which proliferated around the young Prince, heavy with platitudes, but containing some pertinent observations also. Probably the one which stuck most in the minds of the young parents, for it re-echoed their own worst fears, was the suggestion that George IV's follies were due to a faulty education, for which his parents were to blame. The possibility that their own son might take after any of his Hanoverian great uncles haunted their minds, and they resolved that everything possible should be done to prevent it. Alas for their fond hopes–for all the salient features of little Bertie's character, including the best features, did they but know it, were Hanoverian, and he owed nothing to his worthy father.

In brief, Stockmar advocated an education which should be 'truly moral and truly English'; and among other counsellors the Bishop of Oxford, chiming in with an echo of Renaissance doctrine, said that 'The great object in view is to make [the Prince] the most perfect man.' With these comforting objectives in mind, Prince Albert proceeded to study the whole theory and practice of princely education. It would be surprising if he had found in history any encouragement for the view that perfection could be achieved through education; but he was living in an age which had an unbounded confidence in the powers of education, and perhaps he thought that, where so many other parents and guardians of princes had failed, he could succeed. At any rate he set to work on that apparent assumption. The only advice he did not take was the most realistic of all he had received–that of the wise, if slightly cynical, Lord Melbourne–'Be not over solicitous about education. It may be able to do much . . . It may mould and direct character, but it rarely alters it.' By rejecting this warning, he made sure of much toil and travail for his eldest son.

But it would be wrong to give the impression that the Queen and Prince Albert were inhuman parents. Prince Albert, who found it difficult to make friends with adults, was completely at ease with his own children. When they were small he loved sharing their games: we read of him helping to fly kites, playing hide-and-seek, chasing butterflies, turning somersaults on a hay-stack 'to show Bertie how to do it'. As the Queen herself wrote in 1848, 'He is so kind to them and romps with them so delightfully, and manages them so beautifully and firmly.' Looking at portraits of Victorian *patres familiarum*, it is difficult enough to imagine any of them doing this, least of all Prince Albert, so solemn, so immaculate and so heavily clad. But the record proves that he could be light-hearted enough when he chose. His daughters adored him, and even his two eldest sons, who received so much criticism and so much chastisement at his hands, never ceased to be fond of him while he lived, and to honour his memory when he was dead.

As for the Queen, she was fonder of her children than at times might appear. She was never wholly at her ease with the older ones – a curious situation, arising perhaps from her utter absorption in her husband: 'I feel no especial pleasure or compensation in the company of the elder children' she wrote in 1856, '. . . and only very occasionally do I find the rather intimate intercourse with them either agreeable or easy.' Outwardly – and especially after her husband's death – she was often the stern matriarch, who treated her sons like children even when they were grown up – criticizing their clothes and their manners, objecting to their smoking or putting their hands in their pockets, disapproving of their playing cards or going too often to the races – and expected her younger daughters to act as her unpaid attendants, and, if they got married, to choose husbands who did not mind being mere court appendages. But though the failure of the Prince of Wales to live up to her high hopes warped her feelings towards him, she was genuinely attached to her other children, and they were a happy family. A false impression has in some respects been created for posterity by her tendency to write down her criticisms, which have therefore survived, while her spoken words of sympathy and affection have gone with the wind.

Meanwhile, as the experts gave their views, and the memoranda multiplied, the young Prince of Wales, with his brothers and sisters as they became old enough, was enjoying a normal nursery life. His governess, appointed in 1842, was Lady Lyttleton, a widow with grown-up children, who had been lady-of-the-bedchamber to the Queen. She was sensible, motherly and of a sufficiently strong and independent character to stick to and win her point in opposition to both the Queen and Prince Albert, when a controversy arose as to whether the little Princes and Princesses should be taught to kneel when praying. The children liked her, and life in the nursery pursued an even course.

There were three other governesses – sub-governesses they would have been called in an earlier generation–who were specially concerned with languages, Miss Hildyard for English, Mme Rollande de la Sange for French and Fraülein Grüner for German. The young Prince of Wales grew up bilingual in English and German, and in fact as a child preferred German, which was the family language. His pronunciation of English always had a slightly German flavour. French he acquired more slowly: he employed a resident French tutor, the elegant M. Brasseur, for many years in adult life. But the time was to come when his perfect command of the language and his authentic Parisian accent would play their part in cementing the Entente Cordiale.

At this stage in his career the Prince was a confiding, affectionate child, whose fair curls and blue eyes made social relationships easy for him. 'We agreed that he was such a dear little boy,' said his mother afterwards. Lady Lyttleton praised him for his truthfulness and his 'very good principles', meaning perhaps that he knew the difference between right and wrong, but admitted that he was not clever. It was this absence of academic cleverness which precipitated many of the troubles in store for the Prince and his parents. Like many mothers and fathers of humbler birth, the Queen and her husband took their son's cleverness for granted. Before a measure of disillusionment set in, Prince Albert referred to his two eldest children as 'the improved editions', meaning that they were to be like their parents, only better; and the Queen saw the young Prince as a replica of everything she admired so much in his father, including his intellectual ability, which was well above the average. Neither of them could face the facts, when it turned out that the boy had no academic talent. They continued to treat him as if he had, and submitted him forcibly to an education for which he was not suited; and when he failed to respond, the inevitable comparisons, both spoken and unspoken, with his elder sister, the Princess Royal, who had inherited her father's brains, made things worse. The Queen and Prince Albert were in fact caught up in a tangle of a kind familiar enough to every schoolmaster.

But Prince Albert's plans moved remorselessly forward. Much anxious thought was given to the problem of choosing a tutor. The anonymous pamphlet already mentioned quaintly recommended that the tutor should not be a statesman or a clergyman, but 'a man of letters who has passed through the alembic of adversity.' Who could have been intended, one asks oneself. Baron Stockmar was likewise opposed to employing a parson, on the grounds that he would be biased against science. Both the Queen and Prince Albert were well aware of the importance of science (though it was still excluded from the public schools), and arrangements were later made for the Prince to acquire at any rate a smattering of it. But in choosing a tutor orthodoxy prevailed, and, after considering various clerical candidates, among them Dr. Liddell, headmaster of Westminster, later Dean of Christ Church, and Bishop Wilberforce of Oxford, who was not then the controversial figure he later became, their choice eventually fell on Henry Mildred Birch, an Eton master hitherto quite unknown, who had qualifications which his more distinguished rivals lacked – he was, said Prince Albert, 'a young, good-looking, amiable man to whom the child was likely to be attached.' He took up his duties in 1849, when the Prince was seven and a half.

Prince Albert personally drew up his son's first time-table, which in a six-hour day covered nine subjects – religion, English, writing, French, music, calculating, German, drawing and geography, in that order; one hour each for the languages, half an hour each for the other subjects. We are not to suppose that Birch taught all these himself; but his was the guiding hand, and to make sure that he guided aright, Prince Albert (who was no older than the tutor) drew up a document of solemn instructions for his use.

'It will be well,' he wrote, 'to let mental and more mechanical exertions alternate in order not to strain the intellect or wear out the patience of the child.'

'Immediately after the meal in the middle of the day it will be well not to work the mind of the child:'
with other unoriginal but impeccably sound admonitions of a similar kind.

The young Prince liked Birch, and until the novelty wore off things went smoothly. Under his tutor's direction he started writing letters to his relations, and began keeping the far from private diary, which for the next ten years or so his father would carefully scrutinize in search of pointers to his son's development and progress. But steady academic work soon proved too much for the boy. He began to reveal traits unsuspected in the winsome child of only a few years previously – obstinacy, conceit, bad temper, nervous excitability. Birch did his best, but must have wished he had never abandoned his classical teaching in the comparative calm of Eton;

while the distracted parents first tried corporal punishment (administered by Prince Albert himself), and finally went so far as to consult a famous phrenologist, George Combe, in the hope that his diagnosis of the bumps on little Bertie's head might suggest some solution. As was perhaps prudent in dealing with such august clients, Combe diagnosed what was already obvious–that the Prince was excitable, bad-tempered, obstinate and had a high opinion of his own importance. The latter quality, he thought, might in some way be turned to good account. No one seemed to have yet discovered (unless the language governesses had done so) that the Prince learnt best by doing. It might have made a good deal of difference to him if this faculty had been exploited. Meanwhile, unaffected by the struggles which went on in the schoolroom, and unnoticed by his parents, the Prince's real education was proceeding through the people he met and talked to, the places he visited, the lively experiences a boy in his position was bound to have.

After two years Birch was dismissed, ostensibly because of Prince Albert's disapproval of the stress he laid on the catechism in his religious teaching, but really perhaps because it was thought a change of tutor might do some good. Certainly no stigma was attached to Birch's dismissal. He was much missed by his pupils (for by this time he had become responsible also for Prince Alfred, three years younger than the Prince of Wales); and was sad himself at parting from them, despite the trouble they had given him.

The new tutor, Frederick Waymouth Gibbs, took over in 1852, when the Prince was ten, and held office for seven crucial years. At £1,000 a year (£200 more than Birch had received) he was for those days extremely well paid. It was an unorthodox choice in several respects. Gibbs was a layman and an intellectual, a Fellow of Trinity, Cambridge, and a barrister: even more interesting, he was a man of comparatively humble origin, adopted and brought up by Sir James Stephen, Professor of Modern History at Cambridge, along with his own brilliant and later famous sons, Fitzjames and Leslie Stephen. It is not clear why the royal parents thought this clever young man would meet the requirements of their wayward and unintellectual offspring; but certainly Sir James Stephen's remarkably frank assessment weighed heavily with them.

'The moral qualities by which Mr. Gibbs is chiefly characterized are courage and energy,' wrote Sir James. 'He fears nothing . . . and is exceedingly free from all anxious forebodings, and never quailed before the face of any human being. The faults of his character are akin to this temperament . . . He is self-confident and has the strength of will which occasionally degenerates into obstinacy, and these infirmities now and then exhibit themselves in a demeanour which may be described as brusque, peremptory and contemptuous. On the other hand, he is never morose, gloomy or irritable, but opposes to all the vexations and cares of life a cheerful humour, a spirit of alacrity and hope. He is perfectly amiable and good-tempered.'

At any rate it seemed as if Gibbs might be a match for the Prince of Wales. But Prince Albert thought he needed more knowledge of the world, and sent him abroad for some months before he took up his duties, to acquire this, and to brush up his modern languages.

The publication a few years ago[1] of extracts from Gibbs's diary for 1852–56 revealed to the full the sort of difficulties which confronted the new tutor. He had to deal in fact with a thoroughly unpleasant little boy, who refused to do what he was told, spat and made faces at his tutor, threatened and even struck him with sticks, threw stones and mud in his face, and took a sadistic pleasure in tormenting his own brothers and sisters, of whom there were now seven. But Gibbs, showing much good sense and insight, realized that these were symptoms, and refused to be provoked, though Prince Albert told him he ought to box the boy's ears or rap him over the knuckles with one of his own sticks. In 1854, when his chief pupil was thirteen, he submitted to the Queen a frank analysis of the boy's character, in which he saw a conflict between his natural sense of duty and the impulse to violence which arose from his failure to achieve success and win approval. The boy was backward for his age, he pointed out, and found thinking extremely painful. But he had his good qualities, and even a basic desire to learn, which might be expected to prevail as he matured. Meanwhile the struggle to provide him with the essential elementary knowledge must continue. A familiar enough situation, but fraught with peculiar problems, when the backward and difficult pupil was the heir apparent.

Through all this Gibbs retained the full confidence and backing of the royal parents, particularly the Queen, who liked him much better than his predecessor Birch, in whose company she confessed to feeling either that he was in her way or she in his. But there was

[1] In the *Cornhill Magazine*, No. 986 (Spring, 1951).

no relaxation in their treatment of the unfortunate young Prince, though Prince Albert admitted privately that he had come to feel some doubt about this policy of force, and hated being the one who had to administer punishment. Gibbs and his colleagues all recommended less book work. M. Voisin, the Prince's French tutor, even suggested the desirability of a more primitive training:

'Make him climb trees! Run! Leap! Row! Ride!' he wrote. 'In many ways savages are much better educated than we are.'

But the Queen and Prince Albert took no action.

The Prince for his part may have meanwhile found some relief from intellectual strain in the practical accomplishments, which as a prince he was expected to acquire. He was awkward and troublesome with Mrs. Anderson, his mother's old music teacher, who was still doing her duty by the royal family, and he made slow progress as a pianist. He seems, however, to have genuinely enjoyed serious music performed by others, especially opera (in which he took after his mother), and retained the taste even as a grown man, when so many of the enforced habits of his youth were shed; though by that time it took second place to musical comedy in his affections. He enjoyed dancing, in which he eventually became as adept and tireless as his mother; and he showed some talent for acting. In this, as in some other ways, he recalls that other problem child, the future King George III. Like George, he was coached by a well-known actor of the day, George Bartley, and his parents, like George's, made rather a feature of amateur theatricals for their children. Plays were produced in French and German, as well as English, and the young Prince of Wales was able to find some fulfilment for his ego while playing leading rôles in scenes from classics like Racine's *Athalie* and Schiller's *Wallenstein*, chosen, one cannot help feeling, by his high-brow father. Something of the authentic flavour of these productions has been preserved for posterity in a photograph (reproduced in the Cornhill Magazine), in which a somewhat sulky prince is seen seated on a barrel in the rôle of Bacchus, dressed in a leopard-skin and ill-fitting white 'leotards', with imitation grapes in his hair, tipsily brandishing one of those silver cups which used to be given as prizes at athletic sports.

Queen Victoria was something of a patron of drama. Theatrical companies were often invited to perform at Windsor, and in this way her family came to have what was probably a wider experience of drama than any other children of their age in the country. It is said that the Prince of Wales had seen no fewer than fourteen of Shakespeare's plays as a child. As a result no doubt of his own youthful successes as an actor, he continued, again like George III, to be interested in drama all his life; and this part of his education, one in which compulsion had played no part, bore a noble fruit— he became perhaps the greatest single patron of drama in the history of the stage, and, as the first English monarch to knight an actor (Sir Henry Irving), he did much to raise the prestige of the profession, many of whose members were his friends.

One of the reasons for the young Prince's shocking behaviour, in the opinion of all his tutors, was that he had no companions of his own age. This would have been bad for any small boy; but it was particularly so for a boy who was temperamentally gregarious, and, as became clear when he was old enough to choose his own way of life, happiest in a crowd. His parents were very reluctant to allow him to have contact with other little boys, fearing that he might be exposed to corrupting influences. But at length they gave way to the extent of letting a few carefully selected Eton boys attend for an hour or two from time to time to play with the Prince. It is obvious that this could have been no substitute for the rough and tumble of school life, which was what the Prince really needed. His first response was to bully his companions, which brought complaints from the headmaster; and when his father made a point of being present in person at these strange play sessions, the atmosphere at once became strained and unnatural. A further attempt, made a few years later, to bring the Prince and his brother into contact with other boys by allowing them to attend meetings of Pop ended in failure owing to their rude and aggressive conduct. Some good seemed to come of these experiments, however, which after all had good Tudor precedent, and for a number of years the Prince of Wales enjoyed the intermittent company of some half dozen Etonians of selected provenance, who gradually became his friends, some of them friends for life. But one cannot help feeling how much better it would have been if he had been sent to Eton. Among other things, if he had gone to school, he would have played team games like cricket and football with a crowd of other boys, which would have certainly done him good. As it was, what games he did play revolved too obviously round him personally; and though it is reported that his governess's grandson, who was sometimes present, bowled vigorously at the Prince's legs as an antidote to his domineering attitude, it would have been far better to expose him to the force of public opinion.

The Prince's bookish education was in the meantime pushed forward with renewed vigour, as he passed beyond childhood. In 1855 an additional tutor was appointed, the Rev. C. F. Tarver, an Etonian and a Fellow of King's, who had the disheartening task of trying to extend the Prince's sketchy knowledge of Latin and theology; and the following year the claims of modern studies were rather perfunctorily recognized, when he was sent with his brother Alfred to a course of lectures on metals given by Faraday at the Royal Institution, and, along with his elder sister, received lessons in political economy from a privately employed instructor, named William Ellis. It seems doubtful whether either of these well-meaning attempts to broaden the Prince's outlook can have had any lasting effect.

At the same time further steps towards emancipation were taken, when at fifteen the Prince was given a small allowance with which to purchase hats and ties chosen by himself; and at sixteen was allowed to choose all his own clothes. But this first breath of freedom must have blown a little chill, when he was handed a formal memorandum from his mother on the importance of taste in clothes, in which, among other things, she urged her son never to wear anything '*extravagant* or *slang*', and not to imitate those 'foolish and worthless persons', who dressed, as she put it, 'loudly'. As a result of—or should it be perhaps despite these directions?—the Prince later developed an immaculate taste in clothes.

By this time the boy was beginning to hanker after a military career, in which he may have seen the possibility of an escape from books and the restrictions on his liberty which they seemed inevitably to bring; and his father, rather surprisingly, agreed that he should now study for this purpose. He himself would have preferred not to study at all; but any change was probably welcome. This one certainly marked a step forward. The Prince was provided with an establishment of his own at White Lodge, Richmond Park, where he lived with Gibbs, Tarver, and one of three equerries on a monthly rota, whose special duty was to stimulate the young man's interest in military matters, polish up his manners and share his recreations. The three paragons selected for this responsible task displayed between them a fair range of virtues, civil and military. One, Lord Valletort, described by Prince Albert as 'a thoroughly good, moral and accomplished man', had lived much abroad, showed some talent for art and music and had never been to a public school. The other two, Majors Teesdale and Lindsay, were orthodox soldiers of unimpeachable reputation, who had both won the Victoria Cross. Prince Albert was confident that their influence would be salutary. But there can have been little illusion of independence for the pupil.

This time it was the equerries who became the target of a royal memorandum, drawn up for their guidance by Prince Albert. In it he pointed out that the Prince of Wales was now at a critical stage of his development, and stressed the importance of the part they were playing in helping to mould the character of one who was to be 'the first gentleman of the country'. Obviously Prince Albert was still thinking in terms of training the heir apparent rather than preparing a young man for entrance to a military academy. Subsections dealt with appearance, deportment and dress, manners and conduct towards others and the art of conversation. A formidable list of faults to be watched for and checked included 'lounging ways, such as lolling in armchairs or sofas', 'a slouching gait with hands in the pockets', 'dandyism', 'idle, gossiping talk', the use of 'satirical and bantering expressions', and indulgence in practical jokes. On the positive side the Prince must learn to dress according to his rank and station, to acknowledge salutations with the 'appearance of good will and cordiality', to take the lead in conversation, avoiding such banal opening gambits as health and the weather; and his equerries were to make themselves responsible for seeing that the leisure occupations of their sixteen-year-old charge were of an improving character, such, for example, as studying music and art, or hearing poetry, amusing books or good plays read aloud. In practice he was also allowed to ride and row, and frequent dinner-parties were given in his name, at which the guests were all distinguished and mostly middle-aged or elderly. He had no companions of his own age.

When the Prince was seventeen came yet another change. Gibbs passed into retirement, and resumed his practice at the bar, regretted by his now no longer hostile pupil, who kept up a friendly correspondence with him for many years, and honoured by his pupil's mother, who awarded him the C.B. and a pension of £800. It may have been felt that a youth of seventeen needed the firm handling which only a soldier could give. At any rate he was now placed under a governor of proved military reputation, Colonel Robert Bruce of the Grenadier Guards, a dour but cultivated Scotsman of forty-five, known in the army as a strong disciplinarian. He too received an impressive directive from the Queen, which emphasized the importance of the 'momentous trust' he had undertaken, and urged him to 'regulate all the Prince's movements, the distribution and employment of his time and the occupation and details of his daily life', and to teach him also 'habits of reflection and self-denial, the strictest truthfulness and honour, above all, the conscientious discharge of his duties towards God and man'. This was reinforced by yet another memorandum, addressed to the Prince himself on his seventeenth birthday, and signed by both his parents. 'Life is composed of duties,' they said, 'and in the due, punctual and cheerful performance of them the true Christian, true soldier and true gentleman is recognized.'

It is said that after reading this sombre missive the poor young man, overcome by who knows what emotions, burst into tears.

The colonel must have used his discretion in interpreting his instructions: life would otherwise have been impossible for both governor and governed. He found the Prince not unamenable, and under his guidance there was a marked improvement: gradually the bad temper, the self-centred domineering moods of childhood, the idleness and the frivolity passed into the background, if they did not die away altogether. The Prince was coming to terms with his environment, and learning to use again the social charm which had been natural to him in infancy, and which became one of his most characteristic traits as a grown man. People who met him were impressed. Disraeli referred to his 'singularly sweet manner'. His first-cousin-once-removed, the Duke of Cambridge, who met him in the most favourable circumstances, thought him a 'charming and unaffected lad.'

This period of the Prince's youth happened to coincide with the beginning of a popular vogue for walking-tours, a by-product of the 'muscular Christianity' of the day. The royal advisers, and particularly Lord Granville, who was influential with the Queen and her husband, believed that a combination of strenuous walking and earnest talking might be good for the adolescent Prince. The idea was accepted, and an experimental trip was made in 1856. It was a somewhat ill-assorted party—the fourteen-year-old Prince, his tutor Gibbs and one of his father's gentlemen, Colonel Cavendish

–which set forth along the dusty roads of Dorset. The intention was to tramp for a fortnight, staying the night at inns. Unfortunately the Prince, walking incognito as Duke of Renfrew, was recognized, and public excitement along the route became so great that the tour had to be abandoned after a few days.

But the experience was thought worth repeating, and several more tours were organized. In the following year, accompanied by Gibbs, Cavendish, a medical officer (in case of blisters) and four choice Etonians, the Prince visited the Lake District, climbed Helvellyn and narrowly missed chastisement by a farmer's wife for chasing some sheep into the lake at Windermere (an exploit of which he was so proud that he made a permanent record of the scene in water-colour, and presented it to one of his Etonian satellites). He certainly enjoyed himself on this occasion; but his father (now Prince Consort) was dissatisfied with the bald and unreflective quality of his diary of the trip, and laid it down that the next tour should include a programme of work as well as recreation. To make sure that there should be no failure of duty this time, the Prince Consort sent four adults to accompany his son–his secretary, General Grey, one of his equerries and two tutors–though the emphasis on weight and worth was somewhat offset by the usual admixture of Etonians. This was a more ambitious excursion in other ways also. After a month studying German at Königswinter on the Rhine, where the Prince caused a flutter among his entourage by kissing a girl, and where he also met a number of well-known people, chief among them Prince Metternich, now eighty-four years old, in whose imposing presence he became tongue-tied with shyness, he went on to Switzerland. Here, his own personal retinue of eight swollen by the addition of numerous guides and porters, he walked on a glacier and over some passes, but made no actual mountain ascents. Did these artificially controlled and heavily escorted trips serve their purpose? Certainly they aroused in the Prince none of that spontaneous enjoyment of walking, which other young men experienced at that time: as an adult he never walked a step further than he had to. But they did mark a stage in his emancipation: it was a relief for him to get away from his parents and the routine of lessons, and in this way they must have helped him to straighten out his warped psychology. Probably the most beneficial of all was the last, when in 1858 he visited the south of Ireland, alone except for his tutor.

In this year took place also a rather over-organized educational visit to Rome, in the course of which it was expected that the Prince would widen his horizons by studying art, archaeology and international politics, and enjoy carefully controlled contacts with notable people. The accompanying party of seven this time included two ladies, the wives of the Prince's governor and tutor, but no Etonians to distract the student from his labours. No sooner had they arrived in Rome than work started to a set time-table – before breakfast, memory work; 10–11, Italian tutor; 11–12, Mr. Tarver (teaching presumably Latin and theology); 5–6, French; 6–7, private reading or music. This was irksome for a seventeen-year-old boy eager to sample the delights of a new and strange city; and even more so the rigorous programme of sight-seeing under the direction of well-known authorities on art, architecture and archaeology, which filled his leisure hours. The experience must have permanently inhibited his enjoyment of pictures, churches and Roman remains. But, though his father found in his diary no traces of archaeological or historical acumen, something of Rome's charm was able to penetrate the ranks of his learned bodyguard. He enjoyed its teeming life from a safe distance, and found congenial company among some of those he was allowed to meet: others, whose acquaintance he would have liked to make, were kept at arm's length by his over-anxious governor, including the Pope, from whose presence the Prince was prematurely and discourteously snatched away, when it seemed as if the conversation might venture on to dangerous ground. Among those considered fit company for the Prince were Robert Browning and the American historian, Motley, who wrote an account of him which once more recalls young George III:

'The complexion is pure, fresh, and healthy, like that of most English boys, his hair light brown, cut short, and curly. His eyes are bluish-grey, rather large, and very frank in his expression; his smile is very ready and genuine; his manners are extremely good.'
His mother, however, criticized the way he did his hair as 'effeminate and girlish'.

The final stage of the Prince Consort's master plan for the heir apparent's education carried it up to university level. It is very doubtful, to say the least, whether the Prince was fit material for a university. But the Prince Consort, who had himself done well at the University of Bonn, could not accept that his son was incapable of a similar success, and was determined on this grand climax to the boy's education. Before making his mind up as to details, Prince Albert consulted a formidable array of authorities, not only cabinet ministers and Oxford and Cambridge professors, but the President of the Royal Academy, the Director of the British Museum and John Ruskin. The decision meant a complete break with precedent in several ways. No heir to the throne had ever been educated at an English university before (unless we accept the story that Henry V matriculated at Oxford). No English prince (with this one possible exception) had ever entered an English university, though several of George III's sons went to Göttingen. The best arrangement in the circumstances would probably have been to send the Prince of Wales to either Oxford or Cambridge for a full degree course, though it would have certainly needed to be a Pass rather than an Honours course. Instead the Prince Consort seems to have tried to make the most of all possible worlds, and perhaps satisfy all possible claims, by sending the young man, not only to Oxford, but to Cambridge and Edinburgh as well. He thus never really settled down at any of them, and the impact of each was fleeting and superficial.

Edinburgh came first as a sort of prelude to Oxford. Living in Holyrood Palace with Bruce and Tarver, the Prince studied applied science under Dr. Playfair, the Professor of Chemistry, for a few months in the summer and autumn of 1859. He was an amiable pupil, but no great demands were made on either his understanding or his industry. At the same time he worked at modern history and law, which it was intended he should read at Oxford, with a specially appointed tutor, Herbert Fisher (who later became his first private secretary), and Greek and Roman history with Dr. Leonard Schmitz, Rector of the Royal High School, who found him a much more satisfactory pupil than he had been led to expect. It was all rather fragmentary and shallow, if only because it lasted for so short a time—some critics indeed, including *Punch*, described it as mere cramming; nor can it be said that the Prince had really enjoyed the feeling of belonging to the university, for he was there mostly in vacation time. When the course ended in September, the Prince Consort came over from Balmoral for direct consultation with his son's tutors. Their reports were unexpectedly reassuring—'All speak highly of him,' noted his father, 'and he seems to have shown zeal and good-will.' While the subject of their deliberations recovered his spirits deer-stalking at Balmoral, the conference went on to discuss plans for Oxford.

There were difficulties about his entering the University of Oxford, which refused to adjust itself even to the requirements of the heir apparent. The Prince Consort wanted his son to belong to the university, without joining a college, partly to avoid invidious distinctions between colleges, mainly because it would be easier to segregate the Prince from dangerous contact with other under-graduates, if he lived apart. 'The more I think of it, the more I see the difficulties of the Prince being thrown together with other young men,' the Prince Consort had written to Dr. Liddell, now Dean of Christ Church. But the university would not agree, and eventually a compromise was reached, under which the Prince was admitted to Christ Church, but occupied separate premises not far away at Frewin Hall, with the inescapable governor and tutor ever in attendance. The bogey of his possible corruption continued to haunt his parents, and, except for a chosen few, he was not–in theory–allowed to mix with his fellow undergraduates. In practice he managed to meet a good many of a type not approved by his parents, particularly on the hunting field.

The Prince Consort had a very restricted view of the purpose of a university. 'The only use of Oxford,' he said, 'is that it is a place of *study*–a refuge from the world and its claims.' He did his best to see that it should fulfil this function for his son by arranging for the most distinguished scholars to teach him, or to lecture at him–that seems the best way to put it–in the presence of six other under-graduates, brought in, so to speak, to make a quorum, who were expected to rise respectfully to their feet when he entered the room. The Prince was debarred from the ordinary social life of the uni-versity, from which he would have derived both pleasure and profit. For him there were no arguments far into the night, no dining and wining, no clubs and societies (other than the Union, of which he was, naturally, an honorary member). His entertaining was limited to select dinner parties attended by senior dons and clergy. 'I hope,' wrote his father, 'I hope you have begun your little dinner parties again, and are seeing the chief men of the university at your table.' Even his games were confined to tennis and racquets, which had the advantage of requiring a minimum of contact with others. But in spite of these restrictions pleasure would keep creeping in, and the Prince of Wales enjoyed his time at Oxford.

After less than a year, however, his Oxford course was interrupted

by a four-months good-will visit to Canada and the U.S.A., his
first semi-official mission abroad, in which he acquitted himself
with a success which surprised many, not least his own parents. It
was noted for the first time that he had a natural gift for meeting
crowds, and that, whatever his other attainments might be, he was
likely to be a successful public figure. The President of the United
States spoke of him in complimentary terms not entirely dictated
by courtesy:

'He has passed,' he wrote to the Queen, 'through a trying ordeal
for a person of his years, and his conduct throughout has been such
as becomes his age and station. Dignified, frank and affable, he has
conciliated, wherever he has been, the kindness and respect of a
sensitive and discriminating people':

and though his own governor's report of the tour noted faults,
such as weak conversational powers, and an increasing unwilling-
ness to submit to control, there was no doubt that the Prince himself
had moved several decisive steps forward.

After a brief return to Oxford, he entered the University of
Cambridge on somewhat similar terms, as a member of Trinity
College, but resident four miles away at Madingley Hall, under the
eye of his governor (now promoted a general) and Mrs. Bruce, with
an equerry and tutor in attendance. He followed courses in science,
law and history appropriate to a future monarch with various eminent scholars, including Charles Kingsley, Professor of Modern
History, with whom he remained on friendly terms afterwards.
There was little or no relaxation of discipline, and the Prince
Consort continued to receive frequent reports on the work and
conduct of the nineteen-year-old Prince, as if he had still been a
schoolboy. From time to time he visited Cambridge in person to
deliver curtain lectures of the kind known at that time among the
young as 'jobations'. Who can blame the recipient, if, after being
received as an equal by the President of the U.S.A., he felt that the
time had come for him to be treated as an adult by his father?

It may have been as a result of his own protests that in 1861 the
Prince was allowed to join the army for a short period of military
training. He was attached for ten weeks to a battalion of the Grenadier Guards in camp at the Curragh, near Dublin, and for the first
time in his life found himself emancipated from the watchful care
of middle-aged overseers. Even here he had special quarters. But he
mixed freely with his fellow subalterns, and had the novel experience

of meeting men who were not necessarily patterns of moral recti-
tude. He found them congenial, and under their expert tuition his
education proceeded in directions not intended by his parents. In
short, he learnt the meaning of dissipation. The sequel was probably
inevitable in a young man brought up as he had been. Following the
precedent set by so many of his Hanoverian forebears, he became
involved in a scandalous affair with a young woman.

It is a pity this ever became known; but, thanks to some busybody,
the news broke after the Prince of Wales had returned to Cambridge,
and his father was making plans for his next continental visit. Overcome by grief and horror at what his son had done, the Prince
Consort travelled to Cambridge by special train to see him personally.
What passed between them is not known–certainly a sermon on
one side, perhaps contrition and a plea of giving way to temptation
on the other. The Prince Consort returned to Windsor, in the
Queen's words, 'much relieved'.

But all this had come at a time when he was labouring under other
anxieties. There had been a spate of bad news. Several members of
the Portuguese royal family, to whom he was related, had gone
down with typhoid; and word came that the King and two of his
brothers had died. His own youngest son, Prince Leopold, had been
found to be suffering from haemophilia; and when, on medical
advice, he had sent him abroad, the boy's guardian, a retired general
of seventy-four, had died, leaving his charge temporarily stranded.
Then he himself, his constitution undermined by worry, fell ill. At
first it seemed to be no more than a chill. But things got rapidly
worse, and soon it was seen that he too had typhoid. Within three
weeks he was dead.

The Queen always maintained that anxiety over the Prince of
Wales's misconduct had contributed to the Prince Consort's death,
and she never really forgave her son, whose existence and presence
she now seemed often to resent, though he for his part was always
kind and dutiful towards her. She was not consistently prejudiced.
There were times when she recognized and admitted his devotion,'
particularly as old age approached: 'He is so kind and affectionate,
she wrote in 1887. But she never established a proper relationship
with him, either as a mother with her eldest son, or as a queen
with her destined successor. In part it may have been the old
Hanoverian antipathy between ruler and heir rising once more to
the surface. But the death of the Prince Consort had an effect on

the Queen without parallel in the previous history of her race, which further distorted her attitude to the Prince. Obsessed by the feeling that she was under a sacred obligation to carry out her beloved husband's every wish, now that he was gone, she continued to treat the adult Prince of Wales as if he was still a child, denied him all responsibility, and even tried to regulate his behaviour. This prevented him from learning his trade as a future king. But fortunately it was beyond her power to suppress him altogether. His personality proved as strong as hers, though of an entirely different kind, and he developed his own exuberant way of life.

In the adult Prince there was little trace of the ideal which his father had tried painstakingly to realize. Some of the qualities which the Prince Consort had wished his son to cultivate were there – the kindliness, the courtesy and consideration for others, the outwardly cordial manner. But the Prince had revealed these traits in embryo as a child – they owed nothing to his education. Nor again had his education been able to rid him of his major faults, which had also been there from the start – his idleness, his egotism, his love of pleasure, the mildly sadistic delight he took in tormenting others (which in adult life took the form of practical joking). Yet he grew up to be a man of marked and decisive character. His tastes and interests were very definitely his own, though they were mostly not of a kind that tutors try to encourage or parents approve; and through forty years of virtual humiliation by his mother he retained his poise and his dignity. It was a remarkable achievement. Perhaps this was the greatest of all the debts he owed to his father and tutors – that in resisting their pressures he had developed his own vigorous personality to the full.

IO

Reaction

IN SO FAR AS THE FUTURE KING EDWARD VII HAD ANY EDUCA-
tional theories of his own, they were the exact opposite of his father's,
and in educating his own sons his main idea was to make sure they
did not have to undergo the torments he himself had suffered. He
had no faith whatever in the kind of literary education which the
Prince Consort valued so highly; and having scarcely opened a
book since his own painful studies ended, he did not think it very
important that his sons should read books either. Nor did he
believe in keeping the young under constant surveillance, as he
had been kept. His family were allowed considerable freedom as
children—some of their relatives thought they had too much freedom; and as they grew older they were expected to stand on their
own legs. Their mother, the beautiful Princess Alexandra, indulgent
and easy-going by nature, readily fell in with her husband's policy
of *laissez-faire* discipline.

The Prince had two sons, Prince Albert Victor, born in 1865, and
Prince George (later King George V), born a year later. His plan
was that both should enter the Navy, Prince George with a view to
a naval career, Prince Eddy (as he was called) for the immediate
benefits of a naval training. The decision arose naturally from his
own educational prejudices. In the Navy, as he saw it, his sons
would enjoy many things that he had missed—a healthy, active life,
a practical rather than bookish training, freedom from parental
pressures, companionship. It did not strike him that a somewhat
narrow, insular point of view might also result from so specialized
an education. But his mother, the Queen, whose thoughts ranged
back to earlier generations of the family, was well aware of this
danger. Her view was that the boys should be sent to Wellington
College, a new public school in which the Prince Consort had taken

great interest, where, she said, they could live in an adjacent house to escape contamination by other boys, but at the same time enjoy all the advantages of a public-school education.

'Will a nautical education not engender and encourage national prejudices and make them think that their own country is superior to any other?' she asked. 'With the greatest love for and pride of one's own Country, a Prince, and especially one who is one day to be its Ruler, should not be imbued with the prejudices and peculiarities of his own country, as George III and William IV were.' But the Prince had not forgotten his own experiences of books and classrooms, and stuck to his plan of a naval training for his sons.

So the two little Princes were placed under a tutor to work for the entrance examination to the training ship *Britannia* at Dartmouth, where at that time small boys destined for a naval career received their first initiation. It was Queen Victoria herself who chose the tutor, the Rev. John Neale Dalton, aged 32, at that time serving as a curate near Osborne; and there is a pleasing irony in the fact that this pillar of Victorian orthodoxy, whose career, first as royal tutor, later as a canon of Windsor, was to lie so close to the throne, became the father of Hugh Dalton, brilliant leader of advanced undergraduate opinion in the Cambridge of his day, and Chancellor of the Exchequer in a Labour government.

Dalton was an able man, who had gained first-class honours in theology at Cambridge. By temperament conscientious and methodical, he insisted on establishing an orderly routine for the young Princes, and was not afraid to protest to their father when he felt that his pupils were having too many distractions. His influence on Prince George at any rate was strong and lasting; and he remained a devoted friend and counsellor of the royal family till his death at the age of ninety in 1931.

Considering their age, the young Princes were worked quite hard, with preparation before breakfast and before bed, in the accepted public-school manner, work all morning, and the afternoon free for games or riding. Mr. Dalton himself taught all the subjects required for the naval entrance examination, except French, which was entrusted to a native teacher; and kept two large albums, in which his pupils' progress, or lack of it, was fully and frankly recorded from week to week.

This systematic plan of campaign was successful, and in 1877 the two Princes, now thirteen and twelve respectively, passed the entrance examination for the *Britannia*. It cannot have been very difficult – or perhaps the Prince of Wales's sons were given a hidden bonus of marks – for, well taught though they had been, not even Prince George could have been described as a strong candidate, and Prince Eddy was woefully weak.

On board the *Britannia* the two boys had a cabin to themselves, and were somewhat incongruously accompanied by Mr. Dalton. In other respects they lived the same hard, spartan life as the other cadets. Though it was a shock to him after the comfort of home, Prince George made a good start in his chosen profession; but Prince Eddy responded to the challenge of naval discipline with a lethargy which baffled his instructors.

When the two-years course was ended, the Prince of Wales, who looked back on his own early travels as the most satisfactory part of his education, decided to send the boys cruising. There was some public anxiety at the risks involved in allowing the two Princes to go to sea together, but Mr. Dalton argued that, in his own interests, the backward Prince Eddy should not be separated from his brother, and the plan went forward.

In 1879, still accompanied by their tutor, who became honorary ship's chaplain, the boys spent eight months in the West Indies on the naval training ship, H.M.S. *Bacchante*: in 1880–82, during a two-years cruise, they visited Australia, Japan, the Holy Land, Egypt and Greece. Few boys can have enjoyed so varied and so protracted a course of education through travel. This was no holiday jaunt. Prince George went through the mill with the other cadets on board, and both Princes continued to have lessons with Mr. Dalton. But they had many unusual and even dangerous adventures, they visited many strange places, and, when not subject to sea-sickness or home-sickness, as they sometimes were, they must have derived much pleasure and absorbed many unconscious lessons from their experiences. Like their father before them, but perhaps less reluctantly, they recorded everything laboriously in diaries, letters and notebooks. Some years later Mr. Dalton collected these juvenilia, with embellishments of his own, into a two-volume, 1,400-page narrative of the voyage, which Prince George in later life said was the dullest book ever written.

On their return home the two Princes were sent to Lausanne for six months to learn French. Three tutors accompanied them, Mr. Dalton himself, Mr. Lawless for mathematics and a Frenchman,

M. Hua, for French. Not much French was learnt: the Princes, English to the core, were shy of speaking a foreign language, and preferred the company of other English children staying in the same hotel. But Prince George came to think so highly of M. Hua that years later, when his own sons were learning French, he was called in to teach them.

At this point the educational paths of the two Princes diverged, and it is time to consider them as separate individuals.

The elder boy, Prince Albert Victor (later Duke of Clarence), heir presumptive to the throne, had been a seven-months child, and remained physically weak all his life. He had also inherited something of his mother's vague, unpractical character, and possibly, as later developments suggest, his father's penchant for self-indulgence. Not surprisingly, he became a source of worry to his parents from the start. Not that he was a bad boy: on the contrary, he was amiable and obedient – 'such a dear and so good and kind', said one of his female relatives – and his mother doted on him. But even in early childhood he seemed to be the victim of an incurable lethargy. Listless, unpunctual like his mother, uninterested, he drifted through life, as heedless and aimless as a goldfish in a bowl,[1] and almost as incapable of learning. Dalton indeed had found that Prince Eddy needed 'the stimulus of Prince George's company to induce him to work at all', and it had been on his recommendation that the two boys were brought up together. This seems to have been effective after a fashion, and Prince Eddy managed to hold his own with his younger brother. Unlike Prince George, however, he had been out of his element in the Navy, and the most that could be hoped was that, as Dalton said, the disciplined life of a training ship might improve his 'moral, mental and physical development', and enable him to cultivate 'those habits of promptitude and method, of manliness and self-reliance, in which he is now somewhat deficient.'

The hopes had not been fulfilled, and the Prince of Wales found himself faced with some of the same difficulties which had confronted his own parents in dealing with him. Prince Eddy had emerged from his two years naval training and his three years at sea no more than an older, and consequently more difficult, version of what he had been before. Self-indulgence and a love of pleasure,

---

[1] I borrow this rather charming comparison from Mr. J. Pope-Hennessy's *Queen Mary* (1959).

inherited or copied from his father, became his guiding principles. Conscientiously the Prince of Wales tried to give him the breadth of experience appropriate to a future sovereign. He took him round with him as he went from place to place in pursuance of his royal duties. He sent him to India. After intense private coaching at Sandringham, he entered him for a short period at his own old Cambridge college, Trinity, where, though he had more freedom, he achieved even less than his father. None of these things made much impression. Next he tried the Army. Prince Eddy became an officer in the 10th Hussars. But though he adopted the outward guise of a cavalry officer – the waxed moustache, the wavy hair, the slim, fashion-plate figure – he was bored with his military duties, and only appreciated the Army for the opportunities of dissipation which it presented.

In some respects at this time Prince Eddy was an unimpressive, unprepossessing man, tall and thin, with a 'neck like a swan' (as another of his female relatives put it), which necessitated very high collars, and led to his father's nicknaming him 'Collars and Cuffs'. But his large, liquid eyes and a certain languorous charm made him attractive to women, and as a lover he displayed slightly more alacrity than he had done in other fields. In the next few years he was involved in several abortive romances with ladies who, for various reasons, would have been unsuitable brides for the heir presumptive, though there was nothing against them personally – one was a commoner, one a Catholic, another could not face the idea of marriage to so feckless a prince (and incidentally chose instead the future Czar of Russia). But even these affairs were not pursued to any decisive conclusion, and for a time two of them were in progress simultaneously.

When the question of Prince Eddy's promotion in the Army came up, Lord Wolseley, reporting to the Commander in Chief, the Duke of Cambridge, did his best for him:

'I should describe his brain and thinking powers as maturing slowly,' he wrote. '. . . Personally, I think he is *very much* to be liked, has most excellent manners, thoughtful for others and always anxious to do the right thing. He is, however, young for his age' – he was twenty-seven – 'and requires to be brought out.'

The Duke had his own views of his young relative, which he expressed more pungently in private. 'Lamentable ignorance,' 'incurable apathy', 'an inveterate and incurable dawdler, never ready, never there', were the phrases he used. Yet he did not find the situation hopeless. 'He has his father's dislike for a book and never looks into one,' he went on, 'but learns all orally and retains what he has learnt.'

The promotion went through; but by this time the Prince of Wales had come to the conclusion that this problem child of twenty-seven was wasting his time in the Army. 'He has not the knowledge even of military subjects which he ought to possess,' he complained: so Prince Eddy's military career came to an end, and in 1891, alarmed by further evidences of his son's emotional instability, the Prince of Wales packed him off for a long colonial tour, during which he would be at sea and away from temptation most of the time.

Queen Victoria, though not unaware of her grandson's regrettable tastes, inevitably disagreed with the plan for keeping him afloat for long periods. Perhaps she thought it a counsel of despair. At any rate her view was that he ought to be adding to his knowledge and understanding of Europe, rather than of the English-speaking colonies.

'He and Georgie are charming dear good boys,' she wrote to her son, 'but very *exclusively* English which you and your brothers are not, and that is a great misfortune these days . . . You know yourself, who are so fond of going abroad, how it enlarges one's views and rubs off that angular insular view of things which is not good for a Prince.'

The Prince of Wales found it difficult to explain to his mother just why he and Princess Alexandra were reluctant to allow their son to make long sojourns in foreign capitals. Admitting Prince Eddy's incapacity in French and German (due, as he said, to his apathy and disinclination to work), he replied that being too English was 'a good fault in these days', and continued with his plans.

At this point fate stepped in to solve all Prince Eddy's problems with one relentless stroke. On returning from his colonial tour, he had become engaged, amid universal approval, to Princess May, sensible, strong-minded daughter of the Duke and Duchess of Teck, who was eminently qualified in every way to become Queen of England, and might well have shown herself more capable than anyone else of awakening Prince Eddy to his responsibilities. But just before his twenty-eighth birthday, in 1892, the Prince went down with influenza. His constitution, weakened by illness (which had included typhoid as a child and gout at twenty-four) and by the unregulated life he led, proved unequal to the strain. Pneumonia supervened, and within a week he was dead.

Though he was not a popular or a familiar figure, the British people were touched by the tragic death, so soon after his engagement, of one whom they recognized as their future King. There was universal public grief, as there had been when that other heir presumptive, Princess Charlotte, had been cut off unexpectedly in the moment of her happiness seventy-five years before. But the feeling quickly passed, as such public moods always pass; and those who knew the facts of Prince Eddy's character felt some secret relief that they would be spared having as their king one who so lacked all the proper attributes of royalty.

Prince George, who now became heir presumptive, and shortly afterwards Duke of York, was in almost every possible way the exact opposite of his brother: in fact, the one thing the two brothers had in common, and in which they took after their father, was a distaste for books and learning. His character was direct and straightforward, his tastes simple. He was not interested in dissipation, and caused his parents no anxious moments. His father, with whom he enjoyed an affectionate intimacy unusual between fathers and sons of the House of Guelph, must have felt that here at any rate his plans had succeeded.

After returning from the world tour which he and his brother had made together, Prince George went on with his career in the Navy. He took his work seriously, did well in his examinations, and unlike his elder brother in the Army, fully merited the promotion he was given. From being a cheerful, lively child, he grew into a boisterous, high-spirited young man, fond of jokes, and noted for his chaff, or, as his grandfather the Prince Consort called it when seeking to suppress it in his own son, 'the use of bantering expressions' – a habit more congenial to the gun-room than the family circle. If he had been allowed to continue his naval career, he would have been both happy and successful. But the death of his brother intervened, and in 1892 he found himself at the age of twenty-six heir presumptive, yet utterly unprepared for the duties which, as Prince of Wales and King, he would have to perform sooner or later.

Steps were taken to remedy some of the deficiencies of his exclusively naval education. The first, a rather half-hearted one, was to send him to Heidelberg for two months to mend his faulty German. But his attitude to foreign languages was in the worst British tradition.

'My dear old Tut-tut,' he wrote to a family friend, in a style suggestive of sixteen rather than twenty-six, 'Well, I'm working away very hard with old Professor Ihne at this rotten language which I find very difficult and it certainly is beastly dull here, but "in for a penny in for a pound" so I have no English people near me at all and speak nothing but German or rather *try* to speak.'

As his linguistically gifted father prophesied, he did not learn much German; and what he did learn resembled his French in having a strong Britannic flavour.

In 1894, shortly after his marriage to Princess May, his late brother's former fiancée, arrangements were made for him to be instructed privately in the principles of the English constitution by Mr. J. R. Tanner, a fellow of St. John's College, Cambridge. The textbook used was Walter Bagehot's famous work, *The English Constitution*, which contains some uncomplimentary remarks on the educability of princes. Notes which survive show that Prince George, under Mr. Tanner's guidance, made a careful analysis of Bagehot's views on constitutional monarchy; and later as King, he applied what he had learnt. This is one of the few instances in the history of royal education when a king can be shown to have benefited by the theoretical instruction he was given as heir to the throne.

But mostly Prince George learnt, like his father, by doing. The Navy had already set its mark upon him indelibly, giving him, as his son, the Duke of Windsor puts it, 'a gruff, blue water approach to all human problems'. Before all else he was a sailor. His hearty manner, his curt, quarter-deck speech, his practical attitude to all questions, his respect for tradition and his aversion from change (even in the style of his wife's clothes) – all stemmed from the naval training to which he had been submitted during his impressionable years. If education cannot alter a man's character, here at any rate was an instance where it had developed inborn tendencies to the full.

There were disadvantages in this. He himself once confessed as King that he was handicapped by having had a naval training, which had not equipped him to deal with the subtleties of politics; and in this respect he resembled William IV. But a king with the solid virtues of the Navy and no vices was something new in the history of the English monarchy; and King George V's upbringing, with all its limitations, must be put down as one of the most successful on record; it achieved what it had set out to achieve.

In his own way Prince George had carried forward the revolt

against learning which his father, the Prince of Wales, himself had started. His interests–shooting, sailing, philately–were strongly unintellectual. It would be untrue to say he never opened a book; but he certainly did not read much. His hand-writing remained immature. And, when the time came for him to educate his own children, he continued what had now become almost a family tradition, and sent his two eldest sons (the present Duke of Windsor and the late King George VI) into the Navy. Their tutor, Mr. Hansell, himself a typically English product, with his tweeds and his pipe and his firm faith in games and the Christian religion, and certainly no revolutionary, had recommended sending the eldest boy to a preparatory school, which would have been a novel departure. But precedent was all important to the Prince of Wales (as Prince George had now become). 'My brother and I never went to a preparatory school,' he said. 'The Navy will teach David all he needs to know'; so the heir presumptive spent four vital years exposed to the somewhat narrow curriculum and rigorous institutional life of the naval colleges at Osborne and Dartmouth. It was only with the greatest difficulty that his father, by this time King, overcame his distrust of learned men to the extent of allowing the new Prince of Wales to go, as his grandfather had done, for a short spell to Oxford (again on the recommendation of Mr. Hansell, at whose old college, Magdalen, the Prince was entered).

At Oxford, where he matriculated in 1912, and even more while serving in the Army during the 1914–18 war, this most popular Prince tasted a freedom unknown to any of his predecessors. How far this unprecedented escape into the world of common men may have affected Edward VIII's course of action during his short reign is beyond our scope.

But meanwhile there had been a small but significant relaxation in the ancient tradition of royal education by tutors. George V's third son, Prince Henry, later Duke of Gloucester, who was destined for the Army, was sent to Eton, the first son of an English king to attend this ancient school of royal foundation at the very doorstep of the principal royal residence, before going to the Royal Military Academy, Sandhurst. Though there was a reversion to the family pattern, when the King's fourth son, Prince George, later Duke of Kent, entered the Navy via Dartmouth (the only way of doing so at that time), the breach with the past had been made; the son of an English king had been sent to school; and the way was opened for a broader conception of princely education in England.

List of Books Consulted

ASCHAM, R., *The Schoolmaster*, 1570; Cambridge English Classics, 1904.

ASPINALL, A., *Letters of Princess Charlotte*, 1949.

BATHURST, The Hon. B., *Letters of Two Queens*, 1924.

BROWN, P. H., *George Buchanan and his Times*, 1906.

BRYANT, A., *King Charles II*, 1931.

CAMDEN, C., *The Elizabethan Woman*, 1952.

CASTIGLIONE, B., *The Courtier*, 1528: Everyman Series, 1928.

CHAPMAN, H., *Lady Jane Grey*, 1962.

    Mary II, Queen of England, 1952.

    The Last Tudor King, 1958.

Cornhill Magazine, Spring, 1951. 'The Education of a Prince.'

CORNWALLIS, Sir C., *Life and Death of Henry, Prince of Wales*, 1641.

DAVIES, J. G. D., *A King in Toils*, 1938.

Dictionary of National Biography.

ESHER, Viscount, *The Girlhood of Queen Victoria*, 2 vols., 1912.

FITZGERALD, B., *Royal Dukes and Princesses*, 1882.

FULFORD, R., *George IV*, 1949.

    Hanover to Windsor, 1960.

    Queen Victoria, 1951.

    The Prince Consort, 1949.

    The Royal Dukes, 1933.

HIGHAM, F. M. G., *Charles I.*, 1932.

HOPKINSON, M. P., *Anne of England*, 1934.

James I, *Basilikon Doron*, 1598: ed. J. Craigie.

JONES, M. G., *Hannah More*, 1952.

LEE, Sir S., *King Edward VII*, 2 vols. 1925.

MADDEN, F., ed. *Privy Purse Expenses of the Princess Mary*, 1831.

MAGNUS, Sir P., *King Edward VII*, 1964.

McELWEE, W. L., *The Wisest Fool in Christendom*, 1958.

MORE, Hannah, *Hints towards forming the Character of a Young Princess*, 1805.

List of Books Consulted

NEALE, Sir J. E., *Elizabeth I*, 1934.

NICHOLS, J. G., ed., *Literary Remains of Edward VI*, 1857.

NICOLSON, Sir H., *King George V*, 1952.
  Monarchy, 1962.

Parker Society, Original Letters, Vol. I.

PETRIE, Sir C., *The Four Georges*, 1936.
  The Victorians, 1961.

PLUMB, J. H., *The First Four Georges*, 1956.
  ed., *The Renaissance*, 1961.

POLLARD, A. F., *Henry VIII*, 1905.

POLLET, H., *John Skelton*, 1962.

POPE-HENNESSY, J., *Queen Mary*, 1959.

PRESCOTT, H. F. M., *Spanish Tudor*, 1940.

RAYMOND, J., ed., *Queen Victoria's Early Letters*, 1963.

READ, C., *The Tudors*, 1936.

RYAN, L. V., *Roger Ascham*, 1963.

SEDGWICK, R. R., ed., *Letters of George III to Lord Bute*, 1939.

STRYPE, J., *The Life of the Learned Sir John Cheke*, 1705, ed., 1821.

STUART, D. M., *Daughters of George III*, 1939.

TURNER, F. C., *James II*, 1948.

WATSON, F., *Vives and the Renascence Education of Women*, 1912.

WILLSON, B., *George III as Man, Monarch and Statesman*, 1907.

WILLSON, D. H., *King James VI & I*, 1956.

WINDSOR, H.R.H. The Duke of, *A King's Story*, 1951.

WOODWARD, W. H., *Studies in Education during the Age of the Renaissance*, 1906.

Index

Index

Index

Fetherstone, Richard, tutor to Mary Tudor, 47–50

'Field of the Cloth of Gold', 47

Finch, Lady Charlotte ('Cha'), governess to George III's young children, 134, 136

Fisher, Herbert, law tutor to future Edward VII, at Edinburgh University, 184

Fisher, Dr. John, Bishop of Exeter (later, of Salisbury), senior tutor to Princes William and Edward, sons of George III, 122, 125; tutor to Princess Charlotte Augusta, 143–4, 146, 151; bases instruction on Hannah More's *Hints*, 148–9

Fitzpatrick, Barnaby, companion to Prince Edward (Edward VI), 36

Florio, John, teacher of French and Italian to Prince Henry, son of James I, 84; *A World of Words*, and Montaigne translations by, 84

Fontenay, M. de, on James I's virtues and defects, 74–5, 79

Football, Stewart players of, 86; as ancient game, 102

Foxe (martyrologist) on young Edward VI's geographical knowledge, 31–2

Frederick, Prince of Wales, eldest son of George II and father of George III, 99–100; educational theories and directives of, 100, 101–3; favours amateur theatricals, 102–3; on the 'nonchalance' of his heir, 105; attitude of, to Earl of Bute, Hayter, Scott, Stone, 105, 107

Frederick, Prince, second son of George III, *see* York, Duke of

Frederick the Great, 121; *Antimachiavel*, 101

Frederick William of Prussia, son-in-law of Queen Victoria, 157

Fuller, *Worthies* quoted, 33, 34

Fung, Mr., a teacher (possibly of music) to future George III, 101, 102

Gascoigne, George (poet), 77

George I, Elector of Hanover and great-grandson of James I, 97; as wholly Hanoverian, 98, 99; defective education of, 97

George II, as Prince George Augustus (son of George I and husband of Caroline of Ansbach): education and interests of, 98–9; serves under Marlborough, at Oudenarde and Dettingen, 99; as a Hanoverian, 99; his attitude towards Earl of Bute, 108; towards heir, 105

George III (heir apparent at 13 to grandfather George II, *see* Frederick,

Prince of Wales): English education of, 99, 100–3; as heir to throne, 104; attachment of, to Earl of Bute, 107–10; languages spoken by, 111, 117; as actor, 103; early romantic affairs of, 106; virtues and qualities of, 106–7, 110, 111; as 'Farmer George', 111; education of his large family, 112–38; of his sons in particular, 112–19, 130–1; of the princesses, 132–8; continues the old 'preceptor' tradition, 112; enjoys his young family, 113; strife with future George IV, 115–17; his daughters' secret affairs and marriages, 138; mental illness of, 110, 151–2; continuing interest in drama, 177–8; takes a hand in Charlotte Augusta's upbringing, 140–3; at time of this princess's death, 151

George IV, son of George III: education of, 113–17; at strife with father, 115–17, 119; Hanoverian characteristics of, 115–17; 'self-portrait' at 16, 116; attracted to Mary Hamilton, 115–16; and to Mary Robinson, 116–17; as classical scholar, 117; as linguist, 117, 118; as Regent and arbiter of Regency taste, 120; his marriage to Caroline of Brunswick-Wolfenbüttel, 139; their daughter, Charlotte Augusta, 139–49; his anxiety over her public image, 149–150; and the young Victoria, 153, 160–161; Stockmar on education of, 171

George V, second son of Edward VII; early naval training of, 189–91; learning French in Lausanne, 191–2; continues naval career as heir presumptive, 195; learning German in Heidelberg, 195–6; marries Princess May of Teck, 196; receives instruction in Constitution, 196; as primarily sailor, not scholar, 196–7; the education of his sons, 197; sends a son to Eton, 197

George VI, naval training chosen for, 197

Gibbs, Frederick Waymouth, tutor to Prince of Wales (Edward VII), 175 *seqq.*; on walking tours with Prince, 181; retirement of, 180

Gibson, Mr. and Mrs. Richard, art teachers to Mary and Anne Stuart, 94, 95

Giggs, Margaret, in Sir Thomas More's household, 42

Giles, lutanist, teacher to Mary Tudor, 48

Giustinian, Venetian ambassador to London (Henry VIII), 24

Gloucester, Duke of, younger brother of George III, 106

Index

Index

Index